Mediating Catholicism

New Directions in the Anthropology of Christianity

Series editors: Naomi Haynes, Jon Bialecki, Hillary Kaell, and James S. Bielo

Emphasizing ethnographic depth and theoretical innovation, *New Directions in the Anthropology of Christianity* showcases the work of a fresh generation of researchers, as well as outstanding senior scholars, to provide researchers at all levels with rich sources of comparison and new analytical frameworks. The series publishes monographs and edited volumes on a range of topics on Christianity around the world, focusing on a few key themes: politics and Christian nationalism; economic development and humanitarianism; engagement with religious others; gender and sexuality; and environment.

Prioritizing the comparative study of Christianity, the series strengthens a global network of scholars with overlapping interests, while providing a unique vantage point on the growing subfield of anthropology of Christianity.

Forthcoming books in this series:

Christianity, Politics and the Afterlives of War in Uganda
Henni Alava

Pentecostal Insight in a Segregated US City
Frederick Klaits with LaShekia Chatman and Michael Richbart

Mediating Catholicism

Religion and Media in Global Catholic Imaginaries

Edited By
Eric Hoenes del Pinal, Marc Roscoe Loustau, and
Kristin Norget

BLOOMSBURY ACADEMIC
LONDON • NEW YORK • OXFORD • NEW DELHI • SYDNEY

BLOOMSBURY ACADEMIC
Bloomsbury Publishing Plc
50 Bedford Square, London, WC1B 3DP, UK
1385 Broadway, New York, NY 10018, USA
29 Earlsfort Terrace, Dublin 2, Ireland

BLOOMSBURY, BLOOMSBURY ACADEMIC and the Diana logo are trademarks of
Bloomsbury Publishing Plc

First published in Great Britain 2022
This paperback edition published 2024

Series design: Toby Way
Cover image: The Señor de los Milagros processions in Lima, Peru, 2012, by Kristin Norget

A catalogue record for this book is available from the British Library.

Library of Congress Control Number: 2021952911

ISBN: HB: 978-1-3502-2817-7
         PB: 978-1-3502-2820-7
       ePDF: 978-1-3502-2818-4
      eBook: 978-1-3502-2819-1

Series: New Directions in the Anthropology of Christianity

Typeset by Integra Software Services Pvt. Ltd.

To find out more about our authors and books visit www.bloomsbury.com
and sign up for our newsletters

To Alice, Anne, and Judy

Contents

List of Images   viii

List of Contributors   ix

Acknowledgments   xii

Introduction   Mediating Catholicism: Global Catholic Media as a Field
of Anthropological Inquiry *Eric Hoenes del Pinal, Marc Roscoe Loustau,
and Kristin Norget*   1

1   Mediatizing Holy Week: Guatemalan Catholic Experiments with
Radio and Facebook *Eric Hoenes del Pinal*   29

2   NFP Online: The Mutable Religious Space of Social Media
Katherine Dugan   47

3   The Stakes of Catholic Media Practices in Chad *Ludovic Lado*   63

4   "This station only runs on love": Post-Bureaucratic Evangelism
in a Transylvanian Catholic Media Organization
Marc Roscoe Loustau   79

5   A Touch of Love: On Words, Things, and the Global Aspirations
of US Catholics *Hillary Kaell*   97

6   Religious Celebrities and the Expansion of Suffering in the
Philippines and Timor-Leste *Julius Bautista*   123

7   Exorcism in the Media *Thomas J. Csordas*   143

8   Abundance and the Late Capitalist Imagination: Catholicism
and Fashion at the Metropolitan Museum *Elayne Oliphant*   161

9   Miraculous Sovereignties: Mediation and the Señor de los Milagros
in Lima, Peru *Kristin Norget*   179

10   The Mediatization of Catholicism: Some Challenges and Remarks
Luís Mauro Sá Martino   203

Bibliography   217

Index   240

Images

5.1 A collage at Unbound's office depicting Hentzen as a pilgrim, walking hand-in-hand with a child. The collage is made up of the faces of sponsored children in Latin America (photo by author)   101

5.2 Unbound's prototypical sponsors, as displayed in its offices in 2014. Staff used these profiles as a tool to craft new policies and messaging. "Patricia" and "Anne and Andrew" represented markets they hoped to grow, while "Beth" and "Larry and Susan" typified their base supporters. Regardless, sponsorship is pictured as driven primarily by mothers (or mothers-to-be, in the case of "Anne") (photo by author)   110

5.3 Poster of the team of priests who volunteer to promote the program, which has been Unbound's main promotional method since the 1990s. The poster, which featured in several locations around Unbound's offices, is a reminder of the continued role of "institutional" Catholic authority in the organization (photo by author)   115

5.4 Barclay Martin, Unbound's Coordinator of New Channels in 2014, demonstrates how café goers can access interactive videos as they sit amid the photo display (photo by author)   117

9.1 The Señor de los Milagros procession in Lima, Peru, 2017 (photo by author)   180

9.2 Sahumadoras (photo by author)   190

9.3 The Señor de los Milagros procession in the Plaza de Armas, Lima, Peru, 2017 (photo by author)   192

9.4 President Pedro Kuczynski and Vice-President Mercedes Aráoz greeting papal nuncio Nicola Girasoli and Mayordomo of the Hermandad de las Nazarenas, Manuel Orillo outside the Palacio de Gobierno (Lima, October 18, 2017) (photo from Secretaria de Prensa, Presidencia del Perú)   196

Contributors

Julius Bautista is Associate Professor in the Center for Southeast Asian Studies, Kyoto University, and is interested in religious practice in Asia, with a focus on Christian iconography, religious piety, and the relationship between religion and the state particularly in the Philippines and Timor-Leste. He is the author of *Figuring Catholicism: An Ethnohistory of the Santo Niño de Cebu* (Ateneo de Manila University Press, 2010), *The Way of the Cross: Suffering Selfhoods in the Roman Catholic Philippines* (2019), as well as editor of *The Spirit of Things: Materiality and Religious Diversity in Southeast Asia* (2012) and co-editor (with Francis Lim) of *Christianity and the State in Asia: Complicity and Conflict* (2009).

Thomas J. Csordas is Distinguished Professor of Anthropology, University of California, San Diego. He has conducted ethnographic research among Charismatic Catholics, Navajo Indians, adolescent psychiatric patients in New Mexico, and Catholic exorcists in the United States and Italy, spanning topics that include therapeutic process in religious healing, ritual language and creativity, sensory imagery, self-transformation, techniques of the body, causal reasoning about illness, and the experience of psychiatric inpatients. He has published several monographs, including *Language, Charisma, and Creativity: The Ritual Life of a Religious Movement* (1997), *Body/Meaning/Healing* (2002), and edited *Embodiment and Experience: The Existential Ground of Culture and Self* (1994) and *Transnational Transcendence: Essays on Religion and Globalization* (2009).

Katherine Dugan is Associate Professor of Religious Studies. She studies American religions with a specialization in contemporary Catholicism in the United States. Her research interests are in religious experience, women in religion, and the intersection of religious practice and American culture. Her first book, *Millennial Missionaries: How a Group of Young Catholics Is Trying to Make Catholicism Cool* (2019), is an ethnographic study of young adults who commit to two years evangelizing on college campuses in the United States. Her current project is on Catholics and natural family planning.

Eric Hoenes del Pinal is Assistant Professor of Religious Studies at the University of North Carolina at Charlotte. He is a linguistic anthropologist whose work focuses on the role that language, discourse, and embodied communication play in creating religious difference and change among indigenous (Q'eqchi'-Maya). His book, *Guarded by Two Jaguars: Language, Embodiment, and the Contested Meaning of Catholicism in Guatemala* (2022), examines the stakes of language and gesture in an intra-parish rift between traditionalist Catholics and Catholic Charismatics.

Hillary Kaell is Associate Professor of anthropology and religion at McGill University and a faculty fellow at Concordia University's Centre for Sensory Studies. She writes about North American Christianity, often focusing on how Christians make and imagine global connections. She is the author of *Walking Where Jesus Walked: American Christians and Holy Land Pilgrimage* (New York University Press, 2014) and, most recently, *Christian Globalism at Home: Child Sponsorship in the United States* (2020), which was awarded the 2021 Schaff Prize by the American Society of Church History. Her current project explores multispecies ecology and hurricanes on the Outer Banks of North Carolina.

Ludovic Lado, S.J., is an anthropologist and activist from Cameroon. His research concerns social justice in Cameroon with regard to the Catholic Church and Cameroonian politics, particularly the presidency of Paul Biya. His publications include *Catholic Pentecostalism and the Paradoxes of Africanization* (Brill, 2009), *Le Pluralisme Religieux en Afrique* [Religious Pluralism in Africa] (2015), and *Towards an Anthropology of Catholicism in Africa* (forthcoming), and he is co-editor (with R. Yao Gnabeli) of *Etat, Religions et Genre en Afrique Occidentale et Centrale* [State, Religions, and Gender in Western and Central Africa] (2019). He is Director of Centre d'Etudes et de Formation pour le Développement (CEFOD) and of CEFOD Business School in N'Djamena, Chad.

Marc Roscoe Loustau is Managing Editor of *The Journal of Global Catholicism*. His research has focused on Catholicism in Romania where, after decades of official state atheism, there has been a prominent resurgence of religion in public life. His current research focuses on how Radio Maria (a global Catholic radio network) helps constitute the lived religious experiences of Catholics in Eastern Europe. His book about nationalism and intellectual mission among post-socialist Hungarian Catholic educators will be published by Palgrave MacMillan Press.

Luís Mauro Sá Martino is Professor of Comparative Communications in the School of Journalism at the Faculdade Cásper Líbero (São Paulo, Brazil) where he also leads the Research Group "Theories and Processes of Communication." His research seeks to use insights gained from Latin America to problematize and challenge theories of mass media and mediatization developed in the Global North. He is the author of several books in both Portuguese and English, including *Mídia e Poder Simbólico: Um Ensaio Sobre Comunicação e Campo Religioso* [Media and Symbolic Power: An Essay on Communication and the Religious Field] (2003), *Comunicação e Identidade: Quem você pensa que é?* [Communication and Identity: Who Do You Think You Are?] (2010), *The Mediatization of Religion: When Faith Rocks* (2013), and *Teoria das Mídias Digitais: Linguagens, ambientes, redes* [Theory of Digital Media: Languages, Environments, Networks] (2014).

Kristin Norget is Associate Professor of Anthropology at McGill University. Her research has examined popular religious practice, the Catholic Church, and the "progressive" Catholic movements of liberation theology and indigenous theology in Mexico. She is the author of *Days of Life, Days of Death: Ritual in the Popular Culture of Oaxaca* (2006); and co-editor (with Valentina Napolitano and Maya Mayblin) of *The Anthropology of Catholicism: A Reader* (2017), and (also with V. Napolitano) of a special issue of the journal *Postscripts* entitled "Economies of Sanctity: The Translocal Roman Catholic Church in Latin America" (2011).

Elayne Oliphant is Assistant Professor of Anthropology and Religious Studies at New York University. Her research explores the ongoing (and ever-transforming) place of Christian signs and symbols in the public sphere and demonstrates how Christianity is experienced and presented as a sign of secularity. She has published essays exploring the privileged circulation of Christian signs in contemporary art exhibits, museum displays, and European Court of Human Rights rulings. She is the author of *The Privilege of Being Banal: Art, Secularism, and Catholicism in Pairs* (2021).

Acknowledgments

It is not common for academics to directly address the material circumstances in which our scholarship is produced. In this case, however, it seems an apt way to introduce the book you are now reading, which is centrally concerned with how distinct cultural logics and social dynamics shape and are shaped by media. It seems relevant then to note that the first conversation that led the editors to this project occurred during an annual meeting of the American Academy of Religion in the lobby bar of a hypermodern hotel (so modern in fact that it was featured in the blockbuster film adaptation of a bestselling young adult dystopian science-fiction novel). It was there that two of us (Marc Roscoe Loustau and Eric Hoenes del Pinal) discovered that we had both been thinking about the role of old-fashioned FM radio in the lives of Catholics in two decidedly less futuristic settings than the one we were presently in. Just about a year later at another hotel, this time at a meeting under the auspices of the American Anthropological Association a small group convened to give their own papers on Catholic media practices. At that conference, Kristin Norget suggested that we should find funding to produce a stand-alone symposium on the subject. Though the three of us would see each other in person no more than once per year, emails, video and voice chats, and shared virtual documents—that is to say a multiplicity of media services tied to our home and office computers—bound our efforts together over the next five years.

In September 2019, a small group convened at The Monastère des Augustines in Québec City, Quebec, to present early versions of these papers as part of *Mediating Catholicism: A Symposium on Global Catholic Media Practices*. None of this would have been possible without the funds generously provided by a Connections Grant from the Social Science and Humanities Research Council of Canada and a Collaborative Research Grant from the American Academy of Religion. We are also profoundly grateful to the Catholics and Cultures Initiative at College of the Holy Cross, the Centre for Research on Religion at McGill University, and the Department of Religious Studies at the University of North Carolina at Charlotte for the additional funding, as well as to Catherine Lavertu, Edith Caron and other staff at the Monastère des Augustines for their in-kind considerations and invaluable assistance in helping us mount that conference—a memorable time for all. Thanks also to Damián Arteca for his intellectual and logistical support on site throughout the event.

We would also like to express our gratitude to several individuals who were part of the panels and symposium leading up to this publication, but who for one reason or another were not able to contribute directly to this volume. In no particular order we would like to thank Valentina Napolitano, Thomas M. Landy, Jeremy Stolow, Rafael Sanchez, Joanne Maguire, and Mathew Schmalz for their keen insights and the valuable conversations we shared with them that have contributed in ways both large and small to the intellectual project we are proposing here. A final thank you is due to Lalle Pursglove and Lily McMahon at Bloomsbury as well as to the series editors of New Directions in the Anthropology of Catholicism for their support for this project.

Introduction

Mediating Catholicism: Global Catholic Media as a Field of Anthropological Inquiry

Eric Hoenes del Pinal, Marc Roscoe Loustau, and Kristin Norget

Media, Mediation, and Mediatization

Media use is ubiquitous in much of social and cultural life, and religion is no exception. Religious institutions both large and small broadcast their services or auxiliary programming on radio, television, and the internet, and in the process some of their leaders become celebrities known as much for their appearance through mediated channels as for their doctrines or ritual practices. These actors and institutions also produce specialized films, music, books, toys, apparel, and all kinds of material culture that have become part and parcel of people's everyday life. Mediatic forms are also increasingly important to how lay Catholics build a sense of their religious identity, and by making and circulating digital images on social media, they participate in dispersed religious communities and craft new visions of public devotional life. Scholars disagree on exactly when media's ascendancy began to reshape religious life,[1] but whatever religion may have been before media became so central to its workings, clearly it is now irrevocably different because of it. For many, this perceived difference is, in fact, what makes mediated religion so appealing. Increasing access to media technologies has effectively mediatized religious identities, practices, and communities as much as any other aspect of contemporary life. It is thus incumbent on scholars of religion to explore the intersection of religion and media in both the public sphere and people's interior lives.

A comprehensive review of the literature on media and religion is beyond the scope of this essay, especially because several have already been attempted (see Hjarvard 2008; Sa Marino 2013; Lövheim 2014; and Krüger 2018). Nonetheless, it is worthwhile briefly rehearsing some of the key aspects of this field of study. Philosopher Marshall McLuhan is often cited as a key initiator of media theory proper, having famously coined the phrase, "the medium is the message" in his 1964 book *Understanding Media: The Extensions of Man*. McLuhan argued that media technologies are not just technological innovations that reflect social and cultural changes, but are themselves drivers of such transformations. McLuhan and his contemporaries made the case that the media ought to be thought of as an institution with a degree of autonomous agency in shaping society, and that it was thus worthwhile studying them in and of themselves. Building on that insight, scholars turned toward theorizing, and not just describing, how particular media perform mediation. At the same time, it became increasingly common to discuss "media" as a more general category, rather than "the media," which seemed to imply a finite number of mass communications technologies.

As an interdisciplinary field of media and communication studies coalesced in the decades following McLuhan, debates arose around how to best discuss the category of "media" and what its object of study ought to be. Two terms in particular became the focus of scholars' attention—"mediation" and "mediatization."[2] *Mediation*, the broader of the two terms, is used to talk about the semiotic processes (and their attendant ideologies) by which two distinct positions are brought into contact with each other. Hence one can use the term to talk about mediation in a general and colloquial sense afforded by analogies with communication, including how language acts as a medium for communication between people, or how newspapers mediate ideas about national identity between rural peasants and urban bourgeoisies. Mediation also points to approximational processes that are less evidently mediatic, such as how children's games can mediate cultural expectations of labor and kinship, or how ritual specialists mediate the conjunction of natural and supernatural worlds. The more recently coined neologism *mediatization*, on the other hand, accounts for the conditions in which a distinctive logic or "grammar" of mediation has come to pervade social life following the proliferation of media technologies in late modernity. This term usefully draws attention to, for example, how the pace of politics and governance seems to be increasingly responding to twenty-four-hour cable news cycles or the rhythm of Twitter trends, or how pedagogy at various levels incorporates elements of "edutainment" in an attempt to prompt "engagement" with, rather than mastery of, a subject. In these cases, what is important is how various domains of social and cultural life have been altered in order to respond to the media through which people encounter them.

We lay this out and adopt these interrelated terms with the proviso that scholars disagree about their precise lineaments and boundaries. While some scholars argue that they refer to fundamentally different processes and must necessarily be distinguished from each other (see, e.g., Hjarvard 2008), others counter that the distinction only creates confusion (especially outside of the Anglophone literature), and that the intellectual project of media studies would be better served by subsuming these distinctions under a single umbrella concept (see, e.g., Livingstone 2009).[3] We are inclined, by virtue of our empirical focus on Catholicism, toward holding the differences between these terms together in an organic interdependence without fixing them as ontological essences—an orientation which we find at work somewhat intuitively in Catholics' own real-world mediational practices. Indeed, we discern resonances between our ethnographic findings and thought-provoking theoretical statements by Catholics who were themselves scholars of media. McLuhan, for example—who converted to Catholicism at the age of twenty-six—could have been describing the Church's aspiration to form a globally inclusive "society" of its own when he wrote that "The tendency of electric media is to create a kind of organic interdependence among all the institutions of society" (1964: 218).

Although mediation and mediatization theories have a longer history of being used to illuminate questions of politics, identity, and power, as well as cultural and social change more broadly, their application to the study of religion specifically only emerged in earnest in the first decade of the twenty-first century (Sá Martino 2013; Lövheim 2014; Krüger 2018). The so-called "return of religion" at the end of the millennium revealed the prescriptive character of the secularization hypothesis, which seemed to imply that "modern" media would be one of the social forces that would erode "traditional" religion's sway over society. This has proven to be false, and social scientists have increasingly demanded a re-evaluation of religion's place in public life, which of necessity includes its articulation with "the media" and its logics. *Religion and Media*, the 2001 edited volume by Hent de Vries and Samuel Weber, kicked off this conversation and made the case that scholars from across the humanities and social sciences needed to seriously consider how the two broad categories in its title might inform each other. As with the theorization of mediation/mediatization it is possible to identify two ways in which this project has been taken up since then.

The first of these ways examines how religion and media (two broad categories broadly defined) articulate with and inform each other in modern society. Scholars working in this vein have been interested in critically examining how media technologies and media logics have shaped religious institutions, identities, and practices, and vice versa. So, for example, one might link the popularity of sci-fi and fantasy television shows in the United States to changing ideas about the supernatural or concerns about what exists beyond everyday human experience (Clark 2003), or argue that cab drivers in Egypt who consume sermons on cassette tapes are engaged in a project of personal ethical self-cultivation that has also impacted significantly emergent forms of political Islam (Hirschkind 2006).

Scholars in the second camp, meanwhile, have argued, to echo media scholar Jeremy Stolow (2005), that we need to radically reconceptualize religion *as* media. Researchers working along these lines argue that the advent of modern media technologies reveals how mediation has always undergirded much of what we typically call religion or the religious. Supernatural or divine entities, the argument goes, have always made themselves present in human life through diverse media, including texts, totems, clerics, mystics, and mediums (Stolow 2005; Meyer 2015). The work that needs to be done, then, is not so much to examine the interplay of *this* religion and *that* media technology, as it is to better understand the basic semiotic processes, reverberations, and ideologies that constitute religious lifeworlds as forms of mediation themselves. Birgit Meyer, for example, has described Ghanaian Pentecostals' religious practices as revolving around the core idea that human bodies can be inhabited by the Holy Spirit, which is to say that they understand the body as an adequate medium for that transcendental principle to become actualized in the world (Meyer 2011). Although Ghanaian Pentecostals in principle also aspire to a wholly disembodied spirituality, when one observes what they actually do in church it is clear that their religion is organized around specific "sensational forms" that recruit people's bodily and linguistic faculties in ways understood to make Holy Spirit manifest in the physical world. From this perspective, religious praxis is always already implicated in processes of mediation, and as such the scholar's task is to analyze the various semiotic forms and ideologies that people engage in and with when doing religion.

These two broad approaches on religion and/as media stand in relation to (if somewhat roughly and imperfectly) the theoretical orientations to mediation and mediatization discussed previously. Scholars of religion *and* media have tended to gravitate toward the theory of mediatization, emphasizing how the logic of media shapes religious life. Scholars of religion *as* media, on the other hand, find mediation to be a useful heuristic tool for understanding the negotiations of meaning in religious life.

To be sure, there are important stakes in these debates, but we think that both strands of research have merit and thus our goal with this volume is two-fold. First, we aim to document some of Catholics' media practices around the world. Each of the nine essays begins from the premise that an ethnographic investigation of the intersection of Catholic Christianity and media contributes to our larger understanding of religious life in the contemporary world. We would add, too, that examining contemporary Catholics' media practices and imaginaries sheds new light on the importance that Catholicism has long placed on the fundamental semiotic process of mediation. Our second goal, thus, is to offer empirical evidence that other scholars can use as a basis for further developing theories of mediation and mediatization as they relate to religion.

Catholic Media as an Object of Inquiry in Anthropology

While it is a truism that people are increasingly engaging with diverse media technologies as part of their religious lives, much of the anthropological research on this topic has been focused on the media practices and ideologies of Protestant Christians and Muslims, leaving the vibrant ways in which the world's 1.2 billion Catholics use media under-examined. As Birgit Meyer has noted, "turning to Catholicism as an alternative archive" offers scholars fresh material with which to conceptualize key religious processes and critique extant models and narratives about religion in the modern world (2017: 313). In that spirit, documenting some of the world's Catholic's media practices is important, both because there is an obvious lacuna in the ethnographic literature to fill and also because investigating what might be distinctly *Catholic* about Catholics' practices can better illuminate the relationship between religion and media more generally.

While we want to avoid simple reifications or stereotyping, we would nonetheless propose that the rich ideational world of Catholic Christianity and the robust institutional body of the Catholic Church play significant roles in shaping how Catholics engage with and understand the place of media technologies in their religious lives, and our objective is to show that here. This is not simply a speculation along the lines of Andrew Greeley's (2001) thesis that there is a distinct Catholic imagination that unites Catholics worldwide and distinguishes them from all others, but rather a topic for empirical cross-cultural investigation. As ethnographers we are interested in revealing the multiple ways that media in various forms and modalities work to shape the ways that people

understand their faith and senses of themselves as Catholics. We propose that
the question of exactly how processes of mediation might unfold to engender
distinctively Catholic sensibility (which may or may not be relevantly distinct
from those of Protestants, Orthodox Christians, or members of other religious
traditions) is worthy of close attention and analysis. Also, unlike Greeley, we
feel that it is critical to do so with material drawn from distinct parts of the
world, both so that we can see if there is such a thing as a generalizable Catholic
sensibility, and as a matter of resisting the parochialism of using the "North
Atlantic" world as the measure of a global religion.

Anthropologists of Catholicism are particularly well situated to advance
theories of mediation and mediatization because mediation seems to be a
central organizing feature of the religion across its "longitudinal axis" (i.e., its
two thousand years of existence as an institution, and conscious self-elaboration
as an enduring singular church) (Mayblin et al. 2017: 7). One can cite the
doctrine of the transubstantiation whereby the communion wafer and wine
become the body and blood of Christ, the intercessory role of Mary and the
saints, the elaborate aesthetics of Catholic art and architecture, and the cultivated
sensorium of Catholic ritual life, as just a few examples of how mediating logics
are central to Catholicism's practices and beliefs.

The notion that as an institution the Roman Catholic Church is apt to
mediate between distinct categories and realms is also captured by Carl
Schmitt's description of the religion as a distinctive in its work as a *complexio
oppositorum* in which opposites are united, but not necessarily reconciled, to
produce both a Rome-centered magisterium and myriad distinct local lifeworlds Catholicism without apparent contradiction (Schmitt [1923] 1996). An
ethnographic approach to Catholicism and mediation can sometimes make it
easy to lose sight of the global reach of the institution, given that perhaps the
only reminder of it for many people—even Catholics—is the Pope's regular
appearance in the media across the world. Yet Catholicism's status as an
evolving "living infrastructure" (Napolitano 2017) sees it repeatedly stretch and
contract as it moves over time and space; hence a vast institutional bureaucracy,
brotherhoods and lay organizations, public ceremonies and other events,
collective and individual bodies of ordinary devotees, objects and technologies
and their material qualities—all are aspects of Catholicism as a mediating form
at local and global scales. A more deliberate research focus on mediation, we
would argue, helps maintain both of those scales present in research.

Catholicism's globalism has depended largely on its strategies for
communicating the faith to Catholics and those beyond the fold. The Second

Vatican Council was a pivotal point in the Church's "media turn." As Ludovic Lado notes, it was here that the church identified media as "gifts of god," and in various theological statements heralded the capacity of radio, television, film, and printed mass media to enhance the apostolic ministry of the church. A decade later, Pope John Paul II (1978–2005) launched a new globalization strategy for the Vatican's channels of communication within the New Evangelization—"a call to conversion" urging the active re-missionization of the faith by clergy and lay Catholics. This concerted effort to engage with the new media technologies at all scales is part of a decidedly contemporary Church that uses media to compete within an expanded religious marketplace and to confront the many threats of secularism.

Yet long before the Church welcomed such modern modes of communication, the mediation of Catholicism had been part of larger programs of evangelization and missionization which unfolded over several centuries. In many parts of the world, especially in the Global South, saints, such as the Peruvian Señor de los Milagros described by Kristin Norget, were integral to the "emplacement" of Catholicism within local and regional syncretic histories in the context of colonialism (Norget 2011). Still today, within the current project of the New Evangelization, saint celebrations remain sites for powerfully entrenching Church presence and sovereignty. Again, we are reminded of the cyclical and elastic nature of Catholic media flows as new media technologies and platforms (Facebook, Twitter, holograms, laser technologies) today intermingle with the old (saints, relics) and can become refashioned to new ends, and effects.

As mentioned above, Catholic media are also part of the religion's "sensational form" (Meyer 2009) by which the divine is made tangible and experienced as real. Part of Catholicism's alternative archive within the anthropology of Christianity inheres precisely in its focus on what Robert Orsi calls "media of presence," that is, the objects (statues, images, relics, rosaries, medallions, etc.) that act as transmitters and conduits, porous vehicles of the divine (Orsi 2005: 154). As Jon Mitchell (2017) has pointed out, understanding this "Catholic sensorium" as a particular *mode* of porousness is essential to understanding its shaping of the Catholic body and the Catholic self through a particular poetics of sensual and affective experience. This poetics is guided by an "analogical imagination" (Tracy 1998) that works through metaphor, metonym, and ritual performance, revealing a Catholic sensibility that relies on recognizing the continuous ways that God and the saints make themselves manifest.

As Mitchell explains, contrary to Pentecostalism's preoccupation with cultivation of the (individual) body as receptor of the divine (as Holy Spirit), the

Catholic sensorium is "not limited to the body but is 'distributed' beyond the body, and spiritual powers are—at least potentially—immanent in all things" (Mitchell 2017: 214). This porosity of the Catholic body alerts us to the different indirect forms in which incarnation (enfleshment), an enmeshment of the "natural" and the symbolic, may be expressed—as saint or relic, as breath or blood, passion or love—the ways in which these may circulate, and the range of senses through which Catholics may register divine presence in the environment. While it may be problematic to overemphasize differences between Protestant and Catholic Christianities as bounded absolutes, we have here a quite different grounding of religious sensibilities when compared to the de-emphasis on mediation, focus on immediate experience, and "authentic sincerity" typical of other forms of Christianity.

Today, Catholicism's sensational form is becoming ever more complex and multifaceted. The intensification of the mediatization of Catholicism has seen a rise in notably baroque, spectacular public performances and events, with plural cultural referents and heightened emotionalism transmitted through multimediatic forms, allowing Catholicism to be both conveyed and taken in through more expansive modes of experience. The mediatization of Catholicism has led its discourses and forms to permeate new spaces of everyday life and reconfigure the social and the political roles of the institutional church. A new synergy between ancient and contemporary evangelical media, such as in the renewed attention to relics, allows Catholicism to affect and engage devotees in especially compelling ways. At the same time, as several essays in this volume show, lay Catholics are themselves producers of media who replicate received teachings of the Church but also refashion them. Catholicism's emergent sensational forms are not immune to the dynamics of power and authority that delineate and bind the core social relationship between the ordained and the laity, even as this volume's contributors also show that the latter group do find occasions and opportunities to rework media to unanticipated ends.

Outline of the Book

The essays in this volume are clustered into two groups. Essays in the first half of the volume are primarily interested in the role of specific media technologies in shaping contemporary Catholic life around the globe; the essays in the second half tend to emphasize the effects and stakes of mediation and mediatization for Catholicism more broadly. This division is, of course, a rough and imperfect one, since essays in the first group do also seek to theorize mediation and mediatization, and those in the second make their arguments based on analyses of specific case studies. What follows is a brief description of the context and content of the essays, with a more thematic exploration in the section that follows.

In Chapter 1, Eric Hoenes del Pinal examines how Guatemalan Catholics have variously used FM radio and internet streaming video to manage the uncertainties of producing spectacular public rituals during Holy Week. Focusing on the devotional labor that Catholic lay leaders do to mount these events and the fact that the efficacy of that work is not always easy to assess, he asks how their various media practices, which are meant to counterbalance unprecedented social changes, have contributed to the mediatization of parish life. Basing half of his essay on more traditional in-person ethnographic field research and half on research carried out through various social media platforms due to travel bans stemming from Covid-19, his essay also reflects on the challenges posed by conducting research that is itself heavily mediatized.

Katherine Dugan's essay (Chapter 2), dealing with North Americans' use of a social media group dedicated to the discussion of Natural Family Planning strategies (technically the only method of managing family size endorsed by the Vatican), examines how the politics of community and lay authority are mediated. Dugan argues that social media forums, such as the Facebook group she discusses, enable lay people to negotiate what it means to be Catholic and develop structures of authority parallel to those officially sanctioned by the institutional Church. The people who participate in these fora value the ideal of peer-to-peer support and coaching, but also find they must navigate a series of tensions and contradictions that have as much to do with the internal dynamics of the group as with outsiders' discourses about sexuality and family.

With an eye much more sharply focused on the workings of the institutional bodies of Catholicism, in Chapter 3 Ludovic Lado describes the Chadian Catholic Church's media policies and practices. Through this study, he offers further insight into how Catholic media is positioned within larger regimes governing communications media within states. Catholics constitute about a fifth of the population in Chad, and consequently Muslim and Pentecostal Christian media channels predominate in the religious field. Moreover, he notes that most Chadian Catholics' consumption practices tend to be somewhat "ecumenical." Thus, the institutional Church must carefully weigh what purposes their media channels are meant to serve when deciding how to expend their limited resources in that arena. Their solution to this conundrum is to position themselves as something more like a community service, whose programming addresses health, economic, environmental, and cultural issues with more frequency than what we might consider overtly religious content.

Radio Maria Transylvania, an Eastern European manifestation of an international radio network, is a radio station that "runs on love" according to the people who volunteer there. In Chapter 4 Marc Roscoe Loustau examines how the competing ideals about labor, love, and evangelism, as well as other values that this entails, intersect in the organization's broadcasting work. Although the largely female volunteer workforce of the station is sometimes criticized for devoting too much time and energy to the station, they find in that work a sense of purpose and a means through which to practice a kind of "soft evangelism" that they hope will transform not just the broader public, but more specifically members of their own families.

In Chapter 5, Hillary Kaell turns our attention to the transnational aspirations and imagination of North American Catholics involved in a childhood sponsorship charity. Kaell's analysis centers on the ways that the idea of love is variously entextualized in the exchanges of words, things, and money between sponsors in the Global North and the children they sponsor in the Global South. Noting that words and things may be considered to be co-extensive media, her essay explores the difficulties that this organization encounters in trying to mediate care as something that is at once a matter of feelings and of economics—two broad categories which sponsors tend to think imply diametrically opposed values. Nonetheless, this form of sponsorship allows relatively well-off people in the United States to project themselves as members of a transnational community and as moral selves whose love for others is not bound by geography.

Suffering bodies are the point of departure for Julius Bautista's chapter examining the "celebrification" of exemplary Catholics in Southeast Asia (Chapter 6). Bautista takes two case studies of men who have been thrust into the spotlight due to their devotional labor—a layman who performs a public self-mortification in an annual Holy Week Passion play, and an East Timorese Bishop renowned for his humanrights advocacy. These two men personify virtues of humility, self-sacrifice, and suffering, but the fact that they do so publicly also brings them levels of public recognition and fame that can seem at odds with those values. The chapter examines the role of these exemplary figures as media for soteriological meaning in and of themselves, as well as the unforeseen effects that the circulation of their images in news media can have.

Thomas Csordas's essay on exorcism in the televisual realm (Chapter 7) shifts our attention from Catholics as producers of media to how a distinctively Catholic ritual practice becomes mediatized. Csordas examines the social and cultural dynamics between the people who perform the rites (i.e., priests) and those who are subject to them (i.e., afflicted women), as well as how people mediatizing the exorcisms (i.e., journalists and documentarians) put these primary actors into conversation with other parties who have radically different interpretations of what exorcism entails (e.g., psychologists, neuroscientists, and news media personalities). While at the interpersonal level exorcisms enact a therapeutic discourse of healing, their mediatization evokes competing discourses about the nature of evil in the world which in turn, Csordas argues, indexes an "ontological fissure" in contemporary civilization between two very different modes of experiencing the world.

In 2018 The Costume Institute at the New York Metropolitan Museum of Art curated an exhibition that juxtaposed twentieth-century *haute couture* clothing, Byzantine and medieval art works from the museum's permanent collection, and items on loan from the Vatican, with the stated purpose of creating a "dialogue" between the two disparate material cultures of Catholicism and high fashion. As Elayne Oliphant shows in Chapter 8, the upshot of that dialogue was a sort of sacramentalization of the twentieth-century clothes that served to justify the logic of late capitalism. Oliphant argues that in this context historical artworks lent the high fashion clothing some of their sense of excess, abundance, and majesty, effectively making them feel as though they were transcendent objects themselves and occluding the inherent inequalities of the system that produces and displays them, including the fawning press coverage of the celebrities attending the exhibit's opening gala.

Chapter 9 examines the peregrinations that the Señor de los Milagros (Lord of Miracles) makes through the streets of Lima, Peru, each October. Kristin Norget argues that part of the function of these two-day processions is to help establish the political authority of the Peruvian state. As part of the ritual, the *santo* "visits" the head of state and representatives of other important social and political institutions, extending to them some of the exceptional and transcendent power of the image. Though of course news media cover these visits in close detail, her emphasis is on the role that the *santo* himself plays as a mediating power between secular and religious spheres.

In the concluding chapter, communications scholar Luís Mauro Sá Martino offers a commentary on the themes raised by the ethnographic chapters from a Brazilian perspective. As he notes, while neither the study of religion and media nor the Catholic Church's involvement in media are necessarily novel, the cross-cultural ethnographic approach these essays present sheds new light on both those areas. Working from his own insights on the contemporary religious landscape in Brazil and engagement with the study of media, he highlights the complications of defining this volume's key terms (i.e., "media" and "Catholicism") and the implications that our approach to these subjects have for future research.

Collectively, the essays in this volume cover a lot of ground in terms of both geography and pointing to where we might locate the effects of media and mediation in contemporary Catholic life. Although it would be a monumental task to offer a comprehensive account of Catholic media practices everywhere in the world, and we recognize that there are important gaps here (notably the religion's old strongholds in Western Europe), we have made a concerted effort to offer a global perspective on Catholicism by including studies based in Central Africa, Central and South America, Eastern Europe, and Southeast Asia alongside work based in the United States. These cases might also be sorted along a spectrum of high-mediated to low-mediated churches; that is, from those for whom media use is central to their working to those where it is more of a background concern (Sá Martino 2013). Our concern with media extends to things that are readily understood colloquially as "media," such as radio, film, and the internet, as well as forms of mediation that do not always jump to mind when that category is invoked such as saints, museums, aesthetic forms, and suffering bodies. Methodologically, the essays also range from those relatively more empirically grounded in direct participant observation with the producers and consumers of media, to those that build their arguments through a critical examination of mediated forms and representations. In all cases, though, the authors share a commitment to analyzing Catholic media and mediation from an ethnographic perspective, assuming that there are layers of meaning to be discovered through a "thick description" that attends to the infelicities and contradictions of quotidian life as much as it does to its grand narratives and ideologies.

***

Thematizing Catholic Mediation

Having laid out the contents of this book chapter-by-chapter, in this final section we wish to provide readers with some thematic reflections on the core essays. The symposium that gave birth to this book was held on the grounds of one of the oldest continually active convents in North America—the Monastère des Augustines in Québec City, Canada. The convent was originally built as part of the Hôtel-Dieu de Québec hospital, which was founded in 1639 under the patronage of the Duchess of Aiguillon—a niece of the famous Cardinal Richelieu. Completed in 1644, this was the first hospital built in the "New World" north of Mexico, and it has stood overlooking the Saint Lawrence River, surviving wars, fires, plagues, the designation as a cultural heritage site, and the vicissitudes that the passage of more than 375 years inevitably brings. Hundreds of nuns have lived in the monastery and worked in the adjacent hospital over the course of four centuries. As has been the case elsewhere in the Global North, the number of women seeking to enter monastic life declined in the second half of the twentieth century, and so the remaining Augustinian Sisters gradually began a process of transforming the convent into a historical trust. Since 2015, the site has operated a spare but elegant holistic health hotel, museum, and archives on its grounds. Things have undoubtedly changed in many ways—monastic cells are now hotel rooms, the kitchen prepares gourmet organic meals, and the vaults beneath the monastery host yoga classes—but the longue durée of the monastery is also palpable in the creaky floorboards, devotional paintings that hang on the walls, and in the activities of the handful of aging nuns who continue to live on the grounds and meet to sing vespers each day in the chapel.

We chose to hold our symposium at this location because we hoped that by connecting our reflections on media practices in the contemporary world to the transnational history of Catholicism, the space would stimulate our thinking about this religion's long-standing concerns with mediation. In that spirit, in what follows we discuss several features and artifacts of the monastery that help us identify and problematize some of the themes that emerge across the essays. More than a programmatic statement about what exactly we think constitutes Catholic media, or what mediation means in terms of Catholic practice, our aim here is to provoke further reflection on how we might triangulate our research interests around Catholicism, media, and mediation.

The Cloister: The Community and Its Boundaries

The Augustinian sisters were a cloistered order and the women who joined them committed themselves to living the rest of their lives on the grounds of the convent and adjacent hospital. They tended to the infirm in the hospital's wards, ate and slept in the cloisters, cared for the gardens where they grew much of their food and the medicinal plants used in healing, and, of course, prayed in the chapel. Their life was regimented and contained in very specific ways, yet it is worth remembering that well into the twentieth century women's opportunities and agency outside the monastery's walls were also significantly limited and constrained. The cloisters represented one of the few ways young women could escape the strongly enjoined social expectation of marrying young and bearing many children.[4] Dedicating one's life to the Order enabled women to live their lives otherwise, with the cloister establishing its own modes of work and sociality built around the promise that faith and discipline could enable transcendence from this world.

It is easy to imagine the nuns in their cloister as an exemplary version of the sacramental Christian community in which religious imperatives radically transform human society. But it is worth noting that the ideal cloistered life is a precarious one, and that its very structure relies as much on the cultivation of the sisters' wills to produce piety from the inside as it does on the walls that keep the polluting influences of the outside world at bay. The intimate space of the cloister depends as much on the solidarity that is built among those who pass through its doors as it does on those doors symbolically marking a renunciation of the world outside of them.

The leitmotif of the community and the problems of how communities are to be construed, constructed, and maintained are central to several of the essays. As Winfried Schulz has noted, mediatization brings about several changes in how human beings interact with each other because media technologies extend the possibility of communication beyond the natural limits of time and space, which changes the character of existing social activities and social institutions (2004: 88). To take this insight seriously in the context of Catholicism is to raise the question of how the community might be (re-)formed according to new logics and ideologies. Is it possible, for example, to locate the Catholic community in mediatized "virtual" spaces? If so, what shape does it take and what sort of ethics prevail when it is self-consciously mediatized? What possibilities for new forms of sociality and religious belonging might be cultivated by the technical affordances of specific media? Posing these questions also implies asking about the limits of these communities, including both those that they erect as a means of self-formation, and those that are imposed by the form and function of the media technologies they use.

Members of the online group that Katherine Dugan writes about find that a social media platform affords them virtual space to discuss issues at the intersection of gender, family, and religion in ways that they would find impossible in secular society. Their encounters with others through text-based comments allow them to feel a sense of solidarity with what are in effect strangers living in disparate parts of the United States, whom they might never actually meet in person but with whom they nonetheless feel a sense of kinship due to shared moral commitments. Yet these encounters are also marked by a series of tensions—between the intimacy of the topics discussed and the effective anonymity of the discussants; between the shared personal vulnerability the topic engenders and the dispersed authority that produces a "right" way of family planning; and between the sense that what they are doing is both ordinary and extraordinary. Facebook groups like this one function as a "parallel option to more formal religious structures," and create "a space for religious community that is... unavailable in other forms" (Dugan, this volume: 57). However, as Hoenes del Pinal points out, media platforms inherently place certain limits and strictures on how a community can be imagined. Contrasting two instances of a Guatemalan parish's efforts to use FM Radio and Facebook to constitute the sacramental community for specific ritual activities across two decades, Hoenes del Pinal alerts us to fact that media are at best imperfect means for imagining community, and that these social formations often feel precarious to their very members. What holds together a community and what keeps it separate from other ones are thus not always easy to determine.

Several essays discuss the dynamics of media as a tool for defining Catholicism over and against secularity or as something distinct from other religions' communities. Ludovic Lado's essay notes that the Catholic Church in Chad has a vested interest in producing and promoting media because it sees a need to counter-program the media produced by other religious institutions (particularly Pentecostal churches). Entering a plural media marketplace, however, means that the Catholic Church must situate its offerings within a state legal apparatus that distinguishes between radio broadcasters serving primarily commercial, confessional, and communitarian ends. Positioning themselves within this schema entails weighing several factors that have stakes both for the perception of the Catholic Church's place in Chad and for what church representatives actually do on the airwaves. The public spectacle of the Señor de los Milagros's procession in Lima, Peru, plays out as a Catholic ritual in the erstwhile secular public sphere and features distinct moments when the state's power and that of a Catholic *santo* are sutured. In Kristin Norget's analysis of this event, the power of both of these institutions stems from the way the procession disrupts the everyday flow of life, producing as if it were a temporal cloister that performatively subsumes all of Lima into the eventual logic of Catholic miracle. These essays thus prompt us to reflect on the dynamics between state and church and to further examine how the negotiations of power between them sustain the relationship.

Focusing on the ideological and discursive elaboration of "love," Hillary Kaell and Marc Roscoe Loustau's essays (set respectively in a child sponsorship charity in the United States and a radio station in Romania) provide an alternative perspective on these questions by emphasizing the ethics that motivate people to give their time and labor to the project of building a mediated community. The Romanian women who volunteer at Radio Maria Transylvania say that the station "runs on love," which validates their unremunerated work there as an act of piety and a sacrifice made willingly to aid in the salvation of others. However, their investment of time and energy in the radio station is also sometimes read by family members as a disinvestment of love in the home and family; weighing the needs of one's immediate family community against those of the larger mediated community of Radio Maria is thus a delicate balance. The appeal of the latter, of course, is that it is a *catholic* love that is imagined as transcendent—a sentiment that seems to be encoded in the very name of the child sponsorship charity Unbound. Unbound's CEO describes the organization's members as a part of a "prophetic community" whose goal is to transcend divisions of nationality, culture, and class (Kaell, this volume: 95). The organization aspires to the creation of a community bound by ties of intimacy, but dispersed around the world, and various discursive formations and materializations of love become the way of doing so. These essays prompt us to examine not just how media shapes the social dynamics of a community, but also to look at how media might enable them to enact the values that drive people to participate in them in the first place.

In sum, discourses around the notion of community are complicated when we look at the roles of media and mediation in contemporary Catholic life. Mediated and mediatized communities may strive for the ideal of the sacramental community and be conceptualized as a means to construct parallel structures of belonging; in this regard, they are subject to some of the same social and ideological dynamics of the monastic community. Nonetheless, the fact that they are mediated and mediatized, and not the total institutions that monasteries strive to be, also means that they have their own unique qualities that are worth exploring.

The Screen: Communication and Obstruction

When a young woman took her vows to become an Augustinian nun, she did so with the understanding that her life would henceforth be separate from those of her loved ones outside of the monastery. Once a year, though, she was permitted a visit with her family in a specially designed parlor that was divided in half by a wooden screen. The nun sat on one side of the room and her natal family sat on the other. Like the cloister's walls, the screen's primary function was to mark a separation between the physical worlds of the two parties; but the screen was designed in such a way to allow some light and sound to move from one side to the other. As in old-fashioned confessional booths, the screen at once encouraged a particular form of communication even as it unquestionably enforced a physical and symbolic separation of the people on either side of it. The screen was literally a mediator between the nun and her kin, standing between them to at once keep them apart and enable them to communicate through the cruciform holes carved into it.

It is no difficult leap of the imagination to connect the dual function of the cloistered nuns' screen to the ambivalent role of television, computer, and smartphone screens in our contemporary society. Our electronic screens are at once facilitators of mediated communication and often discursively framed as impediments to "real" communication between co-present social actors. Conjure to mind, for example, the last editorial cartoon you saw featuring a stereotypical millennial hunched over their cell phone, or that student in your class whose eyes are fixated on a soft glow emanating from just below their desktop. For as hard as it is to undersell the importance of electronic screens in managing communication across physical and temporal distances, the sense that they are also impediments to other, more "authentic" forms of communication lingers. This may not be a bug so much as a feature, though, since as Kaell succinctly states, "[m]ediation is as much about blockage as it is about transmission and connection" (this volume: 111). Put more concretely, as Katherine Dugan suggests, the efficacy of media may lie precisely in how certain technologies can facilitate intimacy precisely because of the layer of anonymity they provide, so that affective proximity and social distance might in fact be mutually constitutive for members of online groups. A critical examination of mediation thus needs to contend with both the promise that media hold for bridging across distance, and how their material forms may limit the shape that those transmissions and connections can take. Questions about who gets to speak, what they can say, and how they can say it are of course important here; but so are questions about whom is addressed and to what ends. How are mediating forms implicated in the production and maintenance of hierarchies? Or might they rather be important for dissolving and substituting them with other arrangements of social influence and power? Might we also find that cellular screens (whether monastic or the kind made out of LCDs) also work to facilitate affective states such intimacy, passion, awe, fear, or suffering?

Kaell's essay makes these themes explicit in its discussion of how the ideal of love is materialized in childhood sponsorship. Kaell argues that while USA Catholics' childhood sponsorship projects are discursively framed as enabling the circulation of love, it is actually money and material objects that move between persons in its network. Unbound's employees work hard to elide that fact, though, because the American sponsors upon whom the whole enterprise depends tend to associate money and consumer goods with greed and materialism, rather than care or love. From the organization's perspective, to focus on the material is to potentially raise feelings of guilt over the evident inequalities between sponsors and those they are meant to be loving. And yet, people on either side of that exchange seem to long for personalized connections concretized through the exchange of cards and small gifts. As an organization, Unbound has to manage which material forms are deemed appropriate media for personal connection and love, and which seem to dangerously shift the relation to one of economic dependency. Connections between donors and recipients of aid cannot exist independent of mediating objects, but those mediating forms also trouble the idealized ethical and moral stances that child sponsorship is meant to exemplify. The flow of love, that is to say, can get jammed up when it takes concrete form.

Hoenes del Pinal's work with Guatemalan Catholics suggests, however, that technological constraints need not be a bad thing. He argues that lay leaders use marked genres of speech and music in their radio broadcasts to evoke specific ritual contexts, effectively exploiting the inherent technical limitations of an audio-only medium to both establish their religious authority and prompt their listeners to project themselves into the sensoria of Guatemalan Catholic life. Perhaps more dramatically, when faced with a public health crisis that prevented in-person religious gatherings in 2020, they turned to internet videos in the hope that this medium could synchronize the experiences of presence for people in distinct places. The hope was that "live" streaming video would enable some of the Eucharistic mystery of the Mass to be transmitted when co-present participation in ritual was not possible. In these cases, media technologies are not just deemed adequate to the task of communication, but were also understood as having the potential to radically expand the Church's work beyond people's immediate physical contexts.

Marc Roscoe Loustau, writing about Radio Maria Transylvania, notes that his interlocutors likewise see the potential for radio broadcasts to do the work of evangelization in multiple ways. Women tell stories about how exposure to Catholic radio broadcasts at home prepares their otherwise recalcitrant husbands to be open to the possibilities of the miraculous when they are working abroad. By familiarizing their husbands with the "rhythm and flow of the Mass" (Loustau, this volume: 89), these volunteers begin a process of evangelization that they hope will eventually be completed by the efforts of their counterparts working at other Radio Maria stations throughout Europe. The notion that this kind of "soft evangelization" can be transformative extends beyond individuals as well, so that volunteer work in the service of Catholic "love" may itself be a medium for re-negotiating the nature of labor and bureaucracy in a post-Soviet world, even if this may also come at the perceived cost of neglecting domestic responsibilities.

These ambiguities can also be located in larger overarching processes related to mediatization. The "celebrified" Catholics who are the subjects of Julius Bautista's study, for example, are acutely aware of the double bind presented by having their images and words widely circulated by the news media. If, on the one hand, that circulation is potentially a means for advancing their visions of positive transcendent values (i.e., justice and piety), on the other hand, it risks what they do being misinterpreted (i.e., seeing the spokesperson as the locus of suffering) or attracting the wrong kind of attention (i.e., people wanting to emulate pious acts to gain glory for themselves instead of God).

Finally, a different kind of ambiguity of the screen is highlighted by Thomas Csordas's discussion of the films about exorcism. *The Devil and Father Amorth* (2017) in particular stands out because it is directed and narrated by William Friedkin, who also directed the fictional film *The Exorcist* (1973). Though the newer film is as a documentary and the earlier one is an adaptation of a novel, Friedkin discusses the two films as part of a single trajectory that collapses the distinction between the factual and the fictional, with the fictional work positioned as a theological treatise of sorts and the documentary its hermeneutic sequel. The form of the medium, too, leaves ambiguous the nature about what is and isn't recorded by the film. In particular, a climactic encounter that is said to have happened between the filmmaker and a possessed woman is narrated in his voice, but their bodies are not actually shown on screen, creating a sense of indeterminacy about how exactly (and perhaps even if) the event actually unfolded. Moreover, inasmuch as the televisual format enables some of this slippage and ambiguity, Csordas also argues that exorcism itself may be understood as a kind of medium between two very distinct apprehensions of reality—one in which affliction is due to demons and one in which biomedical factors can be used to explain it.

The Reliquary: Materiality and Embodiment

In the historic chapel of the Monastère des Augustines, there is a room containing a display of reliquaries. These ornate vessels of silver, gold, and glass, ornamented with jewels, house the bones of saints and blessed Catholics—the physical traces of lives given over to and elevated by faith. Part of that collection includes a silver bust of Jean de Brébeuf that contains the right half of his skull. Born in France in the waning years of the sixteenth century, Jean de Brébeuf traveled to the new world as a Jesuit missionary and worked to evangelize the Wyandot (Wendat or Huron) nation. Like other missionaries of his time, de Brébeuf's work drew him to conduct linguistic and proto-ethnological research, and he is credited with writing the first Wendat-French dictionary and sometimes dubbed Canada's first ethnographer. The Catholic Church recognizes de Brébeuf and seven other Jesuits who died following a Haudenosaunee (Iroquois) raid on their mission as martyrs, and canonized them in 1930. That version of the story, of course, minimizes the Catholic Church's responsibility in sustaining the French settler-colonial project that has killed or otherwise harmed countless indigenous people over the course of the last five centuries through disease, warfare, economic exploitation, the residential school system, and myriad other forms of violence, abuse, and discrimination.

Mediation cannot exist independent of the material conditions under which it is produced, and these in turn are dependent on bodily human action. At once portable, opulent, and grotesque, reliquaries are a distinctly Catholic medium that serve as a handy metonym for examining the material and embodied dimensions of media and mediation. Reliquaries and their contents invite us to examine the excesses of meaning that emerge at the border of the mundane and transcendent. Their peculiar combination of precious metals, ordinary materials such as linen and wood, the detrita of corpses, and the narrative elaboration of the mythical figures for whom they stand, prompt us to ask about how specific forms of media and logics of mediation work to create and maintain regimes of meaning and value.

The reliquary is a central theoretical metaphor for mediation in Elayne Oliphant's essay examining the New York Metropolitan Museum's 2018 *Heavenly Bodies* exhibition in which high fashion clothing was presented alongside historical Catholic artworks. Oliphant draws on art historian Cynthia Hahn's idea of the "reliquary effect" (Hahn 2017), by which she means that objects acquire value and meaning precisely because of the material excess of their containers. The bone fragments within these boxes become objects of wonder and mediators of divine presence, not because of any inherent quality, but rather because of the way they are contextualized and displayed (and we would hasten to add that hagiographies might likewise be understood as narrative ornamentations of relics). *Heavenly Bodies* essentially presented the commercial clothing items as though they were relics, an effect further compounded by the sense of reverence the names of famous designers elicit from fashionistas. Reliquaries, museums, and other similar containers that purport to contain the extraordinary operate according to a shared baroque logic in which excess itself is a value.

But what of those people whom the relic metonymically represents? Are saints themselves also a sort of media? It is something commonplace in the study of contemporary religion to note that media celebrities are practically beatified and sanctified by their fans, blurring the line between what is entertainment and what is religion (the cult of Elvis would be a prime example).[5] Julius Bautista's essay turns that relationship on its head, examining instead what it means for religious actors to be accorded high levels of media visibility and popularity (i.e., celebrity status) as an unintended consequence of their devotional labor. The ideal of pious suffering links the cases of a Filipino layman who practices self-mortification during an annual Passion play and an East Timorese bishop known for his political advocacy for work. Do these persons become visible as celebrities because they are exemplary Catholics, or does the fact that they are afforded attention make them increasingly visible and thus *appear* to be exemplary Catholics? In the case of the Passion player, the fear that others might seek to emulate him in search of fame and not due to a sense of piety must be weighed against his continued public mortifications. In the case of the bishop, the political value of the international attention his persona brings to the cause of East Timorese independence must be constantly redirected lest the attention become about *him* and not those he purports to represent. In both cases, Jesus is invoked as a model for how to at once be Christ and superstar, how to both suffer and be celebrated. Kaell's essay likewise discusses how the story of Unbound's founder's walking pilgrimages act as an embodied mediation of the organization's ideal that international charity facilitates care across transnational borders.

Finally, in the films Csordas discusses, we see certain Catholic priests emerge as extraordinary figures because of their uncanny ability to mediate between the holy and the demonic, as well as between the natural and supernatural (and, of course, the fact that they are featured on film also lends them some of the transcendent quality as celebrities.)

Kristin Norget addresses a similar dynamic, examining how the Peruvian state draws on the logic of the miraculous to legitimize its political authority. The portable medium here is not the reliquary, but rather a *santo*—El Señor de los Milagros—whose annual procession through Lima leads him to "visit" with both secular and religious authorities. This painted image of El Señor is accorded a sense of agency and animacy (as are other *santos* throughout Latin America), making them part of a larger discursive mode and behavioral logic that Norget calls "*lo milagroso*" or "the miraculous" (this volume, 173). In this case, however, the interactions between state functionaries and the *santo* are not merely interactions between human agents and an object. Rather, as she argues, the ritualized interaction is the medium through which mundane and otherworldly powers are entangled, and so the *santo* becomes an embodiment of the nation, effectively uniting the political and the miraculous in a theopolitics of the state.

As Oliphant notes, "human-material encounters are dialectical processes that form and shape both actors in a variety of ways, according to the particular contexts and communities in which these encounters occur" (this volume: 156–57). Material encounters and concerns are raised in several of the essays. Both Lado and Hoenes del Pinal note the material and monetary implications of Catholic institutions opting to use relatively inexpensive and hence accessible transistor-based media (radio) versus relatively more expensive digital platforms. One of Lado's interlocutors says, "[Internet] connection is too expensive to be used for something you can get at Mass" (Lado, this volume: 68), implying that there may be multiple regimes of value, and that people make calculated decisions about when it is worth it to use media. Such concerns seem to be less present for Dugan's interlocutors in the United States, for whom access to an internet connection through portable devices is much less likely to be a financial burden.

The Signature: Authority and Authorization

The Monastery historical trust maintains a collection of documents chronicling the Augustinian sisters' work and collective memory in a modern, climate-controlled archive built near the old cellars. Included in that collection is the original charter that Sœurs Marie de Saint-Ignace Guenet, Marie de Saint-Bonaventure Forestier, and Anne de Saint-Bernard Le Cointre carried from northern France to Québec in 1639. At the bottom right corner of that charter sit the signature and seal of King Louis XIV of France. There is, of course, nothing inherently spectacular about the signature or seal, but when the staff pointed them out to our group there was a palpable sense of excitement as we crowded around the table to get a closer look. Our shared cultural frame gave these curved ink lines and the blot of wax impressed with a shield and fleur-de-lys a tremendous sense of meaning. Someone viewing the same signature and seal in the seventeenth century would have of course accorded it a different set of meanings and authority than we did in the twenty-first century (or perhaps they would have dismissed it entirely if our prospective viewer was Wyandot and did not recognize themselves as subject to it). Nonetheless, the royal signature and seal are a useful metaphor through which we can think through questions of authority, authorization, and authorship.

These issues may be especially important to Catholics' media practices since arguably one thing that distinguishes Catholic Christianity at the global level from other forms is its "highly centralized 'infallible' core" which nonetheless also seems to be tolerant of local particularity and difference (Mayblin et al. 2017: 7). How, then, does the authority of Roman Catholic Church's ecclesiastic hierarchy assert itself through practices of mediation? Alternately, how might grassroots media practices articulate with official institutional ones? By drawing on the hierarchy's authorizing symbols and practices to co-opt its power? Or might there be ways in which media facilitate the creation of parallel forms of authority that challenge those of the institutional hierarchy? How do practices and ideologies coalesce to establish authoritative forms in the first place? Moreover, how might the legacy of the Catholic Church's long history of involvement in establishing and buttressing political regimes be productively explored through our focus on media?

The role of the Catholic hierarchy in shaping media practices can be seen most clearly in Ludovic Lado's chapter. He notes that the Second Vatican Council described the media as "gifts of God" in 1965, and that subsequently the institutional Catholic Church has guided local churches to adopt various media technologies (Lado, this volume: 59). Yet Lado also shows that despite that dictum, exactly how they should do so seems to be an open question. If Chadian Catholic radio is backed by the institutional Church, it is also clear that the people who operate the station prefer to authorize their status on the airwaves as broadcasters serving a broad public interest, rather than as evangelists for a particular religious viewpoint. That response might seem counterintuitive to the workers of Radio Maria Transylvania, for whom evangelization is precisely the point and what commits them to their volunteer work at the station. Moreover, though their work is aimed at a local audience, its authority stems from the fact that their station is part of a transnational radio network.

Mediated authority might also be construed at a more intimate and local level, a point that is especially salient when we turn our eyes and ears toward lay people's own media products and practices. Dugan's case study makes it abundantly clear that social media, with its ideal of peer-to-peer connectivity, facilitates the construction of horizontal forms of authority that may refer to the Church's hierarchy, but which essentially exist independently of it. These horizontal forms of authority, though, are also invested in establishing their own distinctions between heterodox and orthodox practices. Hoenes del Pinal's discussion of how indigenous lay leaders use radio shows that these forms of authority also depend on culturally specific ideas about who wields it and how it can be enacted.

Although Pentecostal and Charismatic deliverance ministries around the world are arguably the places where demonic affliction is most often treated in the modern world, in popular media Roman Catholic priests seem to have the unique authority to exorcise evil spirits. How that sense of authority is constructed is taken up in Thomas Csordas's essay. There we see the interplay between the priest as a particular kind of authority on evil whose expertise is in part construed by how media producers (be they television journalists or documentarians) place them in dialogue with other experts on affliction such as psychotherapists. The televisual language of cinéma verité, while not necessarily endorsing the existence of demons, nonetheless poses their ontological reality as a possibility at least as worthy of consideration as that of psychological distress and neurological disorder. The exorcism itself, Csordas contends, becomes a mediator for competing understandings of reality—one in which extraordinary distress can be traced to personal traumas or physiological disorders, and one in which it is extraordinary precisely because it is self-evidently diabolic.

In a similar vein, the circumstances of suffering and pain experienced by the subjects of Bautista's essay make them particular kinds of authorities on piety. The raw physical suffering that the Filipino Passion player experiences allows him to act as a mediator between his community and the divine, making him an authority in soteriological matters. It also makes him an object of intense public interest, which he worries might ultimately undercut the efficacy of his devotional work if it attracted people who seek to emulate him because of his fame rather than because of a sense of devotion to God. Conversely, the increased international media attention that Bishop Belo received after being awarded the Nobel Peace Prize facilitated his ability to expand recognition for the suffering East Timorese masses, whom he discursively constructed as the real recipients of the international prize and media attention that comes with it.

The themes of how Catholicism and nominally secular regimes of powers are mutually constitutive are most evident in Kristin Norget and Elayne Oliphant's essays. Norget draws on Giorgio Agamben's ideas about sovereignty and theopolitical power to argue that a Catholic national *santo* participates directly in the construction of Peruvian political power. She examines several episodes when the *santo* meets the state's political representatives, and the public talk that emerged after the latter made gaffes in their interactions, to show that El Señor de los Milagros is a medium through which the sovereign power of the state is legitimized, even if this legitimation is only partial and impermanent. State functionaries who wish to maintain their authority must interact appropriately with the *santo* during these public spectacles, effectively linking their political authority to the transcendent power of the miraculous saint. Here the *santo* himself is the arbiter of all solicitations for legitimation, and yet certain heads of state or of the church can be seen to attempt to mediate him directly, appropriating his miraculous aura for the sake of vindicating themselves or their political position. Elayne Oliphant's chapter, meanwhile, argues that by juxtaposing haute couture and historic Catholic media (which included paintings, sculptures, ceremonial artifacts, and the physical plant of the Met Cloisters museum, which is constructed out of the pieces of several medieval French cloisters), the *Heavenly Bodies* exhibit effectively legitimized the systems of economic and political inequalities that characterize late capitalism. The arrangement of objects effectively "Catholicizes" the high-priced fashion consumer goods, lending them some of the mystique of the Catholic Church's sacramental and hierarchical authority. By treating these clothing items not simply as components of a wardrobe, but rather as quasi-sacred artifacts, the exhibit naturalized an economic system in which rare and largely unattainable consumer products become objects to be revered and understood as indexes of a self-authorizing regime of cultured taste. We might also cite a similar dialectic at play at Radio Maria Transylvania where the slippage between the logics of a professionalized workplace and that of an evangelizing mission is underwritten by the ideal that those who work at the station perform their bureaucratic duties out of a sense of unselfish love for others, and as such do not expect the pay that such labor would entail elsewhere.

Voices: Singing and Silence

Each morning the Augustinian sisters gather in the chapel to sing vespers. There are far fewer of them today than there had been in decades and centuries that came before, but what they do is understood as essentially the same—they coordinate their individual voices and talents to make a unified statement of faith. Collective singing, whether in church or elsewhere, is a profoundly social human achievement that depends on intricate interpersonal and intersubjective coordinations of voices, and its result is always something that evinces a surplus beyond what each singer could do individually, but which can nonetheless only exist when each member of the choir fully "lends" their voice to the project.

While the sisters are singing in the chapel, hotel guests at the Monastère des Augustines eat their breakfasts silently in the restaurant. The restaurant's policy during this meal is a nod to the tradition of the nuns eating in silence, and ostensibly enforced so that guests may begin their days in peaceful reflection—a mode of behavior that is discursively framed as vanishly rare in our media-saturated age. However, as nostalgic and reverential as the image is of Augustinian nuns eating their simple meals in collective quietude and contemplating their works and faith may be, there is an important elision there. It was not historically the case that silence actually predominated in the convent's dining room; rather, meals were accompanied by the sound of the voice of a single nun who read out loud and offered discourses on theological issues setting out for her sisters the subjects for their reflection. That is to say that silent reflection was cultivated as a disciplined response to a specific mediated practice—namely, the lecture— which set the terms for what the nuns ought to reflect upon, what they ought to pray about, and ought to continue to inspire their pious lifestyle.

These dynamics of voices collected, amplified, and muted are worth bearing in mind in our studies of Catholic media practices. Whose voices, exactly, are permitted in the Catholic mediascape? What are the social, political, and economic dynamics that create the conditions for some voices to thrive? And how might this also be predicated on suppressing others or subsuming them in service of a larger collective voicing? What do the voices of individuals and collectivities ultimately contribute to the affective power of the religious media? Concomitantly, what value might be found in silences and absences?

Edited volumes are certainly not the same thing as choirs, but they do share the quality of bringing together disparate voices with their own tones and timbres to produce something more than themselves. We hope that this collection of essays will illuminate the distinctiveness of Catholic media and Catholics' thinking about mediation that our authors have set out to document. We recognize that the asymmetry of our respective positions (which are of course not borne of monastic rank but rather the mediatized form of our interaction through the printed word) allows us authors to speak and enforces a kind of silence on you, our readers. We hope that your silence will be only temporary and that what we say here will generate new thinking about global Catholic media. What have we not engaged with here sufficiently? Whose voices need to be added to the study of Catholic mediation? What have we left unsaid that must be said? Our intention is that this volume can serve as a critical starting point for larger discussions and further debates that we have not yet imagined.

Notes

1   Proposals for this monumental event include the advent of print in the sixteenth century (McLuhan 1964; Anderson 1983), industrial mass production in the nineteenth, and the explosion of electronic communications technologies in the twentieth (see Hoover 2006: 26–7).

2   Related terms such as "medialization," "mediazation," and "the mediatic turn," as well as their various imperfect translations into languages other than English, could also be listed as part of this semantic cluster, though as scholar of communication Sonia Livingstone argues the proliferation of terms seems to further muddle, rather than clarify, our shared objects of study (2009). On the distinction between these terms of art, see Hjarvard (2011), Couldry and Hepp (2013), and Krüger (2018).

3   Livingstone breaks down the distinction between terms somewhat differently than we have, noting that scholars of communication have tended to use "mediation" to talk about situational influence of media, and thus that term is better suited for analyzing the micro-social processes; whereas "mediatization" has more commonly been used to account for media's historical influences, and is thus more useful for talking about macrosocial processes. Nonetheless, she argues, an etymological archaeology of these terms should lead scholars to a broader conceptualization of "mediation" as a term that can encompass these and other uses to avoid confusion.

Others have argued that it is necessary to preserve the distinction between the terms, if only to highlight their complementarity (Hepp 2013).

4   In fact an important service that the Augustinians rendered to Québec was to take in unwanted babies, and the cloister had a special contraption built through which people could hand over infants to the nuns' care without either party seeing the other.

5   For an example of this line of thinking, see Doss (2005).

1

Mediatizing Holy Week: Guatemalan Catholic Experiments with Radio and Facebook

Eric Hoenes del Pinal

Introduction

Guatemala's *Semana Santa* (Holy Week) processions dramatizing the Passion narrative—beginning with Jesus's arrival in Jerusalem, his Calvary march, crucifixion, and ultimate resurrection on Easter Sunday—are spectacularly colorful events. Pictures of men dressed in purple robes girded with golden cords and carrying massive biers upon which stand carved images of Jesus stand circulate widely on postcards, tourism promotions, and have been featured in the pages of *National Geographic* (Scofield 1960).

One of the most distinctive features of these ritual events is the intricate and colorful *alfombras* ("rugs") that carpet the streets over which the processions pass. These rugs are painstakingly created by carefully arranging piles of vibrantly dyed sawdust into decorative filigrees, stars, diamonds, flowers, and sometimes even portraits of Jesus. For all the care put into them, though, alfombras are evanescent testaments to the devotional labor of Catholics in Guatemala (Peña 2011). People spend hours making alfombras, often working through the night as a way of paying homage and showing faithfulness to the *santos* (the saints) who will pass over them. Yet, as soon as the lumbering processions arrive, accompanied as they are by the pomp of a brass band, the explosions of fireworks, and the pungent scent of incense, the alfombras are obliterated. The shuffling feet of the penitent *cucuruchos*[1] drag the sawdust with them transforming the delicate beauty of contrasting colors and shapes into a muddled blur. Later on, the steps of spectators and passing dogs, the treads of automobile tires, and the wind will further scatter the sawdust until some neighbor—very often one of the people who helped arrange the alfombra—will take a broom and bucket of water to the street sending its remnants streaming in a mottled rivulet to the nearest curbside drain.

The delicate fragility of the alfombras seems like an apt metaphor for the processions rituals themselves—painstakingly prepared, spectacular and vibrant for a time, and rapidly dissolved, leaving only the faintest traces of their existence after they have passed. Even though these rituals happen year after year and though their anachronistic aesthetics (e.g., the cucuruchos' decidedly non-modern robes, the faux Roman armor worn by other penitents, and the kinds of music played) lend the events a sort of timelessness, there is a sense of contingency and uncertainty inherent to them every year due to the tremendous amount of resources—both human and material—that need to come together just so to successfully perform them. Over the course of the two decades that I have known and worked with lay Catholics in a parish I call San Felipe,[2] I have heard people wax nostalgic about how the processions used to command wider participation and the difficulties they now face due to dwindling interest. On the other hand, the rituals themselves have largely been resilient, occurring yearly despite changing demographics, political economies, and tastes.

Arguably the accessibility of new forms of communication media plays a role (if not always a straightforward or predictable one) in their endurance and ineffability. While the alfombras themselves are evanescent and meant to be dissolved, their impressions are preserved and circulated beyond their time and place. Guatemalan Catholics do not simply build alfombras and carry saints over them; they also produce, consume, and circulate images of themselves and their co-religionists doing so. By producing and sharing those images, they engage in a process of mediatization in so far as their attempts to capture elements of their religious lives in portable and easily digestible snapshots lead them to adjusting their practices in anticipation of the technological and aesthetic exigencies of modern media-saturated culture (Hjarvard 2013).

The experience of evanescence in ritual is not confined to the colorful sawdust and passing processions, but occurs in other media and ritual spaces, which draw on similar kinds of expertise, expectations, and even concerns about ritual efficacy. In this essay I will explore how San Felipe's Catholics have used communications media—specifically FM radio and Facebook—to manage their celebrations of Lent and Holy Week; in doing so I hope to show how practices of mediatization help offset the contingencies and uncertainties of performing these rites in contemporary Guatemala. Specifically, I will be analyzing two distinct moments when members of the parish used communications media to manage the precarities of Catholic ritual life. The first of these is how the parish

Hermandad (a lay sodality dedicated to the veneration of an image of Jesus) used FM radio broadcasts during Lent in 2005 to manage worries about low turnout to the processions. The second is how the parish used social media and internet streaming video during Lent 2020 to manage a prohibition on public events due to public health risks posed by the novel coronavirus (Covid-19) pandemic. Before doing this, though, a few words about the parish in its national and historical context.

San Felipe's mission since the mid-1970s has been to serve Q'eqchi'-Mayas living in rural and peri-urban areas around the city of Cobán, Alta Verapaz.[3] This region of Guatemala is notable as a place that experienced a "peaceful conquest" in the sixteenth century, meaning that indigenous people there were made subjects of the Spanish empire at the hands of Dominican priests under the command of Bartolome de las Casas, rather than those of Spanish soldiers under the command of the infamous Pedro de Alvarado. Though using this terminology and adopting its discursive framing occludes much of the real violence and suffering that colonization nonetheless entailed there, it is useful to mention because the ideal of a missionary church situated at the borderlands of indigenous and creole worlds figures prominently into the Diocese of the Verapaz's current self-conceptualization. In the twentieth century the combined force of the Second Vatican Council, the advent of Latin American liberationist theology, and the emergence of Maya cultural activism following the country's bloody civil war led local clergy to make concerted efforts to create an "inculturated" Catholicism (i.e., one whose practices respect indigenous cultures and lifeways while being consistent with Catholic theology).[4] Within the context of the modern Diocese of the Verapaz, parishes like San Felipe are conceived as fundamentally formed by the legacy of sixteenth-century missionary efforts and the aims of twentieth-century "inculturationist" Catholicism. San Felipe's leadership—both clerical and lay—orient themselves toward promoting a distinctly Q'eqchi'-Maya Catholic sensibility, although of course exactly what that means has shifted over time (Hoenes del Pinal 2016).

Material factors compound the ideological orientation toward indigenous lay leadership. The parish is large, with much of its population living outside of the urban area in small villages and hamlets dispersed over roughly 60 square miles of mountainous terrain with poor infrastructure. Parishioners tend to be small-scale agriculturalists, and most are relatively cash poor making travel into the city for weekly Masses unfeasible for many. To compensate for this, priests travel to the communities under their care regularly, but may only visit some of them two or three times per year. Absent regular contact with clergy and participation in the Eucharist, most parishioners' religious lives revolve around the weekly lay-led "Celebrations of the Word" held in each of the parish's 122 ecclesial base communities (CEBs, by the Spanish *comunidades eclesiales de base*). Taken together, the ideological emphasis on Q'eqchi'-Mayas' distinct religious sensibilities and the material conditions of the parish mean that there is a strong emphasis on lay leadership in religious life and, to invoke the theological language that predominates there, the clergy strives "accompany" parishioners as they become "protagonists" of their own spiritual lives. What that means, however, is far from fixed as various actors within the parish (clergy, lay leaders, and regular parishioners) and on its peripheries (the Diocesan leadership, for example) each have their own take on what exactly it means to be Q'eqchi'-Maya and Catholic.

I now turn to two ethnographic vignettes that illustrate how San Felipe has mobilized communications media to manage difficulties in celebrating Lent and Holy Week.

2005: Calling Out to Penitents Not Pentecostals

On Tuesday and Thursday evenings during Lent 2005 a handful of the San Felipe Hermandad's (lay sodality) leaders (pl. *qawachineb'*, sing. *qawachin*) met in front of the offices of Estéreo Gerardi[5]—an FM radio station owned by the Diocese of the Verapaz that broadcasts out of the second floor of the eighteenth-century Dominican monastery in the center of town. With the help of one of the station's regular employees they would broadcast a live hour-long show that consisted of procession music, a Bible reading, a short sermon, prayer, and repeated pleas to its audience to remember their duties as Catholics during Lent and into Holy Week. The ostensive purpose of these broadcasts was to offer Q'eqchi'-Maya Catholics outside of the city, but within the broadcast range of Estéreo Gerardi, a means of marking Lent. The program called on parishioners to be mindful of their moral lives during this special time and to prepare themselves for the pious activities of Semana Santa. They reminded people to get organized, pool their CEB's resources, and send representatives with their community's monetary donations and confirmation of participation for the processions to the parish center.

As I have discussed in more depth elsewhere, although the processions had been successful in previous years and there was a reasonable expectation that they would be again, there was nonetheless a sense of uncertainty about them that the Hermandad's lay leadership sought to mitigate by broadcasting their program (Hoenes del Pinal 2019). That uncertainty was borne of major changes in Guatemala's religious landscape since the 1980s which saw Catholicism's near monopoly challenged by the explosive growth of Evangelical and Pentecostal Christianity. In the early 2000s these worries were compounded in San Felipe by the emergence of Catholic Charismatic groups whose members retained affiliation with the Catholic parish but practiced a Pentecostalized form of the religion that was aesthetically quite different from the norm and who abstained from participation in rituals they deemed too tainted by "tradition," which included the processions (Hoenes del Pinal 2017). The Hermandad chose radio as a medium for addressing the issue of (potentially) low participation because it was the one type of mass media they could count on to reach their audience, as well as because the form played to their particular strengths as lay Catholic leaders. The qawachineb' cannily used this audio-only channel of mass-mediated communication to evoke the larger world of Catholic practice banking on the idea that they could elicit certain affective dispositions in their listeners by marshalling specific discursive and aesthetic resources.

As John Peters notes in his historical study of the idea of communication, "Broadcasters, if not quite audience blind, see their audiences through a glass darkly" (Peters 1999: 210). Nonetheless it is also truism that radio broadcasters imagine their audiences in particular ways, and that much of what makes for successful radio talk is a performer's ability to interpellate their addressees into particular regimes of interpretation and understanding—what Erving Goffman calls "frame spaces"—through verbal artfulness (Goffman 1981: 230). A person speaking into a radio microphone can skillfully manage their footing[6] through talk to elicit specific affective responses from listeners across distances and in doing so manage their emotional and intellectual response to the broadcast. Media scholars and linguistic anthropologists have noted that radio personalities can produce a sense of intimacy and solidarity between them and their listeners despite the obvious fact that everything else about the context of their communication that would seem to work against that—for example, the lack of physical co-presence and hence absence of embodied contextualization cues, the one-sided nature of the talk, the grain that modulated frequency transmissions and the quality of the output devices (i.e., the radio's speakers) gives the human voice, its commercial nature, etc. (Scannell 1991; Woolard 1995; Rubino 2016).

The Hermandad's qawachineb' may not have been media professionals, but they did possess certain linguistic skills by virtue of the other roles they played in local religious hierarchy that they could draw on to make their radio speech persuasive. All but one of the men were active catechists in the parish, and the sole exception had formerly been one.[7] Although in many Catholic contexts catechists are understood as primarily exercising a vocation of pedagogy (i.e., teaching the principles of the catechism to children and converts), it is not uncommon for indigenous catechists in Latin America to constitute a kind of organic intelligentsia who play a key role in guiding community life (Wilson 1995; Orta 2004; Chojnacki 2010; Gunderson 2010). The Q'eqchi' term for catechist—*aj tzolotij*—carries sense of someone who teaches Catholic doctrine[8] and in San Felipe they are indeed responsible for preparing members of their community to receive the sacraments of baptism, first communion, and marriage. However, catechists' main duty in San Felipe is to organize, lead, and most importantly "animate" the weekly "Celebration of the Word" (Sp. *Celebración de la Palabra*, Q'. *xNimqehinkil li raatin*) that is the de facto central ritual event for most parishioners. Speech is critical for cultivating animacy in these rituals, and a good catechist must be a skillful speaker. It is not surprising then that the qawachineb' drew on the oral skillset they had developed in their other roles as catechists when performing on the radio.

The qawachineb' employed many of the same verbal markers and discourse strategies that they used in Celebrations of the Word to project a sense of religious authority on the radio program. This was most evident during the short sermons that anchored the program in which they used the same prosodic and poetic features of speech that they would have at a Celebration of the Word—notably a slow and deliberate cadence, line parallelism, and strict Q'eqchi' code consistency. By using this register they evoked the frame space of the weekly Catholic ritual and engaged with their radio listeners as if they were members of the same congregation. Although otherwise stripped of visual, spatial, embodied, and material contextual markers, this form of speech was recognizable as a performance of a familiar and valued genre, one that indexed the speaker as a member of the parish hierarchy with sufficient institutional authority to direct his audience to participate in the Hermandad's Lent project. It was important, too, that the radio program featured several distinct voices and not just that of the catechist giving the sermon, since Catholic rituals tend to be polyvocal, with different actors playing distinct parts in them. As in Celebrations of the Word, the Bible readings that preceded the sermon and the prayers that followed it were performed by someone other than the sermonist, all of which gave the radio broadcast a similar sense of community participation. This is not to say that the radio program strove to reproduce these other rituals exactly— that would have been impossible given the strictures of the format—, but they did evoke them in specific ways. Concomitantly, the polyvocality and use of the ritual genre marked this radio broadcast as something quite distinct from other radio programs, which more often feature only one or two distinct voices using an entirely different set of discursive forms.

One important way that the radio program differed from the CEBs' weekly events was in the music that was played during it. Guatemalan Holy Week processions are accompanied by a distinct genre of music—the *marcha funebre* or funeral march—that can best be described as a sort of symphonic dirge and which is aesthetically in keeping with a sense of mourning Jesus's death. Played by brass and woodwind instruments and featuring sweeping movements and dramatic percussive embellishments, the music is quite distinct from anything else one typically hears in Guatemala, and the sounds of this music are closely linked to the rituals. It is not music that most people listen to in their cars, hear while shopping, nor consume at any other time of the year and it is very different in instrumentation, rhythm, and tone that the hymns Catholics normally sing at Mass or Celebration of the Word. It is also a genre that is distinctly Catholic, and which sounds very much unlike the music of Pentecostals and Charismatic Catholics. Because of their close ties to a seasonal holiday, marchas funebres, not unlike Christmas carols, can elicit strong feelings of reverence and nostalgia from people for whom Semana Santa processions are an important part of devotional life.[9] Playing the recordings of the marchas funebres over the radio thus did a different kind of referential work than the qawachineb's speech in the sense that it evoked the magisterial public processions rather than the more intimate space of the CEB. Nonetheless, it served a similar function in that it evoked a larger ritual sensorium of Semana Santa with the hopes of eliciting an affective response of faithful commitment from listeners in their homes.

The goal of the Hermandad's radio show was to stoke interest in the upcoming processions and facilitate their successful performance. Radio's ubiquity made it an ideal way of communicating with people in far-flung parts of the parish, and the Hermandad's structural position within the Diocese afforded them the opportunity to lease the time to do so. FM radio's limitation of being a sound-only medium seems to have been a boon, rather than an obstacle, to their success since the Hermandad leadership could rely on their audience recognizing the specific genres of speech and music as icons of the larger symbolic regime of local Catholic practice. The cliché that radio is a "theater of the mind"[10] seems apropos here in that the qawachineb' performed and produced the show with the expectation that their audience would hear in it clearly recognizable aspects of local Catholic practice and in doing so would know how to figure themselves as pious participants in "traditional" Catholic life that was distinct from that of Pentecostals and Pentecostalized Catholics.

2020: Semana Santa Goes "Live" on Facebook

The first case of the novel coronavirus Covid-19 in Guatemala was confirmed on Friday March 13, 2020 (Escobar et al. 2020), and by the following Monday President Alejandro Giammattei, who had assumed the office just sixty-two days earlier, announced a set of governmental policies curtailing all public and private sector activities with the aim of preventing the virus's spread. The new law, which took effect the same day, included a prohibition of "events of all kinds and of whatever number of persons" including "all sporting, cultural and social activities" and "in-person religious celebrations" (Escobar 2020). The decree came during the third week of Lent, which in any other year would have been a time when Guatemalan Catholics increased their in-person religious participation. The Guatemalan Episcopal Council issued a statement the following day lamenting the situation while also affirming the state's decision to suspend in-person activities and promising that clergy would continue to accompany the people through social media (Villa y Vásquez and Calderón Cruz 2020). Initially the quarantine was set to be in effect for two weeks with the hope that that would be enough to contain the virus, but as the days passed, although the number of confirmed infections was not climbing as fast as in other countries, it soon became clear that the restrictions of human movement and gatherings would continue well past the law's original expiration date.[11] The Semana Santa processions would have to be cancelled (Associated Free Press 2020).

I would do my best to follow developments in San Felipe from my home office in North Carolina over the course of the next month. My insights in this section come from remote research that, while not ethnographic in a traditional sense, built on my prior ethnographic work in the parish and the relationships I had built face-to-face with people there over the last two decades. Julio, who I first met in Guatemala in 2004 and who was now a lay employee of the parish, confirmed to me via a Facebook Messenger text that there would be no processions this year, and added San Felipe would be closing its church to visitors for the time being. The Hermandad, which was now under different leadership than in 2005, announced via its Facebook page that they were suspending all their Lenten and Holy Week activities for the year to comply with the law. In the following weeks both the parish and the Hermandad pivoted to using Facebook and especially its live video streaming function to observe the holidays. In fact, the Hermandad's initial announcement came in the form of one such video they posted the evening of March 18 that featured the directorate of the group dressed in the cucuruchos' signature robes and headcloths standing around scale images of the santos who would have been carried in the processions. Social media offered a means for Catholics to continue celebrating Lent and Easter and allowed me to follow how they did so from afar.

San Felipe's Catholics were of course not the only ones who took to social media to continue their religious lives in the face of the public health concerns of the Covid-19 pandemic,[12] but it is perhaps surprising that a relatively marginal and cash-poor—"*humilde*" people there would say—parish oriented toward a rural constituency streamed its first Mass online several days before other more affluent parishes in the city did. They were able to do so because a member of the Hermandad's directorate offered to lend them equipment and the expertise he had accrued through his hobby taking pictures and videos of Catholic life in Cobán which he posts on a Facebook page. Although there were some technical issues with the streams (the lighting was dark, their first video is tilted 90 degrees, and music drowns out the voices of the participants for the first few minutes on another), by the time that the Vatican disseminated the text and guidelines for celebrating the "Mass in the Time of Pandemic" on March 30, San Felipe had already live-streamed three events and seemed prepared to continue doing so indefinitely.

In an interview conducted via WhatsApp (a social media platform that allows for video calls and text messaging), Julio walked me through the process that the parish had undertaken during Lent. The guiding principle behind the parish's use of Facebook was that what would be transmitted virtually should become present and immediate for congregants ("*La idea es que lo que se presente virtual se torne presencial*"). To this end, Mass would not be pre-recorded, but rather broadcast live in its entirety as it happened. This was crucial to keeping the pace of the liturgical season, highlighted the notion that even under difficult circumstances religious life progressed, and preserved some of the sense of the Eucharistic mystery even if parishioners could not actually participate in communion. Internet streaming video in this case was meant to be consumed as it happened, ideally by whole households coming together to watch the streams, with the intent of mediating two synchronous experiences of religious presence—one in the church and one in the home. However, my observations suggest that if this was their intent, the process of producing the live streams led them in other directions.

On the last Friday of Lent, San Felipe streamed a modified version of the *Via Crucis* from inside the church. A text for a modified celebration of ritual specifically addressing the Covid-19 crisis came through the institutional Church having been approved of by Pope Francis, disseminated to the Bishop, and then passed on to clergy in parishes. In the case of San Felipe there was the usual work of translation and localization to be done beforehand which included developing a language to talk about the Coronavirus in Q'eqchi'.[13] Under normal circumstances the Via Crucis ritual would have been performed in the streets near the church over the course of three or four hours in the evening; however, under the general quarantine and curfew this year it would be performed in just under an hour in the early afternoon and contained to a space in the church's nave. Instead of convening a large group of people to perform and participate in a public ritual, a small group of the parish's leadership performed it behind the church's closed doors while spectators watched remotely through their cell phone and computer screens. The parish's growing sophistication in video production was on display in the stream as the event was shot using two cameras and featured better lighting than their first experiments streaming Mass. The cameras focused on a single area just in front of the church's main altar, where five members of the parish team—the three resident clergy and two lay employees— took turns reading the stations of the cross alternating between Q'eqchi' and Spanish reflecting the parish's increasingly bilingual identity.[14] Three aspects of the stream specifically drew attention to its mediatized form. Firstly, the video opened with a carefully composed shot of the church's main crucifix and a non-diegetic soundtrack acting as a sort of title sequence. Secondly, by shooting with two cameras the stream mimicked television conventions for making "talking heads" visually interesting. Thirdly, a young woman served as a kind of host for the event and offered brief statements of introduction and closing in which she spoke directly to the camera. Importantly, in those speeches she referred to the event as a "broadcast" ("*transmisión*") rather than celebration or even just event. This is to say that the Via Crucis more so than reproducing the ritual as it might have been experienced in-person was heavily mediatized according to the conventions of television broadcasts.

The Via Crucis was framed as an important event in the parish's announcements and came at a time when people might have been looking for a sense of comfort from religion; however, there were few live viewers. As a form of social media, Facebook Live allows everyone to see who else is watching a stream, and over the course of the forty-four-minute event there were no more than eleven viewers (myself excluded) watching it at any time. Based on how many "reactions" (as displayed by thumbs up, heart, and other emojis) and comments viewers posted during the whole event there were at least twenty-seven distinct viewers. This suggests that most of the live viewers watched only parts of the entire event. Whether people tuned in casually, didn't like what they saw, or had trouble staying connected, participation in the virtual event was significantly shorter and more fragmented than it would have been in person. However, many more people watched the video after it first streamed, with Facebook registering over 350 views of the archived video by Easter Sunday. Thus, although the parish leadership's goal was to bring people in disparate places together as if they were co-present by leveraging the sociality of social media and the immediacy of video streaming, parishioners instead seem to have treated the event as a piece of televisual media to be consumed asynchronously and in isolation, rather than as a ritual in which synchronous co-presence and participation were expected. [15]

The Hermandad celebrated Semana Santa on its own Facebook page by posting a series of videos on the day on which they would have normally carried out their procession. These included short clips of processions from the previous two years, several montages of photos of their processions set to marchas funebres, and two others shot during Holy Week 2020 that bear further discussion. The first was the organization's main video commemorating the day which was composed of a single steady shot of the image of the Lord in Agony (representing Jesus's dying body after he has been removed from the cross) adorned as he might have been for a procession with the sound of a group of women praying the rosary off screen (although one does step into the frame toward the end to wave a censer over the santo). The second video was composed of a single tracking shot of a few blocks where the procession would have passed through had it been allowed. Filmed at dusk that same night one can see that people had put candles out on the sidewalk as a small act of commemoration and devotion to a santo who would not pass by there this year. These videos make clear reference to important local practices and evince some very deliberate aesthetic choices of visual composition that suggest a keen awareness of how things would look on a cellphone or computer screen, but the near absence of people visible in them also makes them uncanny representations of Catholic devotional life.

The Hermandad's videos, even more so than the parish's, augur toward a vision of religious life under the pandemic that is heavily mediatized and geared toward an understanding that for the time being religious life is anything but normal. As I write this, Lent and Holy Week have passed, although the Covid-19 crisis has not. San Felipe's experiments with social media continue and nine months later they are still streaming Mass each Sunday (with the priests sometimes wearing facemasks as a clear reminder of the ongoing pandemic). The parish has also periodically produced videos on other topics (e.g., a two-part series on the parish's history as it approaches a significant anniversary) creating a small but growing library of programming for its parishioners. In the absence of a return to in-person services, increasing numbers of parishioners seem to be watching the videos, with one stream in July (typically a time of low-attendance) registering just over 1,700 views, a number equal to the number of "Likes" their page has. The nature of the comments and shares recorded by Facebook offers evidence that San Felipe's videos are being consumed not just in Cobán, but also elsewhere in Guatemala and abroad.

The growing archive of videos preserved by Facebook shows the parish further experimenting with production values drawn from professional television production so that there is now a chyron title naming the event and location at the bottom of the screen, the camera angles change more deliberately, and the most recent videos also feature an introductory title sequence of still shots of the church's exterior with the priests' missionary order's coat of arms superimposed over them. All of this makes the streams of religious services seem more and more like commercial television broadcasts, and further evidences a mediatization of parish life. Likewise, views of the videos seem to accrue over time, and clearly not all who watch the Masses do so "live." However, the numbers who do so have increased and some participants have been trying to actively participate in the rituals through the platform's chat feature by occasionally typing an "Amén" or displaying the "praying hands" emoji at appropriate times during the streamed Mass. Nonetheless, from a distance it remains hard to gauge exactly how parishioners are engaging with either the live streams or the archive of them that is accruing in the virtual space of Facebook.

What practices may develop around video streamed Masses in the future remains to be seen, but I would hazard to guess that elements of overt mediatization will remain a feature of them. It seems likely, too, that even after the restrictions on gatherings are finally fully lifted, the streams will continue if for no other reason than to maintain contact with parishioners abroad.

Discussion

Brian Larkin reminds us that people's uses of media technologies and the meanings attached to them are products of cultural debate endemic to specific places and social dynamics and subject to change over time (Larkin 2008: 3).

Thinking about how media are incorporated into the religious life of parishes like San Felipe requires that we pay attention not just to how a specific medium is taken up by people, but also the larger political economies which enable or inhibit their use. At some point between 2005 and 2020 a watershed moment occurred that fundamentally reconfigured mass mediated communication in San Felipe from one in which it was largely a product of centralized broadcasting to one in which narrow-casted social media became more common. In 2005 radio was ubiquitous, and few parishioners consumed other forms of mass media other than it and tabloid newspapers that were as popular for their salacious photography as for their material utility as fire starters, food wrappers, and toilet paper. That was also the year the parish office got its first PC (a second-hand desktop unit) and that priests working there could access the internet from home, instead of paying by the quarter hour at internet cafes. Most parishioners then had little if any exposure to the World Wide Web and almost none had email addresses. Fifteen years later, following the expansion of cellular technology things have changed significantly. Parishioners with some means have basic smartphones on which they can access social media, although they may not always have connection privileges for them since most buy network connections *a la carte* rather than as monthly data plans. Data coverage has expanded quickly in rural areas, too, and some villages without running water have clear connections to cellular networks.

One of radio's particular strengths and the reason that the Hermandad found it such a valuable tool in 2005 was the fact that the very low cost of owning and operating a device capable of receiving an FM signal makes these devices ubiquitous. Battery-operated transistor radios have been and continue to be the one consumer electronic that one reliably finds in even the poorest of homes in Guatemala (Cojtí Cuxil 2004). The combination of the devices' low cost, the country's relatively small size, and the strategic placement of broadcast towers and repeaters on mountaintops means that 99 percent of homes in Guatemala receive radio broadcasts (Rockwell 2001: 434). If receiving radio broadcasts is uncomplicated, though, producing them requires significant resources. The Hermandad's leadership was able to disseminate its message in 2005 only because their own goals aligned with those of The Diocese of the Verapaz who had invested significant resources into production and broadcasting equipment and held an operating license from the Guatemalan government. It was telling that when San Felipe experimented with running its own radio station in 2016, financial issues caused the project to falter almost from the start and forced them shut down in less than a year (Hoenes del Pinal 2019). Although the

Hermandad's qawachineb' produced their Lenten broadcast purely voluntarily doing the work as an extension of their positions within the parish's lay hierarchy, the project interpellated them into a tightly regulated mediascape subject at one level to the Catholic Church and at another to the Guatemalan state, absent those connections they would likely have found broadcasting on the radio impossible.

Social media platforms like Facebook entail a different set of economic and regulatory relationships. The initial barrier to entry as a consumer of Facebook is significantly higher than it is for radio, as it necessitates a device with a computer processor and screen (be it a smartphone, tablet, or computer) as well as subscription to internet services of high enough quality to stream video. Moreover, to run one of these devices one needs a reliable source of electricity, which in much of the parish's territory is not a given (although the advent of relatively inexpensive solar panels is changing that). Thus, accessing internet-based media remains difficult for a large portion of the parish, even as the reach of cellular networks continues to expand. On the other hand, once those technological thresholds have been met, it is relatively easy for consumers to become producers, since many of the same devices that can be used to watch a video can also produce and disseminate one. Social media applications like Facebook are predicated on blurring the distinction between consumer and producer of media, with their appeal being that through them one does not simply access content, but also "shares" one's own. Once people within the parish began using Facebook for personal ends, they rapidly latched on to it as a tool for promoting their religious communities as well. Several of San Felipe's CEBs have their own Facebook pages on which they post event announcements, community news, and image macros (i.e., pictures or other pieces of visual artwork with a short text superimposed on top) with religious themes. When the Hermandad and parish turned to Facebook in 2020 it was a natural outgrowth of many parishioner's existing media consumption practices, and as Julio explained to me there was no real debate about which platform to use since parishioners were already familiar with and using Facebook for other ends.[16]

It is tempting to see this and laud the democratic potential of social media; however, we would be remiss if we did not also note that despite the relative ease with which social media platforms can facilitate media production and circulation, they are also proprietary products controlled by multinational corporations whose *raison d'etre* is to generate profit through ad sales. Engaging in religious rituals and maintaining a sense of religious community through that medium laminate the identity of parishioner with that of consumer. This is not, of course, to say that commercial interests aren't present in some form in religious life normally or to reify the distinction between commerce and religion—in fact, Estereo Gerardi is also partially supported by advertising. Nonetheless, it is worth pausing to reflect on how exactly these things might be entangled in this specific case. Facebook makes a profit by selling advertisements targeted to individual users based on information it collects through our devices (technically by our own consent when we register as users). To participate in religious life via Facebook is to willingly, if not necessarily wittingly, entangle one's faithfulness into the neoliberal market's web of consumption, and it is worth wondering what consequences this might have especially in light of the mounting evidence that these systems not only are vulnerable to exploitation but seem thrive on it.[17]

The decade and a half that separates these two vignettes witnessed a significant expansion of the mediascape that San Felipe's parishioners inhabit; however, the advent of Facebook has not displaced FM radio. As one of my consultants noted via Messenger, presenting events like the Via Crucis on Facebook made them accessible to people in Cobán's urban core, but they would not necessarily reach people in rural hamlets who might be experiencing the pandemic in harsher terms due to their economic precarity. To reach them the parish needed Estéreo Gerardi to simulcast the event on its FM radio signal, which they did but only after some cajoling, he later told me. This speaks to the perpetual problem of unequal access to media technologies, and in deciding how to manage this the parish's leadership had to think once again about its core mission. This also invites us to ask whose interests are served and whose sensibilities are reflected in mediatized religious practices. It is important to bear those issues in mind, even as we also note the creative potential that communications media offer Catholics for negotiating and shaping their religious practices in face of life's uncertainties, whether these are borne from changing demographics or a deadly respiratory virus. The media of Catholicism might be evanescent like sawdust alfombras and radio broadcasts, or it might be more permanent like the wooden santos and archived digital videos, but in either case the potential for shaping identities, subjectivities, and lives remains an inextricable part of their form and circulation.

Coda: A Reflection

Writing this piece has forced me to reckon with the subject of this volume not just in terms of the object of study, but also as means through which we conduct ethnographic research. I had intended to travel to Cobán for field research in 2020, but the travel restrictions put in place by the Guatemalan state and my home institution due to the Covid-19 pandemic made that impossible. Those restrictions forced me to adjust my research plans to include Facebook and WhatsApp. Until that point those platforms had been a means of keeping some contact with people in Cobán while I was in the United States, but now they have also become a source of data. While I see value in exploring how people engage with social media as part of our collective endeavor to understand the role of religion in contemporary life, I have misgivings about how doing research through social media affects this. Undoubtedly ethnographic work is always mediated, but attempting to do ethnography through something like Facebook makes it not only more overtly mediated but heavily mediatized, as well. By this I mean that instead of engaging in a co-present, intersubjective, and multisensory experience, research of this kind means that we come to know our subjects only through the tightly restricted means of what the platform shows us. While it is convenient that I can watch a Mass in San Felipe from my home office, streaming video is a poor substitute for the full sensory experience of being physically present in church. WhatsApp may enable me to interview Cobaneros from Charlotte, but it will never enable the myriad unexpected conversations that one inevitably falls into when practicing the art of "deep hanging out." Moreover, the commercial interests of these platforms are by design intrusive and meant to draw our gaze away from our interlocutors (every time I accessed Facebook to view the data that this chapter is based on a sidebar tempted me with images of products to buy), and it is clear that they are subject to commercial and political manipulations both large and small whose consequences are hard to gauge. Likewise, although, both I and my interlocutors have in principle agreed to these platforms' terms of service, I suspect we do not adequately understand them or their implications for the privacy and confidentiality of our conversations through them. I lay this out here not because I think that I have a solution to these dilemmas, but because I think that we scholars need to think more carefully about the epistemological and ethical fallout doing research in this way might have for us as we engage not just in research about mediatized religion but in mediatized research about religion.

Notes

1   This nickname for penitents refers to the style of tall, conical hat with an attached mask traditionally worn by penitents in analogous processions throughout the Hispanic world, although Catholics in Guatemala no longer wear them.

2   All personal names and toponyms below the level of Bishops, dioceses, and cities are fictitious. I have also changed a few minor details to ensure my interlocutors' privacy.

3   Cobán is *municipio*, which in the Guatemalan political system incorporates both a township and its surrounding rural areas, perhaps more akin to a county in the US system than a city.

4   For historical background on the convergence of Catholicism and Maya cultural activism, see Warren (1989), Wilson (1995), Early (2006), and Hernández Sandoval (2018). For anthropological discussion of inculturation elsewhere in the world, see Orta (2004), Chua (2012), and Loustau (2019).

5   This station is named after Juan José Gerardi Conedera (1922–98), who served as bishop of the Diocese of Verapaz between 1967 and 1974. Though he spent much of his career elsewhere, Gerardi's time in the Verapaz was crucial to him becoming an outspoken critic of the military's abuses against indigenous Guatemalans during the Civil War (1960–96). Those experiences were critical to his helping launch the *Recuperación de la Memoria Histórica* (Recovery of Historical Memory) project, which sought to collect and document Guatemalans' experiences of violence. He was assassinated on April 26, 1998, two days after the report was published, and is widely remembered as a martyr by Guatemalan Catholics today.

6   By "footing" Goffman means the alignment that speakers and addressees take viz-à-viz each other and the nature of their interaction (Goffman 1981: 128).

7   He had exercised the office for at least five years but had withdrawn himself from the position due to some personal issues that he felt would undermine his authority.

8   *Tzolok* means "to teach, study or learn," *tij* is "prayer," and the prefix *aj* designates a person who is or does that. So, a literal translation would be "a person [who] teaches prayer."

9   A sample of a marcha funebre is used in a radically different way by *The Howard Stern Show* which broadcasts on subscription-based satellite radio from New York. On that show the marcha funebre's pomp is decontextualized and exploited for comedic effect in a recurring bit in which it interrupts cast member Robin Quivers's news segments. The music made its way on to that program following Quivers's trip to Guatemala in 2010 when she encountered one of the live processions and has been used daily on the show for a decade. There, the music's religious and cultural meanings are stripped from it, and it is completely re-semiotized so that listeners of Howard Stern know it only as Quivers's theme music.

10   For the origins of this phrase and discussion of the concept as it applies to American radio, see Verma (2012: 2–7).

11   As I write this in August 2020, many of the law's provisions remain in place. Despite the governmental restrictions, repatriations of undocumented migrants who had been exposed in the United States and the inevitable movement of people meant that cases continued to climb.

12 By the time Guatemala saw its first case, Italy was already approaching 18,000
    confirmed cases and would see anywhere between 3,000 and 6,000 new cases each
    day through Easter Sunday. By early March the Vatican was making adjustments
    to its practices in light of the virus including streaming videos of the Pope's prayers
    and masses (Vatican News 2020).

13 A key issue that arose here was how to translate "pandemic," for which there was
    no generally accepted term. Ultimately, they decided on the neologism "*kaqi
    yajel*" exploiting the metaphorical associations of *kaq* ("red") as something intense
    to modify the concept of disease (*yajel*). Hence the neologism framed the novel
    Coronavirus as an "intense disease." They also considered "*q'eq yajel*" or "black
    disease," which would have more clearly connoted the potential deadliness of the
    Coronavirus, but ultimately rejected it since they wanted to infuse the terminology
    with a sense of hope that it was survivable.

14 Between the mid-2000s and mid-2010s the linguistic practices of the parish have
    shifted from the almost exclusive use of Q'eqchi' to a bilingual situation where
    Q'eqchi' and Spanish are both used regularly for church business. As of my last stays
    in the field in 2016 and 2017, Mass was celebrated more frequently in Spanish than
    in Q'eqchi', but the Sunday Mass in the Maya language was still the best attended
    and the parish center's signature event. Holding services in Spanish means that
    some non-indigenous people from Cobán's urban core now attend Mass there
    (which was almost unheard of in 2005), but the parish's identity continues to be
    focused on its outreach to the region's indigenous population.

15 Of course, people do not treat all televisual media the same way. One could note,
    for example, that people come together to synchronously watch major sporting
    events like the World Cup finals or WrestleMania; although this may speak more to
    the way in which those special events take on religion-like or ritual qualities than
    anything.

16 Julio also said that the turning to Facebook forced the parish leadership to re-
    evaluate how they talked about social media. He explained that up until then
    the parish team primarily talked about social media in negative terms, warning
    parishioners that it was liable to distract them (and especially for the youth) from
    God and living morally. However, now that the parish was using social media as a
    tool for evangelization, they had had to reckon with how to frame it as something
    that was potentially beneficial to Catholic piety.

17 Facebook's ad sales policy can and has been exploited for political ends (Shapiro
    2017). Moreover, social media seems to be a primary way that misinformation
    about Covid-19 has spread, and one has to wonder about what unexpected
    consequences relying on Facebook for entry into religious life might entail.

2

NFP Online:
The Mutable Religious Space
of Social Media

Katherine Dugan

"Newlywed help, please!"
"We are new to NFP and still learning, and I have a bit of anxiety around getting pregnant right now."

"Teacher popping in . . . "

"I am 12 months postpartum and nursing my daughter."

"I was wondering if someone could help me. I'm trying to figure out which day I most likely ovulated on."

"The way I've always preferred to think of it [NFP] is this: What is God asking of us today?"

These excerpts provide a glimpse into the online life of a Facebook group for Catholic heterosexual couples and single women who already practice or are just learning to practice the only officially Catholic method of managing family size: Natural Family Planning (NFP). There are a range of methods within NFP, but all share a reliance on women tracking various biological markers of their fertility cues on their fertility charts.[1] In 1968, Pope Paul VI re-affirmed the Catholic ban on contraception in his much anticipated *Humanae Vitae* (Tentler 2004). The vast majority of lay Catholics have simply ignored the teaching and Catholic use of contraception has consistently mirrored non-Catholic use (Guttmacher Institute 2012). Yet, since the 1970s, pockets of lay Catholics across the United States have been organizing themselves into formal and informal groups in order to teach one another how to do NFP. These groups rarely involve priests or officials from within Catholicism. Instead, they are women and couples who offer both technical training and emotional support to other women and couples. While originally these groups were local and in-person, NFP communities have followed the trends of the twenty-first century and created an online aspect of their relationships.[2] Much like the offline counterpart, a grassroots, lay-led ethos of NFP knowledge pervades the online community of NFP users that I focus on here.

This chapter uses the case study of an anonymized "NFP Facebook Group" to consider the nature of religious community online.[3] This group is classified within Facebook as a "private group" and is managed by one of several Catholic organizations that teach NFP. There are many NFP groups and the one I focus on in this chapter is one of the smaller ones, with around 1,600 members (larger groups have close to 30,000 members). Staff from a lay-led, explicitly Catholic organization moderate membership lightly, occasionally chiming in with advice based on many years of experience or to advertise an upcoming NFP event. Despite the presence of these "official" moderators within NFP Facebook Group, this group is a product of the members who join, as well as the group's rotating collection of most active participants.

The members of NFP Facebook Group include men, women, and heterosexual couples. Some participants are new to NFP, some are teachers, and others are curious lurkers. Most, though, are women who are either learning to chart their fertility or have a particular question about their fertility chart. Over the course of any two weeks, women post images of their charts (which are detailed accounts of monthly changes in their bodies). They ask for advice about how to interpret their signs of fertility and about details they may have missed. Other women respond with technical answers about the charts, sometimes asking to see previous charts. Frequently, the response is simply reassurance where women share their story of having misread their own chart while on vacation. Men in the group request prayers for their family's efforts to conceive another child. Other men request prayers that their families avoid pregnancy. Young couples counting the days until their wedding ask for help interpreting the trajectory of their charts, in order to anticipate what their first night as a married couple might involve. Prayers for struggling marriages are posted, as are requests for how to measure overnight temperatures with a sleepless infant. Members often respond to posts by first noting how long they have used NFP and if they are teachers. Many teachers spend many comment threads training younger women on the rules and intricacies of this explicitly and proudly Catholic approach to managing family size.

I joined NFP Facebook Group about a year into my larger ethnographic project on how and why some Catholics choose to eschew any form of contraception in favor of methods of managing family size based on basal body temperatures and mucus measurements. I had grown increasingly accustomed to listening to women and couples tell me frank details about sexual intimacy, miscarriages, and infertility struggles. I had logged hours and hours of ethnographic interviews, sitting in living rooms and at kitchen tables and in church basements, hearing careful descriptions of how women's mucus patterns have shaped couple's marriages. I had stopped feeling mildly embarrassed when men told me how hard it can be to abstain until the so-called "fertile window" of a woman's cycle. I thought I had trained myself to be unflappable regarding the more intimate aspects of how this community of Catholics talks about their experiences of NFP.

Even knowing that the subculture of Catholics who practice NFP are quite open about the specifics of their sex lives, the level of openness about personal details that I have encountered in mediated space of this online NFP community has been surprising. Members of the group ask for advice about how to interpret their fertility charts and note that the question revolves around the timing of an upcoming child-free vacation or honeymoon. Imbedded in those kinds of questions is a question about whether or not and when to have sex. Also imbedded in the way this question is framed is whether a couple is trying to conceive or avoid pregnancy. For example, when this woman asked, "Are we truly in Phase 3 as the app says?" she is trying to figure out if they are in the clear to have sex without getting pregnant. She goes on to explain, "We… are TTA [trying to avoid]. I've been charting since March, but I think I may be overthinking things. We are trying to discern whether tonight is safe or if we should wait till tomorrow evening." "Safe," in this case, means that she has passed the fertile window of her cycle—"safe" to have sex without risking pregnancy. Another woman posted a picture of her fertility chart and simply asked, "I'm curious if any teachers could let me know if they think I could be pregnant."

If the posts reveal personal details, the comments encourage this kind of intimate sharing with a tone that reflects an assumption that a woman's chart is simply a matter of course. Comments are often quite technical as experienced NFP charters detail how to interpret a chart. One teacher, for example, looked at a posted chart and explained, "The temperatures clearly indicate a thermal shift. My guess is that you ovulated near CD [cycle day] 11 or CD 14 based on mucus. Your temperature falling on CD 26 may indicate you are about to menstruate. Could you share some of your previous charts to give some context?" In response, the original poster uploaded several previous charts, which detail her daily temperature, mucus, and dates of sexual intercourse. Outside of this context, it might be odd to share one's patterns of menstruation or to share publicly *more* information about one's cycle. Here, in NFP Facebook Group, it is *de rigueur*.

In this particular mediated space, the practice of NFP is understood as an expression of Catholic identity. While the logistics of tracking biomarkers and sexual contact do tend to dominate the group's online discussions, this is not a secular group (several of those do exist, of course—and some women are in both types of groups). Frequently, a post that begins with a focus on the specifics of a particular chart concludes with an emoji of prayer hands or a rosary prayed for that person. There are also regular requests for prayers, like the person who posted, "Prayers please. Experiencing light bleeding all day at 6 weeks. Never had bleeding during my previous 4 pregnancies. No cramping so hoping that's a good sign." Somewhat rarely, someone will reference official Catholic teaching, usually in a way that polices the group's collective Catholic practice with a reminder by reminding one another to be "open to life" and not to fall prey to what many in the NFP subculture refer to as the broader culture's "contraceptive mentality."[4] These references to papal statements and Church teaching—as well as to a range of prayer practices—have the effect of reminding members of the *Catholic* reasons they are practicing NFP. This kind of infusion of Catholic thinking seems to balance the focus on logistics of tracking temperatures and mucus. Some participants jumpstart these theological conversations, like the person who asked this question on an often-recurring theme, "It seems like 'Responsible Parenthood' is primarily a matter of prayer/discussion between God and your spouse. Does anyone have any resources/articles on the topic? Wondering, specifically, when is it legitimate to post-pone [*sic*] a pregnancy?" These snapshots illustrate the ways this online community mediates sexual practices, religion, and marriages.

The ethnographic study of religion and social media has long argued that the flexibility of religious communities online challenges traditional authority roles and upends traditional hierarchical models (Campbell 2012; Campbell and Garner 2016; Hoover 2016). Others have described online communities as "porous" (Dalsgaard 2016) or a "third space" (Murchison 2015) or even "un-sited" (Airoldi 2018), a reference to their lack of physical space. Building on these descriptions of the mutable and unwieldy kinds of religious spaces that are frequently created online, I argue that this online community involves negotiations of the boundaries around and within this mediated religious space. This happens through three tensions that are regularly open for interpretation in this public Facebook group: intimacy and anonymity; vulnerability and authority; the exceptional and ordinary.

These three tensions illuminate the mutable nature of this religious space. That the space is both (and alternatingly) intimate and anonymous means that the way people present themselves here is malleable. One's social media presence is dependent on participants' stage of life, their personal willingness to share in online spaces, and how much in-person community they have (which seems to determine how much online support they are looking for). At the same time, the specifics of their presence are also mediated by the logistics of Facebook, the privacy concerns of online spaces, and in tension with the participants' real-life experiences of Catholic community. That this space can be defined by vulnerability and by authority means that the tone of the space changes, depending on the experience of the participants who decide to log on that day or devote time in that moment to offer expertise. And that the space reflects experiences that are sometimes exceptional and sometimes ordinary means that the kind of sharing that happens here is dependent on the experiences that members bring to this space. Taken together, these three tensions illustrate that when Catholics practicing NFP turn to Facebook communities for support, advice, and camaraderie, they push the boundaries of what constitutes religious community.

Intimate and Anonymous

Late last summer, a young woman posted in the group that she was early in her pregnancy—and quite nervous about it because she had already had one miscarriage. She explained that she and her husband were not telling anyone yet, but wanted advice because she had noted some falling temperatures in the past days.[5] She ended the post with a geotag and pleading question, "Should I worry?" The comments on her post ranged from referrals to specific NFP-friendly doctors in her area to prayers for her pregnancy and references to Saint Gerard, the patron saint of pregnancy. One woman shared her own experience with falling temperatures in the early days of pregnancy. A man chimed in to share the calming anecdote that his wife's temperatures had dropped slightly in the first weeks of a pregnancy that went to full term.

This kind of post and comment chain is not unusual in this group. It is striking not only because these women share the intimate details of pregnancy and miscarriage with an anonymous group of people, but also because it cuts through the cultural taboo around miscarriage in the United States. Recent scholarship has begun demonstrating what women in this group have known experientially for decades: the challenges women and couples have talking about miscarriages and an abundance of reticence to talk about that particular kind of loss in public spaces (Freidenfelds 2020). That this woman was willing to share about her previous miscarriage and then describe her fear of another miscarriage gestures to the power of what I am describing here as an intimacy-anonymity tension. The anonymity of online spaces can make intimacy more possible, less intimidating. The women in Freidenfelds' work describe the layers of shame and embarrassment they feel in telling their friends and loved ones about miscarrying. She points out that even the term—"miscarriage"—seems to place blame on the previously pregnant woman for carrying the pregnancy incorrectly. Being able to do so among strangers, this and its many like-minded posts suggests, is easier.

Yet, this intimacy is also always anonymous. When a woman posts a picture of their fertility chart, she posts a rather detailed record of her body temperatures and mucus measurements, but also a record of recent sexual relations, emotions, and intentions for family size. She shares these details with people she does not know. Her monthly cycle, as well as prescription medicine, moves from private to public in a click.

This tension between intimacy and anonymity makes possible a kind of religious community that can be difficult to find in people's daily lives, in their offline world. Catholic couples who practice NFP are a minority within a minority. NFP-practicing couples are a minority of US couples, but also a minority of Catholic couples. Somewhere around 95 to 97 percent of Catholic women report having used contraception.[6] NFP Facebook Group steps into that vacuum to offer a community of strangers to those trying to do NFP.

Much work in the field of "digital religion" has examined how various forms of media shift the nature of religious practice (Fewkes 2019). Indeed, fertility charts circulated among prayers and prayer requests each day in this group—requests for intentions, gratitude for prayers received, devotions to saints for fertility, notes about upcoming novenas. This mutability—this quick movement between private and public—means that the location of prayer expands with social media. It is not new for Catholics to pray for people they do not know personally. But when a member of this Facebook group posts a detailed record of her fertility with a request for prayer and other members respond, it is not exactly anonymous nor is it exactly intimate. Instead, this religious practice exists in a space between. This social media-based community expands how and why Catholics pray for others.

The encounters between people in this Facebook group are marked by anonymity. This is a different kind of relationship: in-real-life interactions are abundant with the nuances of personal lives, like loud kids interrupting adult conversations and whispered concerns about future pregnancies. However, these in-life interactions are not disconnected from what happens in the online. Every once in a while, someone will post a chart that they suspect indicates pregnancy followed by a quieting request, "If you know me IRL [in real life], this is not shared news." Mediated religious encounters involve layers of anonymity that both run parallel to and intersect with the intimacy of sharing one's life online.

The relationships built in this space have implications for people's real, in-person lives. This seems especially true for one member of the group has been posting somewhat frequently over the past several months. She is in her twenties, a relative newlywed and has one child ("so far," she once noted—a reference to the pro-pregnancy ethos within the group). The range of topics she covers sheds light on the nature of the community created and sustained in this forum. One month she asked several technical questions about how to interpret her chart. A few weeks later, she posted a theological question about NFP within her marriage. She comments on other posts and recently gained the Facebook label, "conversation starter." She occasionally posts her gratitude for the group. It seems clear that this group has, at least in some ways, decreased her sense of isolation in doing NFP.

NFP Facebook Group exists in the blurry boundaries between daily life and online life. Part of the way this group creates religious community is that it does not insist on being either intimate or anonymous. Instead, participants move between the two, sometimes relying on the anonymity to facilitate their intimacy (as in the case of miscarriage worries) and other times acknowledging that the intimacy that can be found in this space has very real implications for daily life lived off-line (as in the young woman in search of an NFP community). For the many ways that this online religious space is separate from and different than those experienced in person, it is also intimately bound into the fluidity of online spaces in the twenty-first century. The mutability of this space remains—people come in and share; they might share little or a lot of their personal details; they might lean heavily on the friendly anonymity of the space or they might pop in for a quick question. This is the shifting, and creative nature, of this religious space, facilitated by the tension between intimacy and anonymity in this space.

Vulnerable and Authoritative

This fall, a young woman with an eighteen-month-old child asked for advice about how to manage her husband's resistance to NFP. She told the group that he "feels that 'since we are married the Church shouldn't be able to tell us what to do in our bedroom.' I do not blame him for feeling that way especially since we have not put any 'restrictions' on our sexual activity in our 6 years of marriage." She continued, explaining that they are new to NFP and that their marriage has become a struggle because of her desire to practice NFP. She told the group, "He has mostly been sleeping on the couch and saying 'tell me when I can come back to bed' and I know he feels like I am rejecting him but that couldn't be farther from the truth. I want us to learn how to express intimacy in non-sexual ways but this will be an uphill climb." She concluded her post with a parenthetical, "(Sorry if TMI... I don't have any other outlets.)."

The vulnerability of this post is palpable. Her marriage is at stake and she seems to lack a local, in-person community of support—or even just like-minded friends—with whom to share her struggles. The new importance of NFP to her, as a full-bodied part of her Catholic identity, is clear. And the responses make clear that she is not alone in this challenge. The responses to her post ranged from prayers to book recommendations to references to Catholic teaching and marital and health benefits of avoiding contraception. A couple of women gave practical advice like having him chart the temperatures while another woman simply typed "F" to indicate that she was following the conversation of the post. One of the group administrators chimed in to cheerlead the couple, reminding the poster of how she understood the value of Catholic teaching on NFP as focused on life. Several women posted stories about their own resistant husband and one woman shared that she had been the so-called "resistant spouse" in her first years of NFP.

What is also palpable in these kinds of posts—posts that portend to be about the logistics of practicing NFP, but are really about marriages and emotions and the vulnerability of family planning—is the complex nature of authority in this space. Though it is moderated by a Catholic organization, NFP Facebook Group is not an officially Catholic forum. Papal documents are sometimes referenced as authoritative, but plenty of other sources that are not particularly Catholic, including wearable devices to track temperatures during the nighttime, a variety of fertility-tracking apps, and books about nutrition are regularly referenced. Couples, soon-to-be couples, and women, not priests or members of the hierarchy, create and moderate the online community of this space. As in many social media spaces, the format democratizes religious experiences (Campbell 2012).

However, this Facebook group is not without hierarchy. But the levels of hierarchy are based on years of experience as an NFP teacher and/or how long a person has been practicing NFP. Couples who have been teaching together for many years have powerful authority in this space. Teachers tend to feel a responsibility to assert their credentials, often prefacing their advice by noting, "Teaching Couple here" or "Twelve years teaching." Conversely, women and couples new to NFP also proclaim their lower rank by noting a lack of experience—"newlywed, please help!" The boundaries around authorial voices within this online community are more flexible than in-real-life Catholic communities, but not without structure. This form of "digital religion" would seem to immerse participants in a seemingly boundary-less community with democratic structures (Hoover 2016). However, members of this community create boundary markers that assert authority among themselves within this virtual space.

As I observed this group over the past year, I began to notice that a second mechanism of this informal authority is through policing Catholic identity. There is pressure to do NFP the "right way"—which is defined as "openness to life" and a willingness to have a big family, "if that's God's plan for your marriage." There are two nascent Others in these comments: Catholics who do not practice NFP and women who use the same methods to track their cycles, but do so from the perspective of the cultural trend toward "natural" in physical wellness. I have not seen particularly nasty exchanges in this forum, but there are occasional subtleties that assert a right and wrong way to be a *Catholic* NFP user as well as a *Catholic* who does not use contraceptives. These take the form of calling out a "contraceptive mentality," which means using NFP as a means of birth control (instead of God-led family planning). Or sometimes a group member will post a meme that is intended to be funny, but is also an authoritative commentary on the value of a big family or the beauty of *Humanae Vitae*.

This policing of Catholic identity means that this group relies on an alternative structure of authority, one that is enforced by self-appointed members of the laity. Despite its self-description and an earnest effort to be a safe space for couples to share the vulnerabilities of being committed to, but also challenged by NFP, this group also exists within several authoritative structures. The vulnerability that couples bring to the group is both affirmed and under potential threat by these structures. To share one's marriage, sexual intimacy, and biology in this space is to take a risk. Social media is a known judgment-filled space. And NFP Facebook Group—while certainly not a toxic space on the internet—does rely on particular definitions of Catholic identity to police its members.

In this online religious space, there is fluidity in how people interact. That this space is defined through a tension that expects both vulnerability and authority from a community of like-minded Catholics gestures to the mutability of this space. A woman or couple, a teacher or a spouse can be in one or both of these roles in their time in this space. Mutability defines how people exist in online religious spaces.

Exceptional and Ordinary Experience

In the spring, a woman in the Facebook group described her negative experience with her medical doctor. She explained:

> Just had my six week postpartum checkup and my doctor brought up birth control, even though she knows my husband and I are practicing NFP. (This is a catholic [*sic*] hospital fyi). She said you can't practice NFP before you get your period again and I told her that you can. She smiled and said 'good luck, I'll be seeing you back here soon pregnant with your second!' I'm feeling very discouraged and worried. My husband and I are not in a position financially to have another child right now, nor am I physically in a position to be pregnant right now according to my Dr. Anyone else been in my shoes before? Needing some positive encouragement!

This post was a popular one that month, receiving more than eighty comments, many of them quite lengthy, most of them indicated solidarity and commiseration. The comments had lots of righteous outrage that trumpeted the medical value of NFP, as one commenter did, "Well congrats on being more knowledgeable than your doctor!" There was also plenty of Catholic policing, "If this was at a Catholic institution, I think I'd seriously consider writing the local bishop about it." A sympathetic Catholic doctor who practices NFP was perhaps most clear, "On behalf of the medical community, I'm so sorry you had this experience!"

This negotiation between their method of family planning and the mainstream medical profession is a frustrating, but also quietly celebrated experience among NFP-practicing women and couples. Their interactions with traditional medicine are unavoidable—the vast majority of these couples have their children in hospitals, with doctors and certified nurse midwives. They access regular pre- and post-natal care. Their standard engagement with the medical establishment illustrates the multiple worlds that these Catholics walk in. However, while they practice many standard medical practices, they engage in a family planning practice that is not, generally, well respected by their physicians. This leads to a sense of Catholic exceptionalism coursing underneath the comments above.

This tenor of Catholic-medical exceptionalism reflects a history of Catholics feeling askew of the broader, contraception-prescribing, medical community.[7]

Many of the developers of the various methods of NFP were doctors in the late 1960s and into the 1970s who saw their work as a direct answer to the call from Pope Paul VI in his 1968 *Humanae Vitae*. In that Catholic teaching, the pope not only re-asserted that contraception is opposed to Catholic teaching, he also appealed to "men of science," pleading that "medical science should by the study of natural rhythms succeed in determining a sufficiently secure basis for the chaste limitation of offspring" (*Humanae Vitae*, para 24). While the woman and her commenters are frustrated and angry about the Catholic hospital's response to NFP, there is also a sense of pride in being Catholic in this post: they are better Catholics than their contracepting peers because of their adherence to *Humanae Vitae*.

At the same time, the reality is that Catholics in NFP Facebook Group are not alone in rejecting contraception in the twenty-first century—and Catholics practice NFP not *only* for Catholic reasons. The "all-natural," "organic," and "free-range" health-conscious movement of the past decade has made some secular women nervous about the birth control pill. Catholic women are not the only women who are deciding to go off the pill for what sound like the same reasons they buy organic meat: values around health. A 2018 survey by *Cosmopolitan* of 2,000 women under forty found that "70 percent of women who have used the Pill said they'd stopped taking it or thought about going off it in the past three years" (Vadnal 2018). A 2018 commentary in the *New York Post* referenced this survey and then surveyed the many apps and smart technology options for "Fertility Awareness Methods" and suggested that millennial women are just no longer interested in the birth control pill because "hormonal birth control isn't just unnatural. They are also worried about its long-term effects, from depression and digestive disorders to—on the more extreme end of the spectrum—stroke, blood clots or breast cancer" (Laneri 2018). This survey suggests that the members of NFP Facebook Group are part of a larger cultural hesitancy with contraception. It is possible that for the first time since 1968, Catholics are *part* of a reproductive trend, rather than resisting it. I have come across Catholics working in women's clinics where they teach a method of NFP alongside a doula, tarot-card reader, and acupuncturist. A dual frame of "Catholic" and "crunchy" permeates the contemporary NFP world.

But there is a way in which this dual frame threatens the Catholic exceptionalism. Feeling sidelined by the larger medical community is scary and vulnerable, as the post at the start of this section suggests. Yet, that shared sense of fear of being misunderstood also creates a sense of community—bonding through hardship. Within NFP Facebook Group, a tension between exceptional experiences of practicing NFP and a growing ordinary-ness of their experience raises questions about the implications of this online community as participants move in their daily in-person lives. How does sharing this individual experience of being shamed by her doctor in the mediated space of a supportive Facebook group really affect her daily life, off-line? She still has to deal with her NFP-unfriendly doctor and worry about her ability to do NFP well in the complicated postpartum period. And, yet, a sense of pride in navigating the experience of being a medical outcast seems to create a network of relationship within this group. In the work of sharing her experience online, her exceptional experience shifts from being isolating and scary to a source of shared connection.

This tension maintains the mutability of this space, as evidenced in the way that the original post began with a sense of worry about how to navigate the traditional medical system. By the end of the thread, her experience had been re-interpreted as a source of pride. The emotions of the post moved from outcast to normalized in the course of a couple of hours. What this means is that this online religious space has the potential to transform how people move in their daily lives. That kind of transformative mutability creates this online space as an alternative to the kinds of religious communities these members are able to find in person.

Conclusion

I wrote the first drafts of this chapter before the Covid-19 pandemic radically reworked the fabric and expectations of virtual religious community in the United States. As so many religious communities moved online and into Zoom in the spring of 2020, there is a way in which NFP Facebook Group was more prepared than the other religious forms that scrambled to find ways to make virtual connections among community members. I noted an uptick of activity in this group—more members, more links to online trainings, and previously infrequent discussion about daily family life. Members of the group wondered about the impact of pandemic stress on charting their cycles and traded tips on how to manage remote education for their children and how to set up for streaming Mass in a living room. When Pope Francis offered public prayers for an end to the pandemic, it was shared in this group. Perhaps because NFP Facebook Group became just one mediated religious space among many, its ability to exist as an alternative space became even more pronounced. The group did not collapse into other online spaces, nor did the prayers and requests for information merge into the myriad options for mediated religious practice. It continued in its form, as parallel option to more formal religious structures, even when so much of religious life moved online. This lends credence to the proposal of this chapter that NFP Facebook Group really does create a space for religious community that is unavailable in other forms. Even when religious life became primarily an online experience, this Facebook group remained an important space for its members.

That this group can navigate the tensions I have outlined in this chapter reflects how this community flourishes as a mutable space on-line. When Catholics practicing NFP turn to Facebook communities for support, advice, and camaraderie, they follow the example of many who have pushed the boundaries of what constitutes religious community.

In early July 2019, the online magazine, *The Outline*, published an article about this and several other Facebook groups where NFP is the primary point of discussion. The author, Mary Meisenzahl, argued that the spaces are not safe for women because they use Catholic teaching as a "bludgeon" to make Catholic couples feel shame about sex. She describes women's comments about fear of pregnancy and concern about doing NFP correctly as heavy with panicked anxiety. Meisenzahl argues that this panic is a sign that these women need better and other birth control options. She quotes one poster's worry about conceiving a child amid health concerns and then comments, "No matter how dire the circumstances or how clearly the poster expresses her anguish, some commenters are quick to admonish her. 'Just pray; the pill and tube tying fail too!' one wrote" (Meisenzahl 2019). The article's conclusion argues for a change to Church teaching that would allow contraception, so that the women in these groups feel less shame and like they have more control over their reproductive choices.

Several days later, the Catholic News Agency published a counter article, arguing that the Facebook groups create an important network of support. Mary Farrow's article, "Why Some Catholic Women Say an NFP-shaming Article Was 'Off the Charts'" first argued that *The Outline's* article had done damage to the sense of safety that women feel in the groups. There was, among the woman interviewed for Farrow's article, new nervousness about posting in the groups, lest their comments end up in a news story. She quoted the administrator of one Facebook group who told her that "some women have been afraid to post openly in groups they had previously assumed were friendly to NFP and all that it entails" (Farrow 2019). This points to the role that mediated religious spaces play in people's lives—they are not denigrated as a second-class religious community, but another way to learn, discuss, and practice religious ideals.

These competing interpretations of the online NFP spaces illustrate the variable roles of NFP Facebook Group: this is a space that intends to support women and couples, but the very nature of the Facebook form means that it is under constant negotiation. Significantly, that negotiation happens not by these outside observers, but by those within the group. The tensions I have outlined here—between intimacy and anonymity; between vulnerability and authority; and between exceptional and ordinary experiences—make the online space a mutable religious community.

Notes

1 The different methods choose different biological markers, but the most common are a woman's "basal body temperature" (which a body's temperature at rest, best taken first thing in the morning), her mucus pattern throughout the month, and the shape of her cervix. The Archdiocese of Boston offers a clear explanation of the various forms of NFP, "What Is Natural Family Planning," https://www. bostoncatholic.org/nfp/what-is. Couples interpret the chart based on whether they are TTA (trying to avoid pregnancy) or TTC (trying to conceive).

2 It is worth noting that the Covid-19 pandemic further sped up the move to use remote and online instruction for NFP. This was underway before the pandemic, but took on an increasingly important role when being too close to people for too long posed health risk. This also, I noted anecdotally, caused an increase in the numbers of people in the Facebook group as well as a shift in the kinds of questions asked—many more questions about the impacts of stress on tracking a cycle and fewer questions about how to manage cycles affected by weddings and honeymoons.

3 I conducted this research under IRB approval from my institution and all names, details, and titles of the group are anonymized.

4 This term comes from Pope John Paul II and is generally understood as not being open to pregnancy (John Paul II, *Evangelium Vitae*, 1995).

5 When "charting" biomarkers of fertility, a woman's Basal Body Temperature (BBT) is elevated while she is fertile and drops when that shifts. A BBT that stays high is one early indication of pregnancy.

6 The number of Catholics following this teaching is small, but the actual numbers are unknown because of the way the question on survey data is collected—many

women in my research, who now practice NFP, were at one time using some form of contraception. Estimates by the Guttmacher Institute find that 96–98 percent of Catholic women either have been or are using oral contraception, "Guttmacher Statistics on Catholic Women's Contraceptive Use," February 2012, https://www.guttmacher.org/article/2012/02/guttmacher-statistic-catholic-womens-contraceptive-use. See also Tentler (2004), Miller (2014), and McClory (1995).

7 This is most evident in some of the early journals about NFP, especially the *International Review of National Family Planning,* which has published articles like "Natural Family Planning: God's Plan for Fertility" (1980) and "Spiritual Care of Couples Practicing Natural Family Planning" (2013), in addition to more biological-minded articles like "Continuous Mucus in the Use of the Ovulation Method" (1983) and "Natural Family Planning and the New Technologies" (1989).

3

The Stakes of Catholic Media Practices in Chad

Ludovic Lado

Introduction

For the past two decades, Pentecostal media practices in Africa have drawn the attention of researchers in sub-Saharan Africa (Oha 2002; De Witte 2003; Ukah 2003, 2015; Meyer 2004, 2009, 2015; Baugh 2011; Müller 2014; Asamoah-Gyadu 2015; Pype 2015; Adesokan 2017). But on the other hand, Catholic media practices in Africa remained understudied. Edited volumes on religions and media (Douyère, Dufour, and Riondet 2014; Hackett and Soares 2015) rarely feature a case study on media and Catholicism on the African continent. The only exception I am aware of is Mouthe (2015). But this preferential option for Pentecostalism over Catholicism as object of study is not limited to the field of religion and media. It is a recent development in religious studies in Africa. This paper aims to contribute to a better knowledge of media practices in the Catholic Church in Central Africa, with a focus on Chad. It appears that on the one hand, compared with other cases studied in this volume (see Kaell, Loustau, and Dugan's chapters) which present a broad and more unstable picture of multiple actors with varied interests operating together in Catholicism's media field, the Church's official institutional actors exert total control and monopoly of the Catholic media field in Chad. On the other hand, critique, dissatisfaction, and aspiration to better Catholic media services dominate grassroots perspectives on Catholic media practices in Chad. The Catholic Church is perceived as lagging behind on media performances, compared to non-Catholic churches more generally.

Following the Second Vatican Council (1965), the Catholic Church described the media as "gifts of God" and prescribed to "adopt a fundamentally positive approach to the media" (Pontifical Council for Social Communication 1971: 1). "Communication therefore is of the essence of the Church" (Pontifical Council on Social Communications 2002: 3), writes the Pontifical Council for Social Communication in a more recent document entitled "Church and Internet" that spells out the stakes for the Catholic Church of the emergence of internet. In Africa, the Symposium of Episcopal Conferences of Africa and Madagascar (SECAM) has a secretariat for social communications of which the replica at countries level are national or diocesan commissions for social communications. These institutions have the mission to implement the media policy of the Catholic Church in local contexts.[1]

How is Catholicism mediatized in Chad and what are the reverberations of its media forms at the grassroots level? Has the advent of new information and communication technologies changed the media practices of the Catholic Church in Chad? These are the main guiding question of this paper which seeks to explore the stakes of Catholic media practices in Chad for both clergy and faithful. The paper is based on an empirical study of Catholic media practices in Chad, with a focus on the Archdiocese of N'Djamena. Chad is located in central Africa with a population estimated in 2018 at 15 million inhabitants[2] of which the majority are Muslims (about 55 percent) and the rest are Christians (40–45 percent) or adepts of a variety of traditional religious groups. Catholics make up about 25 percent of population. The Chadian Church is one of the youngest on the Continent. It is only in the early 1930 that the first Catholic missionaries arrived in the south of Chad. Established in 1947, the Apostolic Prefecture of Fort Lamy (later renamed N'Djamena) became a diocese in 1955 and an Archdiocese in 1961. Today, it has around 221,000 faithful spread over 25 parishes, 58 priests and deacons, 109 religious, and 15 major seminarians (see Archdiocese of N'Djamena, *Yearbook 2019*: 1).[3]

I locate this paper within the field of religion and media. But, as Stolow rightly points out, "The problem with the phrase 'religion and media' is that it is a pleonasm" because "'religion' can only be manifested through some process of mediation" (2005: 125). He advocates for the concept of "religion and/as media" to point out the limits of exclusively instrumentalist approaches to the study of religion and media. This paper also acknowledges the value of current debates around the conceptual delineations between "mediation" and "mediatization" (Couldry 2008; Morgan 2011; Hjarvard 2014). According to David Morgan, "The literature offers three different uses of the terms in relation to one another: the two terms may be interchangeable; they may refer to altogether different phenomena or mediatisation may be a special instance of mediation" (Morgan 2011: 138). For the purpose of this paper, media refers here predominantly to media technologies (printing, radio, television, and the new media such as internet and the related social media). "Media practices" as used in the title of the paper therefore encompasses the many ways in which the Catholic Church mediatizes itself through modern media technologies in Chad. In this sense mediatization is here understood as a special instance of mediation which is the use of any medium (words, texts, body, sounds, spaces, gender, foods, dress, movements, sounds, etc.) to express religious forms (Morgan 2011). The paper has three main sections: the first spells out the context and the methodology of the study; the second presents the empirical data; and the last attempts to interpret the data so as to spell out the stakes of media practices in Chad for both the clergy and the faithful.

Context and Method

To understand Catholic media practices in Chad one needs to locate them within the wider context of the recent evolution of the media world in Chad as a postcolonial country. Printed materials in both local and Western languages were one of the main communication mediums for Christian missionaries in Africa. Missionaries and colonial administrators were also a main vector of the diffusion of the radio in colonial Africa. The first radio transmitters in West Africa occurred in 1940 (Ilboudo 2014). The first radio station was established in Chad in 1955 by the French colonizers and was taken over by the Chadian state as public media at independence in 1960. Until 1990, there were no private radio stations in Chad because of the repressive nature of the state, which saw them as potential laboratories of political dissent. But thanks to the wind of liberalization that blew over Africa from the late 1980s, Chad experienced a blossoming of private media in both the field of printing press and audiovisual productions (Ngardiguina 2013).

Since independence in 1960, the Chadian state has promulgated a number of legal texts to regulate the creation and functioning of the media in Chad. During the period of the dictatorship (1960–89), the legislation was restrictive and the media were subordinated to the ideology of the single party system. From the 1990s, however, new and more liberal laws were introduced to regulate the functioning of the media and to promote freedom of expression.[4] This led to the mushrooming of private newspapers and radios alongside public media. The state has however sought to limit the creation of private television channels in order to keep dissenting voices under control. Social media are also occasionally blocked by the state to control a potentially subversive mass communication.

Today besides sixteen private and public newspapers, the Chadian media landscape includes fifty-five private radio stations, one public radio station with about twenty-four branches scattered throughout the country, a public television channel with national coverage, and four private television channels whose coverage is limited to the city of N'Djamena and its surroundings.[5] There are about ten Christian radios, five of which are Catholic. The Catholic Church in Chad has no newspaper and no television channel. Radio is the main mass media used by Church authorities. Each diocese has at least one radio station. For this reason we have chosen in this study to focus on this predominant use of radio by the Church in Chad.[6]

In the city of N'Djamena are located the public television channel, the four private television channels, the public radio channel, and ten private radio channels, one of which is Catholic (Radio Rainbow), one Protestant (Radio the Voice of Hope), and one Islamic (Radio FM Al Bayane). The other private radio stations belong to individuals or local communities and associations. The Chadian law distinguishes three categories of private radio: commercial, community, and confessional. Radios belonging to religious organizations are generally categorized as "community" or as "confessional" depending on the nature of their programs. In general, the location of these radios is urban or semi-urban for the sake of a better access to energy.

The collection of data for this paper targeted media practices of both the church's hierarchy and the faithful. The main data collection method consisted of semi-structured interviews with directors of two Catholic radio channels, with priests and with members of the faithful of the Archdiocese of N'Djamena. The two Catholic radio channels are owned by two different dioceses: the Archdiocese of N'Djamena and the diocese of Pala in the southern part of Chad. Interviews sought to capture not only the mode of operation of selected radio but also the self-positioning of each radio in the Chadian media landscape. Concerning the Catholic clergy, a survey was carried out on a group of sixty-one priests from eight dioceses of Chad on how they relate to information and communication technologies in their ministry. Ten Catholic faithful of the Archdiocese of N'Djamena were interviewed on their media practices especially in relation to their Catholic identity.

Media Practices of the Institutional Church

The Bishops' Conference of Chad, which includes a National Commission for Social Communications, adopted in 2004 a document entitled "Charter of community radios of the Catholic Church in Chad." The charter aims to clearly formulate the "identity and spirit" of Catholic radio stations, whose mission is to inform and educate people in light of Gospel values. Catholic radios, according to bishops, are

> to be a visible and effective Christian presence in the current media world, to be a means of free expression of the Church in order to reach as many listeners as possible, to be the voice that brings peace, joy, hope and love in the name of Jesus Christ in an ecumenical spirit and is open to other religions. To be a tool for Christian formation, prayer and information on the life of the Church and society in the light of faith, to be radios at the service of those who, in our society, have no voice.
>
> (CET, Community Radio Charter of the Catholic Church in Chad)

The charter is signed by all the bishops of the National Bishop's conference to serve as the framework for the establishment of Catholic radio channels in Chad.

Radio Arc-en-Ciel (Rainbow Radio)

In 1972 the Catholic Church set up in N'Djamena a recording studio called "Radio Presence Antenna" to produce and broadcast religious programs on the public National Radio of Chad. The content of the programs focused on Sunday sermons and on the news of the Catholic Church in Chad. After the advent of democracy in Chad in the early 1990s, the Catholic Church founded a multimedia center called Radio Television Presence (RTV-Presence) which now houses Radio Arc-en-Ciel established in 2005 but no television channel yet. RTV-Presence has the status of a private association and operates as a private multimedia center. Radio Arc-en-Ciel broadcast every day from 06:00 to 10:30 a.m., and in the afternoon from 15:30 to 20:30 p.m. Because of a financial crisis in the Archdiocese of N'Djamena, Radio Arc-en-Ciel suspended its activities in 2013. But in 2017 the diocesan commission on social communications restarted the radio. The radio staff initially worked on a voluntary basis, but since December 2017, it is now a team of eight permanent agents, assisted by a dozen volunteers. The radio is led by a diocesan priest who studied media in Rome. He is also the general manager of the Multimedia Center. Regarding the status of Radio-Arc-en-Ciel, the director states, "We are not a confessional radio but rather a community radio. (…) As a community radio, we have a variety of programs to reach our diverse audience. We run social, political, economic, educational, cultural, health, environmental and religious programs. 10% of our programs are devoted to religious issues" (Interview conducted on March 27, 2019). Regarding the future, the director of Radio Arc-en-Ciel hopes that there will be more collaboration between Catholic media across the country for more visibility and vitality. The main sources of funding are subsidies from the archdiocese, the radio's own revenue from commercials, and a few local donations. According to the director the annual budget of the radio is about 35 million FCFA (70,000 USD). The main expenses concern energy supply, staff salaries, and secretarial and computer equipment.

Radio Terre Nouvelle (Radio New Earth, Interview Conducted in May 2019)

Radio Terre Nouvelle was founded in 2000 by the Diocese of Pala in Chad. The Italian priest who is the current director has been in office for the last four years. With regard to human resources, Radio Terre Nouvelle collaborates with a team of thirty-five people, nine of whom are permanent and the others volunteers. Among the nine permanent members, "five have graduated from journalism schools, four are interns including two journalists and two technicians from journalism schools in Chad and Cameroon. We broadcast in nine different languages to reach all our targets" (Director, Radio Terre Nouvelle).

As for the sources of funding, they are mainly sponsored programs from humanitarian institutions, diocesan collections, advertisements, and some limited external support. The revenues are spent primarily to pay salaries, purchase and maintain appliances, power the generator which is the main source of energy, given that the National Electricity Company supplies energy only three days a week. The radio has not received public funding for the last four years. The radio broadcasts six to seven hours per day except on Sundays when it runs from 8:00 a.m. to 21:00 p.m. As for the content of the programs, according to the director,

> our programs revolve around social issues (health, education, environment, culture…) and, of course, the Gospel. We are one of the most active radios of all the dioceses in the country because of the quality of our programs. Less than 10% of our programming concerns the Gospel, in line with the status of community radio as stipulated in Chadian law. Unfortunately the aid promised us in return has never reached us. And that is regrettable. (Director, Radio Terre Nouvelle)

Table 3.1 Comparison of Catholic and non-Catholic radio stations

Areas	Catholic radios	Non-Catholic radios	Observations
Legal status	Preference for "community" status with less than 20 percent of programs dedicated to specifically religious content	Pentecostal preference for "confessional" status with more than 50 percent of the programs dedicated to religious content	The Lutheran radio like the Catholic radio prefer "community" status
Ownership	Institutional	Institutional	
Leadership	Clergy	Lay	In both cases they are appointed and supervised by the church leadership
Personnel	Few permanent and professional staff; predominance of amateurs and volunteers	Idem	Because of financial reasons
Finances	Local contributions and services are the main source of revenues	Idem	In both cases, occasional foreign subsidies especially if the church has an international outlook. All struggle with the issue of financial sustainability
Major expenses	Salaries, fuel for the generator, ordinary operations	Idem	
Collaboration	Collaborate with the public media but not with other Christian media	Collaboration between Pentecostal radios	Little collaboration across denominations
Nature of programs	Mixture of religious content with predominance of development/ secular of content	Predominance of religious content for Pentecostal radio	The Lutheran radio like the Catholic radio gives more space to development/ secular content

With regard to future challenges, the director hopes that the faithful and other partners will make more efforts to financially support the radio and that Catholic radio channels will be able to take up the challenge of fighting corruption:

> for the media belonging to the Catholic Church, I propose that we work together to be able to counter corruption because, our first mission is to announce the Good News, to be at the service of justice and truth and not sell ourselves to the highest bidder. It is sad to see that corruption has reached us and is killing our founding values. We must fight with strength, trust and faith against the corruption that plagues our media. (Director, Radio Terre Nouvelle)

For comparative purposes, three protestant radios, *Radio Mon Ami* (Pentecostal), *Radio Voix de l'Espérance* (Pentecostal), and *Radio Evangile et Développement Globale* (Lutheran), were also explored.

Media Practices of the Clergy

Concerning the Catholic clergy, a survey was carried out on a group of sixty-one priests from the different dioceses of Chad on their relationship to information and communication technologies: 95 percent have access to a computer and use it mainly to typewrite, to watch movies, and for internet access; 65.5 percent effectively use their computer for accessing internet; 100 percent own a phone that they use mainly to make calls, send/receive messages, and take pictures; 90.1 percent have access to the internet through their phones; 96.7 percent declare having an e-mail address that they use more or less regularly; 88.5 percent have a Facebook account that they use more or less regularly. All declare using various media technologies, especially radio and phones, for pastoral purposes, inter alia, to communicate with parishioners for a variety of reasons. In view of these statistics, it can be said that although the Chadian clergy is familiar with the new information and communication technologies and does use them for pastoral purposes, these media have not significantly changed their pastoral practices.

Media Practices of the Faithful

The analysis of data collected from the grassroots led to a number of conclusions. The first is that the parish setting remains the privileged space of access to information on the life of the local church. Most of the interviewees are informed about church's activities through announcements in the church at the end of Sunday masses which remains the major weekly gathering at parish level. Some parishes also produce weekly magazines through which information is disseminated. Central to communication practices among the faithful is the use of the telephone. For example, Maxime is the coordinator of youth movements in his parish. To communicate with other members of the movement, he uses phone calls, phone messages, announcements, and posters.

The second conclusion is that the Catholic media most known to the faithful of the diocese of N'Djamena is *Radio Arc-en-Ciel*. Most interviewees listen to it more or less frequently and for a variety of reasons (religious music programs, programs on the word of God, daily news, etc.). Some are very critical of the performance of the radio. It is the case, for example, of Pulcherie, a faithful from the Cathedral parish of N'Djamena who works with the United Nations. She says:

> It was doing well at the beginning, but I came to realize that it's no different from other radio programs because it broadcasts worldly music. The content of their programs is not rich and has little connection with the Gospel and the activities of the Church. There is still a lot to do for this radio to achieve its purpose and to honor its identity as a Catholic radio.
>
> (Interview with Pulcherie, faithful of the cathedral parish)

Loustau's paper in this volume portrays Radio Maria Transylvania as a locus of a creative synthesis of secular and Catholic values within the framework of the New Evangelization movement in Romania. Chad is less secular than Romania and a number of Catholic listeners are not comfortable with a Catholic radio airing secular music. The secular is here construed as mundane and therefore not compatible with Catholic values.[7]

Pulchérie adds that she regularly follows a children's program on the Protestant radio "Voix de l'Espérance." She is also a regular viewer of some religious programs of the French Catholic TV channel *KTO* and of Protestant channels like *Bénie TV* and *Parole de Vie*. On the internet, she visits Catholic sites such as *Hosanna, Etoile Notre Dame, Gospel.Net, AELF* and Protestant sites like *Top Christian* and *Know God* "to interact with pastors and Christians, Protestants and Catholics alike, around the world. For example, on Protestant sites, I am asked questions about the way Catholics see this or that religious festival, how they celebrate this or that... there are often very heated and rich debates like the one about the holiness of Mary" (Interviewed on 10/4/2019).

The third conclusion is that, like Pulcherie, a number of Catholics at the grassroots have ecumenical media practices. Many interact with Protestant and Pentecostal media. For example, Ferdinand is a student at the University of N'Djamena and he listens to the Protestant radio "Voix de l'Espérance" for the following reason: "It is an evangelical radio that offers very good songs of praise programs. I am inspired to write songs in local languages for our choir Ste. Faustine of which I am in charge." This ecumenical acquaintance is also practiced by Biyada Allo who is a faithful of St. Josephine Bakhita parish where he is a choir member. He listens to Radio Arc-en-Ciel especially for the daily news. About his ecumenical media practices, he says: "I usually watch *LMTV*, *Emmanuel TV* and *KTO* which are foreign TV channels. Here, I follow Electron TV of Pastor Djégoltar Armand. There is also Radio Arc-en-Ciel that I listen to. As a singer, I listen to Voice of the Angels on FM Bonne Espérance to improve my voice. You should never be ashamed of copying a good example." Still on the topic of ecumenical openness, Grébé Achim is a high school student and faithful of the Cathedral parish of N'Djamena. On Catholic media, he is more familiar with the French Catholic television channel KTO. He is less acquainted with Radio Arc-en-Ciel of which he is not happy with the content of the programs. He thinks they should be improved to adapt to the youth. However, he is viewer of the LMTV Protestant television channel and is fascinated with the teachings of Pastor Irvin Baxter: "This is a very good show that I advise all Christians to follow as well. This pastor, he is so powerful! Of course he is Protestant but he says a lot of good things about Catholics. I advise you to follow his show on 'The Apocalypse', the end of time." Grébé Achim would like the Catholic Church to improve the quality of its programs and increase its media presence to maintain its leadership position in the Christian landscape in Chad.

The fourth conclusion is about the minimal use of the internet and social media for religious purposes. It should be noted that internet is expensive in Chad, which limits access to social media at the grassroots. Periodically, access to social media is blocked by political authorities, allegedly for security reasons. But in reality it is to limit grassroots critiques of the rampant poor quality of governance. Grebe Malachie is a university student and a faithful of the Cathedral parish of N'Djamena. About accessing religious content on television, he says: "When I do not go to church on Sundays, I follow the mass on KTO TV. Especially during the rainy season because our road is flooded almost from June to the end of September." As for the internet, he uses it for purposes other than religious, partly because it is expensive: "No, no! When I connect it's a lot more to chat with friends. The connection is too expensive to be used for something you can get at mass. I visited the diocese website two or three times but it discouraged me."

There is also the generational factor. Alyem Yvette is a faithful of the Sacred Heart parish of Chagoua. She is in her sixties and is a nurse by profession. About religious programs on television and on the internet, she says: "I do not have a TV, my son. Even electricity I do not have. I will follow the TV with what (laughs)? Internet business at our age, this is no longer possible. We did not know it in our time so it's hard to use it for me." She mentions with some nostalgia the days when European missionaries project religious films in parishes.

As for expectations and future prospects about Catholic media practices, most interviewees believe that the Catholic Church in Chad is not doing enough in light of current evolutions. These Catholic Christians believe that their church is late compared to Pentecostals. Memadji Honorine, student and member of the Saint Charles Borromeo Parish of Farcha, says: "I want them to talk more about the gospel and singing on Radio Arc-en-Ciel, as it is the only Catholic medium that I know. No, in my opinion they are not doing enough. We must also create other media, including TV channels." One of the main issues seems to be the competition from Pentecostals and Islamist fundamentalists. Both streams have a reputation for making the best use of the latest information and communication technologies. Bénédicte is a journalist by training and a faithful of the cathedral parish. Concerning prospects for the future, she says:

> First, the diocese needs to create Catholic media like a TV channel and enhance Radio Arc-en-Ciel broadcasting capabilities. They are distracted by programs that have nothing to do with the word of God. I agree that it should feature social welfare programs, but more time must be devoted to the Word of God to further strengthen the faith of Christians who are perpetually threatened by newcomers. Scholarships should be established to train Catholic journalists to be at the forefront of new information and communication technologies because communication is essential to winning the war.

In the same vein, Grébé Achim, a high school student and faithful of the Cathedral parish, believes that the Catholic Church investment in media is essential, among other things, to counter or balance what he perceives as Pentecostal and Islamist threats:

> But imagine the number of young Chadian Catholics who are tempted every day to convert to Islam in order to be recruited as a civil servant, or to have a job somewhere. How many are wanting to join the new so-called born-again churches, especially women and young people who follow them in the hope of finding a husband or a job. If they follow good media programs, they will realize that all that is promised them there is vanity. We need constructive debates, real

debates about youth, religion and the future. Otherwise we are moving back to the last place in terms of numbers. Is it true that Muslims outnumber Catholics in 2018, do you see that? But we have not done anything to keep the first place, and we continue to plummet with problems of pedophilia, homosexuality, and priests impregnating Mass servants and women every day… that too must be discussed. There must be programs on "For or against the marriage of priests."

Empirical data seem to suggest that the institutional Church in Chad has not decisively professionalized its use of media and new information and communication technologies. On the other hand, data suggest that media practices are more ecumenical at the grassroots where there is demand for more quality Catholic media content. The interpretation of data attempts to explain this deficit of professional engagement with the new media in terms of negotiating tensions between vertical modes of communication predominantly institutional/clerical and the horizontal modes of interactions prevalent at the grassroots level.

Discussion: Vertical and Horizontal Communication

Pype (2015: 116) states that "Of the diverse religions on the offer on the African continent, Pentecostal movements are the most significant media players." They thrive on television and on the new media through which they access the public sphere (Hackett 1998; Meyer 2004). Indeed numerous studies show that the use of films, videos, recorded materials, television, and the new media for religious purposes is far more pervasive in Pentecostal churches than in the Catholic Church (Oha 2002; De Witte 2003; Ukah 2003; Müller 2014; Asamoah-Gyadu 2015; Pype 2015; Taiwo 2015; Adesokan 2017). One major hypothesis which seeks to account for this particular fascination of Pentecostalism for media underlines the ability of televisualization of religious practice not only to create and reproduce charisma but also to mediate the experiential (emotional) dimension of religion central to Pentecostalism (Pype 2015). Also, as argued by Marleen De Witte, "the creation of religious subjects outside the church by the televisualization of church members' emotions and reactions to sermons widens the notion of 'religious community' to include different audiences" (De Witte 2003: 176). Religious content in media has the ability to create ecumenical or interreligious audiences which escape the control of hierarchical structures such as the Catholic Church. This shed some light on the ecumenical media practices of Chadian Catholic at the grassroots.

Asamoah-Gyadu (2015) argues that whereas the historic mission churches use the internet in a limited way, contemporary Pentecostals use the same medium in more evangelistic ways. Indeed Pentecostal radios in N'Djamena tend to more "confessional" and therefore to feature more religious programs, whereas Catholic radio tend to prefer the "community radio" category in order to include more secular programs. The findings of the present study tend to confirm that the advent of new information and communication technologies has not yet substantially changed media practices in the Archdiocese of N'Djamena in particular and of the Catholic Church in Chad in general. The parish remains the main source of information for most Catholics, the telephone the main tool of interpersonal communication, and local Catholic radio channels the major medium of mass communication for the institutional church.

Gildas Mouthe has noted in a study on the uses of internet in the Catholic Church in Cameroon that "While the church has often emerged as an expert in group communication, it seems less adept in its use of electronic media communication" (Mouthe 2015: 6). The hypothesis is that the Catholic Church as a very hierarchical institution is more at ease with a vertical mode of communication. The challenge therefore for any hierarchical structure engaging the new media is to adapt to a mode of communication that is predominantly horizontal. Angela Anzelmo conducted a study on Vatican media practices on social media and concluded that the Pope's communication strategy is indeed more vertical (top-down) than that of the Vatican Secretariat for Communication perceived as more horizontal (egalitarian). As she puts it, "Ultimately, the discourses are different according to whether they emanate from the Secretariat for communication or the pope. In fact, for the dicastery it is a question of carrying out a corporate communication strategy, invested with a marketing dimension, thus promoting its 'brand image' ... " (Anzelmo 2017: 8) in order "to disseminate a new modern institutional image" (Anzelmo 2017: 10).

I pointed out in my previous work on the charismatic phenomenon in the Catholic Church that the latter was able to absorb the former only by domesticating it, that is by institutionalizing its charismatic aspects in its hierarchical apparatus (Lado 2009, 2019). Just as it is difficult to reconcile the hierarchical dynamics of the Catholic Church with charismatic predicaments, the Catholic Church is struggling to adapt to the horizontality that characterizes communication on social media. Indeed one of the particularities of the new technologies is that it promotes the emergence of an ecclesial public opinion, in the sense that they allow "the faithful to express their opinions on the current concerns of the Catholic Church" (Mouthe 2015: 15). Internet and the social media have the ability to democratize, intensify, and level the production and circulation of information, making it possible for voices from the grassroots to challenge authority and doctrine. Technological changes lead to social changes and each type of media shapes the communication experience in a particular way. Eric Maigret (2015) distinguishes three dimensions of the act of communication: the functional dimension which makes it possible to exchange information, the sociocultural dimension as an instance of construction of meaning and identities, and the political dimension that brings into play asymmetrical power relations between stakeholders. He emphasizes the idea that besides technological dimension, communication is also a cultural and political practice (Maigret 2015: 8).

The new media by subverting the hierarchy of sources and promoting free speech constrain religious institutions to reposition themselves in the public space. The institutional Catholic Church, which has a long-established tradition of face-to-face communication through parish communities, fears that virtual communities will take precedence over physical communities. This fear of losing control of the "Catholic" label and faithful in the new media is clearly captured in the following excerpt from a Vatican official document which is worth quoting in length:

> The proliferation of web sites calling themselves Catholic creates a problem of a different sort. As we have said, church-related groups should be creatively present on the Internet; and well-motivated, well-informed individuals and unofficial groups acting on their own initiative are entitled to be there as well. But it is confusing, to say the least, not to distinguish eccentric doctrinal interpretations, idiosyncratic devotional practices, and ideological advocacy bearing a "Catholic" label from the authentic positions of the Church. We suggest an approach to this issue below. One area for research concerns the suggestion that the wide range of choices regarding consumer products and services available on the Internet may have a spillover effect in regard to religion and encourage a "consumer" approach to matters of faith. Data suggest that some visitors to religious web sites may be on a sort of shopping spree, picking and choosing elements of customized religious packages to suit their personal tastes. The "tendency on the part of some Catholics to be selective in their adherence" to the Church's teaching is a recognized problem in other contexts; more information is needed about whether and to what extent the problem is exacerbated by the Internet. Similarly, as noted above, the virtual reality of cyberspace has some worrisome implications for religion as well as for other areas of life. Virtual reality is no substitute for the Real Presence of Christ in the Eucharist, the sacramental reality of the other sacraments, and shared worship in a flesh-and-blood human community. There are no sacraments on the Internet; and even the religious

experiences possible there by the grace of God are insufficient apart from real-world interaction with other persons of faith. Here is another aspect of the Internet that calls for study and reflection. At the same time, pastoral planning should consider how to lead people from cyberspace to true community and how, through teaching and catechesis, the Internet might subsequently be used to sustain and enrich them in their Christian commitment.

(Pontifical Council for Social Communication,
Church and Internet, 2002: 8–9)

This approach contrasts with those of many Pentecostal churches which tend to value virtual communities precisely because of their ability to transcend denominations. Asamoah-Gyadu highlights the global nature of Pentecostalism, the ability of the new media to help Pentecostals reach "denominationally disenchanted persons outside their weekly captive constituencies" and to generate new communities that challenge the traditional ideas of parish communities (Asamoah-Gyadu 2015: 167). They value the interactive potential of computer-mediated communication that allows feedbacks from potential converts. The interactionist approach sees the media as instances of interaction between various actors pursuing various interests. From this perspective the media is also a space of religious competition between denominations (Moute 2015). It has been noted that the youth is the most tech-savvy social category, especially with respect to information and communication technologies (October 2014) and a denomination which does not engage the new media run the risk of losing touch with the youth or of losing them to those other denominations which are more present on the media. The Catholic Church media practices in Africa are today located in a plural religious context where it does not have the monopoly of the media.

Notes

1   National Episcopal Conferences assemble bishops of the same country while the Symposium of Episcopal Conferences of Africa and Madagascar (SECAM) brings together all the regional episcopal conferences of the continent. The purpose of these platforms is to work together in order to provide answers to the common problems facing the Church in a particular country or on the continent at large. Both at national and continental levels, there are departments dedicated to media and communications. Their role is to provide guidance on how to make the best of media technologies in the Church.

2   Cf. data of Institut National de la Statistique, des Etudes Economiques et Démographiques (INSEED), http://www.inseed-td.net/index.php/thematiques/statistique-demographique/population, consulted on August 20, 2019.

3   In the Catholic hierarchy, a diocese is headed by a bishop who runs the diocese assisted by priests who usually run parishes; deacons are one stage below priests that they aspire to become; seminarians are lay people studying for the priesthood. At the bottom of the hierarchy are the lay faithful. In the diocese of Chad, media are controlled by the clergy who hire lay people to run them.

4   Cf. Law 029 / PR / 94, repealed in 2010 by the law 17 / PR / 2010 of August 31, 2010, on the freedom of the press; Law 043 / PR / 94 on the freedom of the audio-visual communication and the right of the Chadian citizens to the services of audiovisual communication. It, too, will be repealed by Law No. 009 / PR / 2010. The most recent law is Ordinance No. 016 / PR / 2018 of May 31, 2018, on the organization and functioning of the High Authority for the Media and Audiovisual (HAMA). The text on HAMA was ratified by Law No. 32 / PR / 2018 of December 3, 2018.

5   See 2019 annual report of Haute Autorité des Media et de l'Audio Visuel du Tchad (HAMA), the official watchdog of media in the country.

6   A parallel can be drawn here with Eric Hoenes del Pinal's chapter in this volume on the crucial role of FM radio in the communication landscape in rural Guatemala. In most rural Chad, which makes 80 percent of the country, radio is also the "most widely accessible and reliable form of mass mediated communication."

7   See also Norget's chapter in this volume on the many ambiguities of the articulation of the secular and religious in the celebration of the Señor de los Milagros in Lima, Peru.

4

"This station only runs on love": Post-Bureaucratic Evangelism in a Transylvanian Catholic Media Organization

Marc Roscoe Loustau

Introduction: "This station only runs on love"

For its tenth anniversary in 2016, the Catholic media organization Radio Maria Transylvania invited newspaper reporters, television crews, and online news correspondents into its headquarters to see the station in action and interview the staff. In ten years, Radio Maria Transylvania had gone from a tiny one-person startup to one of Romania's largest Hungarian-language broadcasters, serving the country's ethnic Hungarian minority with four regional broadcasting stations, fifteen paid staff, and five hundred volunteers (Ozváth 2011; Balázs 2016). Radio Maria Transylvania is also a member of The World Family of Radio Maria, a global network founded in 1998 with branches now spearheading the Catholic Church's "New Evangelization" initiative in seventy countries around the world. Although anthropologists have noted that Christian evangelism in North America and Europe often takes shape through subtle, background constructions of faith, the tenth anniversary celebrations marked a departure from this norm. Typically, European secularism discourage the expression of faith as the imposition of private interests on the public sphere (Casanova 1994; Asad 2003; Kaell 2016). Many contemporary evangelists plot paths around this injunction by embedding ambiguous material signs of Christianity in public spaces to make what Mathew Engelke calls "ambient faith" (Engelke 2012, 2013). Although Engelke shows how evangelists put a lot of work into picking an appropriately ambiguous angel design and finding the right out-of-the-way spot to hang it in a British shopping mall, the invisibility of this labor seems to be a precondition of the highly mediated evangelism called ambient faith. The angels are ambient because the evangelists are so subtle as they go about designing and hanging them. To paraphrase the saying, dramatically performing "how the sausage" of ambient faith is made would somehow make it too obviously evangelical and thus be a violation of secular norms.

Radio Maria Transylvania certainly recognized Western European norms, even as the network has taken advantage of successive post-socialist Hungarian governments' support for Catholic cultural production (Loustau 2021). While the state has frequently sought to burnish its legitimacy by promoting "Christian values," the tenth anniversary coverage served multiform and contradictory purposes, among them the need to skirt injunctions against showing how mediated evangelism is done. When a newspaper reporter asked Radio Maria Transylvania's founder, Ferenc Szatmári, to speak about the network's challenges, Szatmári responded, "For me, because I handle our administration—which is invisible to our audience—the greatest challenge is providing for our everyday needs. Let me say a bit about how we do this" (Berecski 2016). Szatmári's contribution to the tenth anniversary coverage implied that the conditions of radio evangelism in secular Europe contribute to his administrative work's invisibility. Yet he also sensed that he should show the public what managerial tasks are involved in evangelism, and that Radio Maria Transylvania's work might even benefit from this.

In this essay, I examine contemporary Radio Maria Transylvania workers' discourse about and practice of evangelism. My material comes from three years of ethnographic research in Transylvania's ethnic Hungarian communities as well as fieldwork at the Csíksomlyó Catholic shrine. Located in the Ciuc Valley, widely known as a bastion of Catholic and Hungarian ethnic identity, Csíksomlyó is the Hungarian world's most popular religious site and home to one of Radio Maria Transylvania's regional broadcasting stations. During my fieldwork, I conducted interviews with twenty different Radio Maria volunteers at Csíksomlyó and elsewhere in Transylvania. My participant observational research with workers at the Csíksomlyó Radio Maria branch included handling clerical duties like answering the phones and recording donations. I also observed other volunteers as they did these and other tasks. Finally, I joined Radio Maria Transylvania's on-air workers in the booth as they broadcast from Csíksomlyó. In the article's first section, I describe the historical context of Romania's post-Second World War state bureaucratic expansion and then, following the collapse of state socialism, the recent emergence of highly critical views of bureaucratic work. This historical context, I show, creates an unstable atmosphere for evangelists' understanding of their work, since in addition to working in the station's office many Radio Maria Transylvania volunteers undertake bureaucratic evangelistic labor in domestic contexts that, in today's post-socialist milieu, have come to be associated with nonmonetary values of care, honesty, and authenticity.

In the next section, I turn to media coverage of the network's fifth and tenth anniversary celebrations during which Radio Maria Transylvania's officials described the organization's managerial style with the catchphrase, "This station only runs on love" [*Ez a rádió csak szeretetből működik*]. By drawing attention to the practice of evangelistic labor, Radio Maria Transylvania's leaders synthesize Catholic ethical values with the increasingly authoritative, quasi-secular discourse of "holistic management theory." According to sociologists Luc Boltanski and Eve Chiapello, holistic management theory emerged in Western Europe and North America in the 1960s to advocate for workplaces based on conviviality, informality, lateral relations, availability, and receptivity—qualities that appealed to managers who increasingly felt cramped in and oppressed by rigid, cold, and hierarchical firms (Boltanski and Chiapello 1999). Holistic management theory took shape alongside the "time-space compression" of globalized fast capitalism, which Marxist geographer David Harvey has identified with conditions of dispersed production and instantaneous consumption that increasingly destabilize cultural and religious time-space barriers and categories (Harvey 1989). Post-Second Vatican Council Catholicism and the Cold War were also crucial backdrops to Radio Maria Transylvania's embrace of an organizational principle of love. In the first case, many European and North American Catholics heard calls to "modernize" coming from the Second Vatican Council, the early 1960s global gathering of bishops in Rome, to be a critique of Catholicism's bureaucratic and hierarchical institutional structure (Dulles 1974). In the second, holistic management theory's originators saw Eastern Bloc communist parties as the primary example of "bad," rule-bound organizations (Boltanski and Chiapello 1999: 65; Gonzalez 2015: 328). By speaking of a workplace based on love and evoking holistic management theory's ideal of the anti-bureaucratic firm, Radio Maria Transylvania and other Catholic evangelists carve out a position for themselves in a story about an emerging post-Cold War, post-Vatican II, and post-bureaucratic European modernity.

While Radio Maria Transylvania's volunteers embrace the administration's holistic management theory–inspired image of a Catholic and loving workplace, many of them also portrayed their work in terms reminiscent of the "old" vision of a rigid, rule-bound, and hierarchically bureaucratic firm. Based on interviews and fieldwork with volunteers, this paper will describe their general view that radio evangelism work requires precision, regimentation, punctuality, and, above all, a serious attitude. These views were not simply an anachronism or holdover from their experience working in the socialist-era bureaucracy. Rather, volunteers selectively and strategically used these ideas to negotiate the specific incongruities entailed by prevailing views about gender, family, and work. This did not save Radio Maria Transylvania's volunteers from encountering other kinds of contradictions and incongruities as part of their evangelism work. Women were especially challenged to reconcile the idea that they were doing work in a domestic space defined by opposition to bureaucratic values. I conclude by branching out to describe how the practice of evangelistic work influenced views about one of the Ciuc Valley's most popular jobs. The Waberer's trucking company, one of the region's largest employers and Europe's third biggest freight company, has used a recruiting office in the Ciuc Valley to attract over three hundred drivers from this area. By describing interactions between two truck drivers and their wives who volunteer for Radio Maria Transylvania, I show how these volunteers use the notion of seriousness to win recognition for their evangelism work.

The Radio Maria Bureaucracy in Historical Context

Since its founding in 2006, Radio Maria Transylvania faced the task of managing a growing group of workers and volunteers when many Transylvanian Hungarians held mixed views about bureaucracies and bureaucratic work at best. Bureaucracy was a universal feature of the post-War Romanian socialist state's centrally organized economic and political system, and the tension between ideal-typical procedure and actual practice as set out by the government's five-year plan defined jobs in a variety of sectors (Kligman and Verdery 2011). For many socialist-era citizens, having a job in a favored sector of the bureaucracy that redistributed large pools of resources was a sign of social advancement and influence (Verdery 1996: 46). Many of Radio Maria's older female volunteers had once held positions in the socialist government bureaucracy as clerical workers, taking these positions as part of the state's official commitment to gender emancipation through universal employment. But many Transylvanian Hungarian women complained that the socialist state bureaucracy had exacerbated various social problems, either by virtue of an imperfect design or by practical incompetence. In line with their comments, anthropologist Gail Kligman has argued that, despite its propaganda claims, the Romanian state bureaucracy failed to create the institutional conditions necessary to ensure that women and men bear equally the labor of social reproduction (Kligman 1998).[1] During my fieldwork, when I asked women about this double burden, some said their male kin often refused to perform domestic tasks (Kligman and Gal 2000: 75–6). Others offered accounts that implicitly blamed these burdens on a practical failure to follow proper procedure: they cited the socialist state's constitutional recognition of minority rights and European Union minority protections and claimed Romanian politicians' preference for other Romanians and animosity toward Hungarians led them to violate them both. In their view, the state bureaucracy was blameworthy not because it was inherently wasteful or inefficient, but rather because powerful bureaucrats had used their positions to make ethnically partisan decisions (Brubaker et al. 2007: 116; Bottoni 2008).

In the 1980s, the Romanian socialist government also began exporting most production to pay down its foreign debt, resulting in long lines in front of state grocery stores and widespread shortages of basic consumer goods. Katherine Verdery calls these lines the visual index of the state's "etatization of time," a system by which the government organized its domination by making citizens wait for hours for even the most basic necessities (1996: 48). To pay the state's "time tax," families often mobilized kin who were otherwise unable to work: the elderly and children. In addition, the costs to families' time were heavier in cities than in villages, since urban residents had little direct access to the farms that produced food and, in addition, often had to wait in processions and parades to honor visiting politicians and dignitaries (49). These lines, in Katherine Verdery's words, "immobilize[d] bodies for hours, destroying their capacity for alternative uses of time" (1996: 48). And for all Verdery describes an "experience of humiliation, of a destruction of dignity," that the waits created (Verdery 1996: 49). Food queues and shortages were the prototypical context in which everyday people interacted with a corrupt, exploitative, and humiliating state bureaucracy (1996: 45). Today, many remember interactions with the low-level bureaucrats who doled out scarce resources—store clerks and ticket-sellers—as frustrating and degrading.

In my own work as well as that of anthropologists Susan Gal and Gail Kligman, I found that post-socialist subjects tended to figure the family as a world apart, as completely separate from the dirty business of government (2000: 69). This view also contributed to the phenomenon of urban and middle-class women in post-socialist societies who prefer not to perform wage labor (Funk and Mueller 1993; Ferge 1997; Szalai 2000).[2] Lingering memories of women's double burden and unpleasant and unfair workplace environments led to a sense that the ideologically driven socialist state had "forced" urban and middle-class women into the workplace. During my fieldwork, the urban women who gave voice to the view that domestic sociality was an unchanging and traditional locus of nonmonetary, loving, and caring relationships were often middle-aged and retired. They used a discourse of "heterotopia," which Fehérváry follows Foucault in calling an oppositional spatial and social construction, to speak about their professionally employed daughters (2013: 16–18). The retired mother of a government bankruptcy lawyer, for instance, described her daughter's work as "sordid" (*piszkos*) and full of "falseness" (*hamisság*). Sitting in her urban apartment's living room, she told me, "Here it's like we're in a little heaven, and then she goes to work and it's like she's going to hell." As Gal and Kligman (2000) point out, ideas about work in Romania are also gendered, and women I spoke with identified the market as masculine—cutthroat, dangerous, and unwelcoming to women (Gal and Kligman 2000: 69; Fehérváry 2013: 56). Radio Maria Transylvania began seeking out volunteers among Catholic devotees of the Virgin Mary—a most female population—at a time when many post-socialist subjects were navigating between these contradictory views about bureaucracy, work, and gender.

Nevertheless, Catholic women I spoke with in Transylvania still found ways to embrace new post-socialist professional values of initiative and ambition. Many reported that organizing in cultural NGOs was an appealing way to win recognition for their accomplishments. For instance, village governments and tour companies paid women to recruit home hospitality for Hungarian tourists visiting Transylvanian Hungarian villages on vacation. This was an especially popular form of volunteer work as the annual Csíksomlyó pilgrimage event approached, as the site could expect 100,000 visitors needing places to stay in the area. Local organizers worked at the intersection of the market and the state bureaucracy but were able to say they were advancing the cause of building cross-border, state-transcending national solidarity. Like pilgrimage hospitality organizers, Radio Maria's volunteers associate their work with values like initiative and ambition in the service of the broader community. To drum up financial support and awareness for Radio Maria Transylvania in Ciuc Valley parishes, volunteers travel to different villages for "promotion work" (*promóciózni*), in which they spoke about Radio Maria and the New Evangelization. On one occasion I traveled to a parish 20 kilometers north of Csíksomlyó with three volunteers. In charge was Eszter, a middle-aged woman who lived on the fifth floor of an apartment building in the Ciuc Valley's largest city, Miercurea Ciuc, directly adjacent to Csíksomlyó. During the event, Eszter gave a short speech about her volunteer work that she began with an adage about the importance of desire and ambition: "You're never going to get somewhere if you don't want to go in the first place." Eszter went on to explain that she works for Maria Radio because she loves it, and that she feels this love especially strongly when other tasks and obligations get in the way. At such times, "I thank God that He helps, and I feel he is next to me. He gives me bodily and spiritual strength to do everything." When I asked another volunteer named Réka what kind of work she did for Radio Maria, she laughed and said that it was "meager" (*csekély*). I sensed that her humility was partly due to the village priest's resistance to Radio Maria Transylvania. According to Réka, he had refused her entreaty to have Radio Maria Transylvania broadcast a Mass from the parish church. Yet when we were talking about the parish's new choirmaster and organist, she allied herself with this man's initiative and drive: "I'm happy to say that we have a young organist, who came about a year ago, who works enthusiastically. He came here to my house to encourage [my work with Radio Maria] and give me some support." Réka went on to describe the organist's new initiatives, including a new village brass band, and she called him an "enthusiastic, young, and ambitious person." Through her work in Radio Maria Transylvania, allied herself with this ambitious Church leader and claimed his support.

While conducting fieldwork in the Ciuc Valley, I observed Radio Maria Transylvania's volunteers perform a wide variety of clerical tasks for the organization. They collected and mailed monthly membership dues and distributed Radio Maria Transylvania monthly newsletter. They organized and participated in Rosary prayer groups, and brought members of these groups to the Csíksomlyó station to pray on the air. Activists also kept detailed membership and financial records. They were required to be at regular planning meetings at the Csíksomlyó station, where they also staffed the front desk, took phone calls, and recorded prayer requests. Many of these bureaucratic tasks took Radio Maria Transylvania's volunteers into domestic spaces. The organization's workers faced the additional contradiction that their evangelical labor was caught up in the production of entertaining, uplifting, and informative cultural goods. Their evangelical work was mediated through products that were supposed to be key parts of creating nonwork, leisure-oriented atmosphere.

Managing and Mediating Bureaucracy

In 2011 and 2016, on its fifth and tenth anniversaries, Radio Maria Transylvania opened up its headquarters in Oradea to television and print reporters from secular media networks and the Transylvanian Archdiocese's official media outlets. Radio Maria Transylvania's staff collaborated with these visitors on a series of interviews and reports about the organization's administration to help the audience visualize this aspect of evangelism work.[3] In an article for the Archdiocese's weekly newsletter, *Vasárnap* (*Sunday*), Director of Programming Tibor Karácsony broke down Radio Maria Transylvania's broadcasts into three primary and three secondary types: prayer, evangelization, and assistance followed by news, entertainment, and music. Karácsony explained to the interviewer that opening listeners' hearts and minds to Christ's light requires "building a well-structured program." Thus the program's structure has a higher purpose: responsiveness to the needs of its listeners. As Karácsony explained, the staff's production process prioritizes "personalization" (*személyre szabottsága*) and sensitivity to the audience's everyday rhythms and habits. In line with holistic management theory's critique of mechanical bureaucracy, these principles ensure that the organization's product does not feel artificial: "While planning the broadcast," Karácsony insisted, "it is of basic importance to take into account the audience's everyday rhythm so that the programming is not artificial but rather responds to the audience's concrete life situation." If these articles' goal, as Ferenc Szatmári said, was to make visible Radio Maria Transylvania's bureaucracy, in the process Szatmári's colleagues highlighted the organization's commitment to a programming process that ensured a personalized, non-artificial product.

About his organization, Ferenc Szatmári often says that it runs only on love, or in Hungarian *csak szeretetből működik*. In his 2011 interview with an archdiocesan reporter, Szatmári revealed that love is the reason that Radio Maria Transylvania uses only volunteer workers: "This is precisely why it's important that we are not allowed to pay money for this work" (Ozsváth 2011). He told a story about two volunteers who stayed at the company even though they showed such talent they were offered more lucrative positions elsewhere. "Both of them," Szatmári declared, "let it be known very clearly that they won't leave because their place is here and there is no way to replace this spirit." The notion that workplaces are defined by a "spirit" (*lélek*) or "atmosphere" (*hangulat*)— another term used in Radio Maria Transylvania's literature—is a staple of the ideology that sociologists Luc Boltanski and Eve Chiapello call "the new spirit of capitalism" (Boltanski and Chiapello 1999). According to Boltanski and Chiapello, the discourse of workplace spirit emerges from a nineteenth-century Romantic critique of "mechanistic capitalism" and advocates greater emphasis on "intangibles" like feeling and the soul as a way to blunt the alienating effects of labor (1999: 93). I gathered the impression during my fieldwork that the line between Radio Maria Transylvania's volunteers and official staff was often blurry, even for regulars at the organization's stations. But according to the administrators this is a designed ambiguity. In one interview, Szatmári specified Radio Maria Transylvania's employment policy as an outgrowth of its volunteer-centered model. All employees, in all positions, he said, had to be volunteers first. In another interview, Szatmári cites the rules of evangelization to justify Radio Maria Transylvania's alternative notion of "professionalism." "It is a rule that one cannot evangelize for money," Szatmári told an interviewer in 2011, "We consider people who sacrifice their time for others, from the perspective of evangelization, to be 'professionals' already" (Ozsváth 2011). If the machine was the compelling trope of industrial Fordism as well as state socialism, such that what anthropologists often call everyday practice was treated as "disruptive" and "confusing," fast capitalism incorporates ambiguity directly into the rules that govern its bureaucratic organization.[4] Employment categories and concepts of professionalism are intentionally blurred in holistic management alternative to bureaucratic hierarchy (Gonzalez 2015: 76).

Most discussions of Radio Maria Transylvania's finances draw on and promote ideas about new caring and compassionate post-bureaucratic workplaces. For Szatmári, one story exemplifies how affect, caring, and money come together in the life of Radio Maria Transylvania's workers. According to Szatmári, he once ran out of money and could not afford to pay the employees. "Our situation was totally hopeless," he recalled, but then he had the idea of asking Radio Maria's listeners for help. The donations they received more than covered the needed expenses. Radio Maria Transylvania's volunteers, Szatmári says, remember this as a "cathartic experience" to this day. The outpouring also proves Szatmári's point that Radio Maria Transylvania is a family: "In fact, this is precisely why we are a 'family,' so that we can share our problems and troubles with each other" (Ozsváth 2011). This story about overcoming challenges embraces seemingly capitalistic values of ingenuity, growth, and success. But this event, in Szatmári's version, actually illustrates a practice of shared caretaking. Szatmári is therefore able to embed Radio Maria Transylvania's narrative in a long-standing Catholic theological critique of overly individualistic forms of capitalism, especially the idea that business success was solely dependent on individual qualities of the mind, character, and temperament.[5] Love, spirit, caring, and other concepts ally Radio Maria Transylvania with both a Catholic theological anti-capitalism and a post-Vatican II effort to modernize a supposedly old-fashioned bureaucratic Church. In the process, Radio Maria Transylvania's leaders also tap into the popularity of holistic management theory and its vision of a post-Cold War office based on conviviality and informality. Contradictory secular and Catholic values seemingly meet and merge in the Radio Maria Transylvania workplace.

Serious Work at Radio Maria Transylvania

While Radio Maria Transylvania's volunteer workers embrace the administration's image of a loving bureaucratic family, many of them also portrayed their work in terms reminiscent of a mechanistic bureaucracy. Evangelism required precision, regimentation, punctuality, and, above all, a serious attitude. These views were not simply an anachronism or holdover from their time in the socialist-era bureaucracy. Rather, volunteers selectively and strategically used these ideas to negotiate the contradictions that evangelization *qua* bureaucratic work entails. Many Radio Maria volunteer workers have internalized a job description-style knowledge of their tasks. When I asked them to describe their work, they often provided an exhaustive list of responsibilities. They recited precise numbers of newspapers received and delivered as well as dates and deadlines for submitting donations. The volunteer named Júlia told me that,

> My work includes newspaper delivery [*újsághordás*] and keeping the account books in which are recorded our monthly supporters. I collect the monthly donations, and I deliver them to the post office each month, paying attention very precisely to the amounts and notations. As for delivering the magazines every second month, there are eighty-three copies and forty members.

Other volunteer workers performed detailed record-keeping to support Radio Maria's most popular broadcast, a prayer request call-in program. Emma, for instance, teamed up with several other volunteer workers to keep track of the prayer requests that listeners were constantly calling in to the office. They kept two hardbound ledgers, identical except that one was black and the other blue, in a desk drawer. When listeners called with prayers for the hosts to read on the air, Emma answered the phone, drew out one of the ledgers, and entered information in precise and legible handwriting. The entries had to fit in small squares for the caller's name and location, as well as a larger section for the text of the prayer. Radio Maria's bookkeepers were scrupulous about making sure this information was filled out properly and then crossed out when the hosts read the prayers on the air. Some volunteer workers insisted that callers include information for all three fields and would sometimes press callers for data. One of Emma's coworkers, Csilla, picked up the phone when I called to offer a prayer for a friend whose sister died in a car accident. I was reluctant to give my name and hometown in the United States, since it would have been obvious that I had offered this prayer. But Csilla would not allow me to leave these fields blank. We reached a compromise that I would be called "an everyday listener" and list my hometown as Miercurea Ciuc, where I was based at the time. There were two levels to this conflict. First, a prayer from Boston would have confirmed Radio Maria Transylvania's identity as both a global and evangelistic organization, since many Christian organizations increasingly see evangelism as an access point to the transnational circulations of people and prayers that define active participation in a global community (Coleman 2000; Oosterbaan 2011). But most importantly, Csilla responded to my reluctance by asserting her bureaucratic obligations. She insisted on filling in the blank in her ledger book as Radio Maria Transylvania's regular procedure required.

The ambiguities of doing bureaucratic evangelical work in familial contexts fuel many everyday conflicts and disagreements about Radio Maria Transylvania. A middle-aged volunteer named Klára once told me that her family members, especially her deceased husband, chafed at her enthusiasm for listening to Radio Maria. When poor health forced him to stay at home, Klára simply turned off the radio lest it antagonize him. The conflict had saddened Klára and colored her experience of evangelizing in the family:

> I've tried to find an explanation for it. My husband drank a lot. He was a good worker, but religion, church, and prayer, that was difficult. For some, they get enjoyment [*élmény*] from living their faith. Especially in the family. To give children an education in faith. And so on. It's a great blessing to have a joyful experience of faith in the family. But this wasn't so for me. It was always hard work.

Klára's recollections evoke one side of the leisure-work contradiction that destabilizes many Radio Maria Transylvania volunteers' beliefs about their work. On the one hand, domestic devotional labor, when it is proper and good, should be joyful and bring enjoyment. The word for "enjoyment" (*élmény*) Klára is tied to the concept of leisure and is closely related to words like "amusement park" (*élmény park*). When Catholic women properly train their families in the faith, Klára suggests, their families should experience a joyful and pleasurable integration of prayer and domestic contentment. Klára took the fact that her devotional labor felt like work to be a sign that something was wrong and her family was not properly faithful.

On the other hand, Radio Maria volunteers often complained that their daughters or daughters-in-law were not "working" when they neglected to teach their children about Catholicism. "It's unfortunate. My daughter-in-law Kamilla doesn't choose to make this effort, but a mother's first responsibility is her children. To raise them spiritually. It's not good, but I try to understand." In this complaint, devotional labor is a form of work and a duty to be fulfilled, rather than a type of leisure activity that engenders enjoyment and pleasure. Radio Maria Transylvania's volunteers also feel pulled in two directions when their bureaucratic values—punctuality, professionalism, and precision—come into conflict with their obligation to provide domestic care. An older volunteer named Dorottya mentioned that her daughter often complained when she stayed at home to do Radio Maria Transylvania business rather than visit to watch her grandchildren When Dorottya repeated her daughter's complaint, she said she felt accused of shirking her work: "I don't go to their house to take care of my granddaughter, so my daughter-in-law says, 'Why aren't you here to do this work?'" Dorottya told me she tries to compromise by hosting her granddaughter at her home, but this had not satisfied her daughter. Other times, Dorottya's volunteer work requires that she be away from her village at the Csíksomlyó broadcast booth when her family would prefer she be at home. This also seemed to interfere with Dorottya's domestic responsibilities.

> There are times when she notices that taking care of my granddaughter is not as important, because for instance I have to go out to Csíksomlyó... . If they say they want to come here to my home, then I have something to do right then for Radio Maria and I need to leave. They ask why I don't stop this work. Why don't I make time for them to come here? That's why they argue with me.

These comments show how the values associated with domestic childcare and evangelism come into conflict. Women may be doing bureaucratic work to advance Radio Maria Transylvania's program of evangelism, but their kin do not perceive this to be valuable labor, especially when it comes into conflict with domestic responsibilities. When volunteers show up at Csíksomlyó for a work shift, the family members who would benefit from childcare perceive the duty of care to contradict the demand to be punctual. In most circumstances, Radio Maria Transylvania's volunteers avoid or ignore questions about whether their volunteer labor is truly bureaucratic work. But sometimes they are forced to find some clarity, like when Dorottya needs to be in two places at once—at Radio Maria Transylvania's Csíksomlyó station and at home with her grandchildren.

Seriousness between Evangelizing and Trucking

Like Klára, Júlia hoped one day her family would be interested in Radio Maria Transylvania. She told me once, "They haven't felt [*átérezni*] the significance of it deeply yet, my family members." The word *átérezni* suggests one has come to a transformative new understanding of a problem. Júlia herself had become a volunteer after listening to broadcasts during a prolonged illness, and she articulated her evangelical hope for her family in similar terms. My long-term experience getting to know another Radio Maria Transylvania volunteer, Eszter, demonstrates how evangelization can produce knowledge of others' deep and serious experience. When I first met Eszter, she was already a dedicated volunteer, having signed on the first day Radio Maria Transylvania opened its station at Csíksomlyó. She was an occasional on-air personality, and was also the woman whom I recorded at a Radio Maria Transylvania promotion event speaking about ambition and wanting "to go in the first place." Eszter constantly listened to the broadcasts at home. She too hoped that the programs would leave her husband with an intuitive knowledge of the Mass that, when the time and need arose, would incline him to convert and discover faith. Eszter complemented this subtle education in faith with more assertive acts of evangelism, even though these efforts left her deeply frustrated at her husband's continuing resistance. In a 2011 interview I conducted with Eszter and her mother, Eszter spent a long time lamenting her husband's lack of interest in Mass. "My family life is very hard," she said, attributing her difficulty to Ádám's lackadaisical faith, "We have been praying for over twenty years for my life to turn better." This was not the first or last time Eszter had sacrificed for her husband's faith. She often reported commissioning Masses in his name and fasting in hopes God would turn his heart. Through all this, Eszter seemed to be struggling to find a rational and meaningful explanation for her husband's resistance to Catholic practice. She once suggested that her husband was simply too bored to sit through a Mass. On another occasion, she said that he simply could not tolerate the embodied aspects of the Catholic Mass. "He says that he can't get the wafer down his throat," she told me. What flummoxed Eszter was that Ádám was still resistant despite having been born to Catholic parents, baptized as an infant, and confirmed. Over the years, she often cited these explanations, found others, and then returned again disappointed. Once Eszter told me that she had hit on a foolproof solution that would avoid all these objections. If sitting through Mass would bore him and taking communion was disgusting, then maybe praying at the statue of the Virgin Mary would be tolerable. She asked him to stop by the

Csíksomlyó shrine with her to offer a brief prayer, but he refused, letting her go in with their children while he waited in the car. "He didn't even step in the church," she lamented once again.

Over the years, I began to sense that Eszter's search for a rational explanation for her husband's reluctance was doomed because Ádám himself was not acting according to the rules of causality or rationality. Attiya Ahmad and Devaka Premarwadhana have both argued, in studies of religious conversion, that the absence of ideological formulations and reasoned justifications for these transformations should prompt cultural anthropologists to look beyond the "explanatory impulse" to reduce this fundamentally embodied phenomenon to some sensible pattern of cause and effect (Ahmad 2017; Premarwadhana 2018: 23). But Premarwadhana and Ahmad go too far in mapping the explanatory impulse onto the concept of "outsider," just as Michael D. Jackson is too quick to speculate that "it is probably the separateness of the observer from the ritual acts" that leads anthropologists to search out for reasoned justifications from our informants (Jackson 2013: 59). The notions of insider and outsider, so central to the tradition of cultural analysis in anthropology, seem to muddle rather than clarify our understanding of the emerging dynamics of the Catholic Church's New Evangelization. Although Eszter was as "inside" the New Evangelization as anyone I met, when she was driven by Radio Maria Transylvania to convert her husband she sounded like the anthropologist Jackson as he pestered his informants with questions, consumed by a fervent search for clues to hidden meanings lying "behind" or "underneath" the ritual performances she was witnessing (Jackson 2013: 59). Ultimately, Eszter's questions were just as fruitless as Jackson's because, in Pierre Bourdieu's words, rituals underline the mistake of "treating movements of the body and practical manipulations as purely logical operations" (1977: 116). Eszter's references to Ádám's physical complaints about boredom and indigestion thus came the closest to the "ontological metaphors" or "analogies of the body" that subjects often use when forced to linguistically evoke inchoate, pre-verbal, and embodied experiences of profound discomfort (Lakoff and Johnson 1980).

When I returned to Csíksomlyó for a brief visit in 2016, Eszter invited me to her home to share something important. After I rang the doorbell, she urged me into the living room of her fifth-floor apartment in Miercurea Ciuc, a city of about 40,000 adjacent to Csíksomlyó. The big news, she told me, was that Ádám had "converted" (*áttérni*). Ádám had taken a job as a long-haul truck driver for the Waberer's freight company. "Once he was in Italy," she recalled excitedly, "and it happened that we were talking on the phone, and he said, 'You won't believe what I'm listening to.' He held the phone over to the radio, and it was a Mass. He knew because he heard the word, 'Gospel,' or something like it. And he started praying with the radio."

Eszter's story suggests that Radio Maria Transylvania's ideas about volunteer work may help Catholics make sense of the new working conditions they encounter in the emerging transnational European labor market. Volunteers' responses to truck driving actually challenge stereotypical views about the experience of neoliberal mobile labor. Sociologist Steve Viscelli argues that truck drivers' conditions demonstrate how neoliberalism has undermined collective bargaining rights, isolated laborers, and deepened truckers' experience of tensions between "home" and "work" (Upton 2016; Viscelli 2016). Medical anthropologists would concur that truck driving exacerbates parental abandonment (Lichtenstein et al. 2008; Adumitroaie and Dafinoiu 2013; Thakur, Toppo, and Lodha 2015); HIV/AIDS exposure (Orubuloye, Caldwell, and Caldwell 1991); male aggression and intimate partner abuse (Bolton 1979; Kalanit and Shoham 2013); and cardiovascular disease (Mitler et al. 1997; Robinson and Burnett 2005; Chen and Zhang 2016; Garbarino et al. 2016; Hege, Lemke, and Sönmez 2018). The dominant trope of truck driving's risks, dangers, and harmfulness rests on a more fundamental notion that, when viewed from the perspective of truck drivers' kin, trucking poses risks to the domestic unit's "ontological security" and that drivers' female relatives prize conservative values associated with security above all else. Yet Eszter did not perceive truck driving as a threat to her security but rather as an opportunity for Ádám to take advantage of the background training he had undergone when Eszter played Radio Maria at home. Chance and Radio Maria Transylvania's multilingual broadcasts eventually led Ádám to faith. During Ádám's long-haul trips, Eszter told me, he was constantly running across Radio Maria broadcasts. "You know what," she said, "he goes to Belgium, England, Ireland, everywhere. And he's been saying that, totally accidentally, it's always Radio Maria here, Radio Maria there. Radio Maria wherever he goes." By broadcasting the Mass at home, she had prepared Ádám to recognize familiar words—"Radio Maria" and "gospel"—when he heard them recited on the radio. The broadcasts also taught him to recognize the rhythm and flow of the Mass so that, at the right moment, he could recite the same words in Hungarian. This experience also drew Eszter's attention to positive personal characteristics that she had not noticed in a long time. "You know," she said, "Italian is a lot like Romanian. And Ádám has an especially good feeling for languages." It was one of Ádám's positive attributes I had never heard her talk about before. Eszter's domestic evangelism had seemingly prepared Ádám to pray as he had not done during Eszter's time in Radio Maria Transylvania.

The increasing authority of New Evangelization discourses about conversion in Transylvanian Catholic communities resonates in a greater willingness to view truck driving as a source of transformative experience that deepens one's sense of the seriousness of devotional practice. One Radio Maria volunteer, Hanna, spent the bulk of a joint interview with her husband Zoltán trying to underscore the seriousness of a road accident he had experienced, early on in his career as a truck driver. At the time of his accident, he was hauling agricultural produce for a small company based in Miercurea Ciuc. When Zoltán called his escape "good luck," Hanna jumped in to offer several other details that underscored the incident's seriousness:

> But it was you who came home to give me the news that the truck had flipped over. That was also a big thing. That *you* told me. If I had heard the news from someone else, imagine what could have happened. I was still pregnant at the time, remember? And if someone had come and said that you had tipped over, then it's possible I would have gotten so startled that I could have given birth to the child right there and then.

Hanna then explained why she had added this detail. She felt that it contradicted an interpretation that minimized the import of such accidents. "They are big things," Hanna insisted, "Some people don't believe in miracles. They don't take these accidents seriously. They say, 'Oh, you had some luck. Don't worry about it.' But I say that I trust in the Virgin Mother." She concluded the exchange by indicating how experiences like Zoltán's could lead one to feel grateful to the Virgin Mary for her assistance. "When you have experienced as much as I have. And I have experienced this help. More times than I can count. Then you won't speak like this." Radio Maria Transylvania's volunteers like Hanna urge their family members to take Catholic media seriously, and some try to highlight experiences that they might lead them to appreciate Radio Maria Transylvania in this manner. Júlia embraced a subtler and more indirect approach to this evangelical hope. She waited and trusted that an event would happen to draw their attention to Radio Maria Transylvania. Others like Eszter felt joy that truck driving could bring workers into contact again and again with Radio Maria Transylvania's broadcasts where their direct and willful attempts at evangelism had failed. Debates about Radio Maria Transylvania's volunteers and their work were not confined to people directly involved in Catholic media production but influenced conversations about other important forms of work in the region, as well.

Conclusion: A Post-Bureaucratic Catholicism

This article has invited readers to explore a seeming paradox: Modern Western Catholic radio evangelists who draw the public's attention to their evangelical work. Radio evangelization in Romania's ethnic Hungarian minority engages with a framework of secular norms that both destabilize and animate spreading the word about faith, even as Radio Maria Transylvania has also benefited from the material support of Hungarian governments seeking to ally themselves with a post-socialist Christian culture. Anthropologists Mathew Engelke and Hillary Kaell have shown that although Christians are by definition called to publicly express their personal faith, often-implicit norms deem such expressions an inappropriate imposition of private interests in the public arena. British bible activists and Quebecois Catholic artists creatively take advantage of this contradiction by spreading God's word in a highly mediated manner, placing paper angels in shopping malls and crosses on rural roadsides to constitute a background atmosphere of daily life or "ambient faith." But where I did fieldwork in urban Romania, the nearest shopping mall was a three-hour drive away. And although many urban transplants remained a part of their natal village social networks, artistic endeavors like repairing a roadside cross were not a popular way to sustain these connections. In Romania, bureaucracy is a crucial social form through which secular norms are both constituted and legitimized as well as challenged and destabilized, as when Hungarian government bureaucracies provide funding to Catholic charitable organizations. The notion that Radio Maria Transylvania "runs on love" works within and targets bureaucratic norms while also helping the group's officials and volunteers hold together multiple ethical contradictions and conundrums encoded into the practice of media evangelism. When they make visible the cathartic, lateral, and personalized practice of funding and producing evangelical broadcasts, Radio Maria Transylvania's officials echo in a muted manner the anti-bureaucratic critique of post-Vatican II theologians like the prominent twentieth-century ecclesiologist Avery Dulles, who famously wrote, "In an age when all large institutions are regarded with suspicion and aversion, it is exceptionally difficult to attract people to a religion that represents itself as primarily institutional" (1974: 44–5). Pre-Vatican II theologians' emphasis on finding the ground for the Church's hierarchical institutional structure in God's power, holiness, and eternity, Dulles charged, had led to "unfortunate consequences in Christian life:" "While some virtues, such as obedience, are strongly accented, others are not" (Dulles 1974: 43). These other de-emphasized virtues include some of the very concepts that Radio Maria Transylvania's officials place front and center in their portrayal of everyday life in the station's workplace: love, spirit, care, receptivity, and openness. Radio Maria Transylvania draws attention to its evangelical practice to integrate Catholic ecclesiology with holistic management theory, creating a synthesis that allies the field of Catholic media production with a post-bureaucratic European future.

Notes

1   In his study of socialist-era urbanization and modernization in Miercurea Ciuc, the nearest city to Csíksomlyó, Demeter states that the government's daycare services were constantly inadequate, making childcare a significant problem for families in which both parents were required to work (Demeter 2011: 66). Kligman estimates that childcare facilities accommodated 8.7 percent of children aged one to three in 1985 and dropping to 7.4 percent in 1989 (Kligman 1998: 82–5). See also Laki and Bíró (2001).

2   Kligman and Gal warn against essentializing this view without acknowledging its social causes; they point to the fact that this view prevails mostly among the urban bourgeoisie.

3   See also Ozsváth (2011), Péter (2011), and Balázs (2016).

4   Verdery's voluminous writings about socialist-era organizational culture in Romania often rely on the Weberian trope that everyday practice created unplanned inefficiencies, cross-fertilizations, and corruptions of bureaucratic designs, rules, and structures. See, for instance, this statement about the Romanian secret police bureaucracy: "With this, the contradiction—so common in ethnography—between rules and their practices comes clearly into view" (2013: 141).

5   This critique goes back to Pope Leo XIII's 1931 encyclical, "Quadragesimo anno." In his 1891 encyclical "Rerum novarum," Pius XI also based his critique of industrial capitalism on the principle that Catholics must recognize private property, both individual and social, but only so that common goods like nature may be ordered for the common good.

5

A Touch of Love:
On Words, Things, and the Global
Aspirations of US Catholics

Hillary Kaell

This chapter is about love. More specifically, it has to do with the multiple entextualizations of the word "love" that I noticed during my research on child sponsorship plans. Each year in the United States, millions of donors use sponsorship as a platform through which to support a child abroad. Such programs generally cost between 30 and 50 dollars a month, and include the opportunity to exchange letters, photos, and small gifts. Entextualization is baked into the process. It refers to how texts are made available for circulation in new contexts, often through the interaction of multiple forms of media (Eisenlohr 2010). In this case, I am interested in how one fragment text— the word "love"—circulates through a variety of sites including theological statements, sponsorship organizations' YouTube videos, figures of speech in American English, and homemade Christmas cards.

Theories of entextualization are one facet of the turn in media studies away from earlier assumptions that spoken language was "the most 'immaterial' of all media" (Eisenlohr 2011: 267) and, by extension, that "materiality" referred to everything else (Gershon and Manning 2014: 540). As anthropologists of evangelical Protestantism have noted, it is more fruitful to consider words and things as coextensive media (Coleman 2000; Keane 2003). Doing so requires defining "mediation" broadly, along with David Morgan (2013: 351), as "any practice of communication that intermingles the body with the world around it such that modes of embodiment become the measure of what people claim to know or feel as true." What I consider in this chapter is how a word or concept, such as love, can become the vector for that intermingling, and how its power is related to material things, including bodies, and electronic media.

I explore this theme in the context of Unbound, the largest Catholic sponsorship organization in the United States. My larger project on sponsorship spanned more than six years and covered a variety of Christian organizations; my work on Unbound was mainly concentrated from 2014 to 2016 when I conducted fieldwork in its offices in Kansas City and with sponsors who live there and near Albany, New York.[1] In what follows, I focus on how the organization's founders and current staff discuss and entextualize love, especially in their attempt to shape a theology of sponsorship for US donors. From a Catholic perspective, it is not very surprising that Unbound has adopted the language of love. Indeed, love is a native term in contemporary Catholicism, as is the idea that love takes embodied form.[2] As I note below, Unbound's founders adopted the child sponsorship model in the early 1980s from Protestant organizations that also emphasized love. While they kept the word's association with humanitarianism and the Christian Gospels, Unbound redefined sponsorship as a distinctly Catholic endeavor in part by entextualizing love within Roman Catholic social teaching.

In anthropological work, there has already been some attention to Catholic love as "a theological principle or ontological premise" (Mayblin 2012: 246). Anthropologists have shown how, for Catholic laypeople, human love—that is, for family and friends—may seem to channel divinity (Moore 2015) or appear as flawed, even impossible, compared to a perfect relationship with God (Lebner 2012). They have interrogated how aspirations for societal love may promote civic volunteerism (Muehlebach 2013b: 509). Theologians have also examined Roman Catholic love talk in personalist, Thomistic, and Augustinian thought. The first set of anthropological studies inspires my focus on informal, culturally rooted lay theologies; the second set of theological ones inspires my emphasis on love that exceeds particular, face-to-face relations in service of what sponsorship organizations often call "the world" or "one human family" (to quote Unbound's Statement of Core Values). This kind of love sutures, more or less successfully, the "irreconcilable tension between universalism and localism" that is inherent in the Catholic Church (Napolitano 2016: 69; Norget 2017: 189).

At a basic level, my primary questions are twofold: What *is* love in Unbound's theology of sponsorship? And how is it conceived as circulating even when the bodies of sponsors do not? In what ways do some people's bodies and actions become visible to others as channels for love? To answer these questions I examine the context for Unbound's views on love, its relation to family, motherhood, and material objects, as well as the organization's use of certain media to distinguish itself as lay Catholic. Of importance throughout is how the word love's capacity to bundle qualities, and therefore entextualize across many forms of media, helps give Unbound a certain flexibility in terms of organization identity as it balances between being Catholic yet distinct from the institutional Church, being humanitarian yet divinely guided, or being voluntary yet authoritative. To begin, however, let us turn to a brief discussion of the love I have in mind and the contexts in which it emerged.

Embodying the "Journey from Power to Love"

When I met Unbound's new CEO Scott Wasserman in July 2014, we were in the cafeteria eating rice and beans. Inspired by its beginnings as an intentional community, Unbound still offers its staff a free daily lunch featuring the simple food that founders Bob Hentzen and Jerry Tolle ate in Latin America as missionary priests in the 1950s and 1960s.[3] Both men left the priesthood in the early 1970s and returned to home to Kansas City where, with help from three of Hentzen's siblings, they co-founded the Christian Foundation for Children in 1981. It was the first major organization to promote child sponsorship by and for US Catholics. Today, it is called Unbound and has about 300,000 sponsors, nearly all of whom are US Catholics.

Hentzen and Tolle, who served with the Christian Brothers and Jesuits respectively, embraced the "preferential option for the poor," a phrase first used in 1968 by the superior general of the Jesuits and adopted by Liberation Theologians in Latin America. As we ate our rice and beans, Wasserman told me that although Unbound does not use that language any more—it sounds too Catholic and obscure for unchurched sponsors—they still abide by the principle, as interpreted over the years by Hentzen in particular.[4] For Unbound, it means trying to nudge sponsors on "the journey from power to love"—the title of a song Hentzen composed and often performed—where "power" refers to having money and "love" refers to solidarity and mutual respect. Hentzen characterized this journey as something that exceeds logic or human agency. In a quasi-mystical moment, the comparatively wealthy American individual connects God to humanity and becomes flooded with a feeling of loving connectedness. In the song's best known lines, Hentzen described his experience in Latin America: "Then it happened, oh, Lord. I fell in love with your people, I could not leave."[5] Later Wasserman clarified for me: "We want our sponsors to feel that they aren't just financial contributors, they are members of a prophetic community of compassion in which people… bridge national, cultural and economic divides."[6]

I never met Hentzen, who steered the organization as President until his death in 2013 at age seventy-seven, but his spirit lingered everywhere in Unbound's offices during my fieldwork. Unbound employees characterized him as an idealized "worker–priest" who personified social justice (Schneider 1991: 188; Muehlebach 2013a: 454). They told me multiple times how Hentzen was born on a humble Kansas farm in the throes of the Depression (1936, to be exact) and grew up in a family of fourteen. He was educated in local schools before joining the Christian Brothers in 1953, after which he taught in Colombia and Guatemala until 1970 when he left the order. After three more years in Guatemala, he returned to Kansas with his new wife, Cristina, to work in the nonprofit sector. In Unbound's portrayals of Hentzen during the second half of his life—as president of the organization he co-founded—he is no longer the farm boy, but he is still a humble servant who embodies the figure of traveling pilgrim and apostle (of love, not the evangel). During my time there, the corporate office displayed photos of Hentzen on his epic 4,000-mile overland pilgrimage from Kansas to Guatemala in 1996 and his 8,000-mile pilgrimage from Guatemala to Chile in 2009. One large image was an artful collage where his body was composed of hundreds of photos of sponsored children (Figure 5.1). Another zoomed in on his tattered shoes, which Unbound also used for his online obituary. "When asked why he walked," reads the obituary, "he said it was simple: 'I walk because I love them.'"[7] In YouTube videos from 2009, Hentzen himself elaborates:

> The most vulnerable people in this world feel isolated. The first message, then, in this walk is that you are not alone. We are walking with you. We are the group that not only walks, we are the group that really relates to the poor... .There have been some close calls [along the road]. Our greatest vulnerability out there on the road has been our smallness, our flesh and bones versus a 4,000 pound piece of steel flying down the highway at break-neck speed. But to submit to the dangers of the open road is a tremendous statement.[8]

Hentzen's actions were epic, but also comprehensible in Catholic terms. The pilgrim uses his body as an instrument through which to mediate and cultivate humility, piety, and reparative sacrifice. His actions embody humanitarian metaphors—"We are walking with you," "It is a journey from power to love," and "Walk the road to the heart of God... [as] pilgrims on this earth together," to quote some of Hentzen's songs. Metaphor becomes cramps, blisters, and breeze-ruffled hair. Love is mediated through the body: the pleasure, sweat, and pressure of touch as Hentzen embraced the families of sponsored children along his route

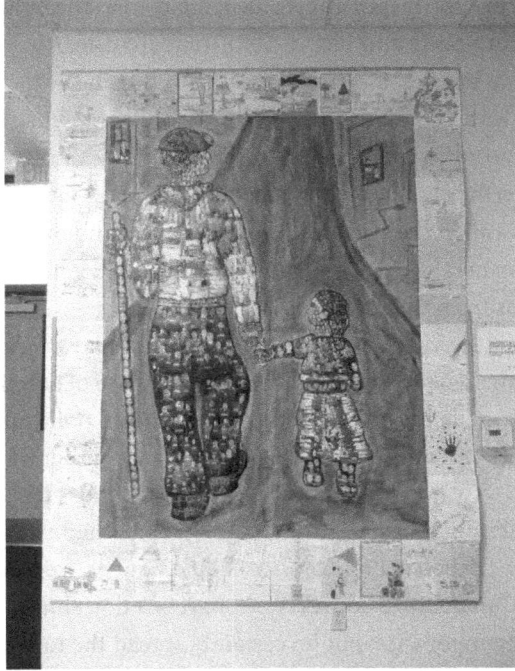

Figure 5.1 A collage at Unbound's office depicting Hentzen as a pilgrim, walking hand-in-hand with a child. The collage is made up of the faces of sponsored children in Latin America (photo by author).

(mediated twice over for US people at home through videos and photos). The walk, as the video explicitly states, also embodied Unbound's inverted model of power by showing how even its president uses his feet—the humblest form of transportation.

Though Hentzen's status as a former priest is unstated, it is hard to ignore. His life, available to audiences through YouTube and photographs, is one of sacrifice, spirituality, moderation, and even privation—he is gaunt yet calm and cheerful, wearing out his shoes on the trek. The mediatization of the pilgrimage highlights this priestly aura, whether or not it was evident to people during the walk itself. What I mean is that the camera's lens focuses on Hentzen; literally, it often sharpens the focus on him in contrast to the blurry mass of people behind him. Even without this sharpening and blurring effect, the videos and photos often show him walking or standing slightly in front of the (usually local) groups that walk together or in pairs as they accompany him for portions of the journey. It is hard not to see the priest leading his flock. His touch, as he meets laypeople on the route, is not a priestly blessing since he no longer has the power to transfigure bread and wine into body and blood. Yet it remains a marked act of corporeal immediacy, which implies the transmission of blessings—the friendship and funds that come with Unbound sponsorship. Indeed, my sense is that Hentzen's epic pilgrimages were powerful precisely because they were events featuring a layman who nevertheless retained the power of priestly authority. Hentzen was both much greater than the average Unbound donor, and one of them—the son of Midwestern farmers who loved regular folk—emblematized through home-movie style videos from the road.

The quote from the video, noted above, underlines how Hentzen's love-walk also embodies human beings' shared "smallness" in face of literal machines (cars and trucks) and metaphorical machines, like unjust political and economic systems that seem to flatten humble people in their wake. Hentzen's kind of love echoes mid-century US Catholic social teaching: the worker-focused personalism of Dorothy Day and the intensely embodied pacifism of Thomas Merton—the two Catholics Pope Francis singled out as "representatives of the American people" in his 2015 address to Congress. I don't know if Hentzen cited these famous contemporaries, but he certainly spread the love-talk that, for the US Catholic left, seemed to hail a new Catholicism in the mid-twentieth century, as I elaborate below.[9] Hentzen, and his sponsorship organization, circulated love-talk to a wide swathe of charitably minded US Catholics, many of whom were older, Midwestern, less political, and more devotional.

Hentzen's pilgrimage as a form of *embodied mediation* introduces one of my key questions: How does Unbound view love's trajectory for sponsors who, in contrast with Hentzen, are not physically present with those they purport to serve? "Bob's office was on the road, and the homes of the families were his boardroom," was how Unbound's director of US outreach put it rather poetically in a *National Catholic Reporter* obituary (Fincher 2013). Hentzen moved back and forth across national borders in the Americas all of his adult life. His and Tolle's vision for their organization, which Unbound promotes today, is that US sponsors learn to "walk alongside" the people they support so "a relationship would blossom across international boundaries, and people would simply learn to love one another, even at a distance, and be committed to help each other as brothers and sisters" (Hatrup 2019).[10] But whereas Hentzen actually walked and developed relationships with people far away, these hopes for Unbound sponsors rest entirely in the mediated and imaginative sphere. According to Unbound, fewer than 1 percent of sponsors meet the child they support. Their average age is fifty-five and, if my fifty-two interviews are any indication, relatively few have traveled outside the United States and even fewer have traveled beyond a few locations in North America and Western Europe. So how is love mediated through these comparatively stationary US Catholic bodies?

Making Love: A Backstory

Before returning to this question, let us consider how love came to circulate so freely, and so often, in sponsorship media. Child sponsorship was first introduced to raise money for Protestant missions in the early nineteenth century. Love language came directly from the Gospels; "love thy neighbor" was a major theological premise upon which Protestants justified expending resources on foreign missions. However, love talk had another source too: child sponsorship was linked to a rising trend in "sentimentalism" among White middle-class Americans, which celebrated the moral worth of pious emotions, especially during motherhood (Kaell 2020). "The cult of motherhood," as historians dub it, integrated mother love as fundamental to the paternalistic family unit (cf. Muehlebach 2013a: 465), and therefore a basic building block of society as a whole.

According to this view, good Christian families circulated love through "reciprocal sentiments" between unequal parties, such as men and women or parents and children. For example, a mother nurtured her child in faith while her own heart was also "enlarged" in love for God by observing the child's simplicity and responsiveness (Corrigan 2002: 174–5, 292; Stoler 2002: 81). Scholars, many of whom use mediation as a theoretical apparatus, have tracked the rise of these social norms in mid-nineteenth-century US Protestantism and, by the 1870s, in US Catholicism (Alvarez 2016: 9). Bourgeois American ideals melded easily with a Catholic devotional culture that already celebrated Mary as loving mother (McDannell 1986). Put in these terms, the link between godly love (*agape*) and mother love was less an inherent feature of "Christian cultures" (Mayblin 2012: 248) than it was a reflection of emergent properties within particular modern, class-based societies.

Through sponsorship, American donors were told they could circulate their love much further than their own family or even nation. In that respect, sponsorship was typical of a class of nineteenth-century charitable activities that linked Christian sentimentalism to humanitarian aspirations. This introduces another entextualization of love with a slightly different valence. Humanitarianism is rooted in early modern European moral philosophy (Fassin

2011) that viewed all people as sharing basic traits through their relation to a single Creator. As a result, it was assumed that an individual could examine his or her conscience to intuit natural laws that governed the self and, extrapolating, humanity as a whole (Poovey 1998: xv, 148–9). While Catholic thinkers at the time had a complicated relationship to individual conscience, they also viewed inherent regularities in human nature as reflecting the work of one Creator (Napolitano 2016) and, in the Thomistic tradition, understood this nature as regulated by a *caritatis ordo* (order of love). According to this "ordered" view of love, it was natural that a Christian would feel emotions within her family as the most vital, since these structured her primary experiences. From family love one should then nurture a wider love that could sustain feelings of connection within the global Catholic church and fuel one's duty to support foreign missions (Pope 1991).

Versions of these ideas are the conceptual bedrock in every US Christian sponsorship organization I have studied, and they long predate Unbound's founding in the early 1980s. From the start, Hentzen and Tolle were undoubtedly aware that love language saturated the media produced by Protestant (and non-Christian) sponsorship organizations. Throughout the 1980s, Unbound staffers filed and kept clippings from advertising campaigns by Protestant organizations World Vision, Compassion, and Christian Children's Fund. Hentzen and Tolle even toured Compassion in 1980 as the model for their soon-to-be program. At Unbound, then, love was used (and likely successful with sponsors) because of its long association with gendered sentimentalism, American humanitarianism, and Christian missions. But for Unbound's founders, and perhaps its sponsors, love also evoked trends within mid-twentieth-century US Catholicism.

At the time of Unbound's founding, God had become much more "likely to be defined [by Catholics] as infinite *agape*—a forgiving, loving father/mother type" (Mayblin 2014: S271n.1). As noted briefly above, love talk was especially prominent on the Catholic left, notably in the Catholic social teaching that served as Hentzen's and Tolle's earliest inspiration for Unbound. The United States Conference of Catholic Bishops (USCCB) pastoral letter *Economic Justice for All* was a key articulation of these ideas at the time Unbound launched its sponsorship plan. The USCCB elevates love to a central premise; the word appears seventy-seven times in its ninety-six pages. At base, it argues that "love is made real through effective action" and defines economic justice as both "a manifestation of love and a condition for love to grow." Two kinds of love are made manifest when people act for justice: divine love and human love. The first is God's "creative love," referring to the Creator's design for humanity to flourish materially and spiritually. The second is each person's love for God, which should then become love for God's (human) creation in fulfillment of God's design. This "dual command of love that is at the basis of all Christian morality," writes the USCCB (1986: 11, 14). It is only by linking human and divine love that economic action becomes truly generative as the basis for more love "to grow."

In order to reify love through the economic action of transferring money from North to South America, Unbound's founders chose a tool—one-to-one child sponsorship—that was highly individualized. Sponsorship grew enormously in the 1970s and 1980s, not least because it appealed to a broadly American sensibility at the time that viewed effective humanitarianism as an opportunity for personal growth in both donor and recipient. For Unbound's early staff, however, it was axiomatic that their donors learn to see one-to-one sponsorship through the lens of Catholic social teaching that said every person is always, inherently social. It is almost certainly why Hentzen emphasized walking with others during his pilgrimage (a journey that otherwise could be mistaken for an individualistic quest for personal growth). This focus on human connection brings us to another key mid-twentieth-century Catholic concept related to Christian bodies, and the love and redemption that could be shared between them.

"Mystical body of Christ" refers to the union of believers through their common connection to Christ, as embodied in the central ritual of ingesting Christ's body in the Eucharist. In 1943, Pope Pius XII's encyclical *Mystici Corporis Christi* popularized the term and tied it to the institutional Church, stating that "the mystical Body of Christ... is the Catholic Church." However, the concept broadened in the atmosphere surrounding the Second Vatican Council. The Vatican did not forgo the idea that believers were mystically joined through the Eucharist as administered by a priest, but it also described various degrees by which all "people of good will" could be related to the Church. Under the influence of Hentzen (and likely Tolle), this idea became critical to Unbound, which defines its sponsors as "people of good will" who are joined through love to become a unified, even prophetic, community.[11] In this formulation, the Eucharist is no longer the (only) mediating ritual through which love travels; Unbound sponsors also create channels for love's circulation by giving money and, ideally, exchanging letters.[12] In ideal terms, sponsorship integrates economic action and spiritual connection, with love as the impulse. On its website, Unbound's Statement of Beliefs reads, "When we [sponsors]... love as equals, we are doing more than alleviating material poverty. We are also creating the bonds of lasting peace and unity among [diverse] people."

In my conversations with Unbound staff, they often expressed concern that sponsors mistook their loving connection to others as arising *ex-nihilo* from their own actions; that view could move the sponsor back into an individualistic and prideful conception of their own self-worth. Instead, they wanted sponsors to view loving connections with their "sponsored friend" as a direct outcome of each party's *already existing* link to God. The importance Unbound places on this ordering of love seems to draw on two main ideas in Catholic social teaching. The first one, which we have seen articulated by the USCCB, states that it is only through the full integration of human/divine love that economic action can become a generative basis for more love to grow. Redefining the popular metaphor in American English that the "economy grows," Unbound wants its sponsors to understand that growth can only occur when love comes from within, but also from beyond, the human. Another aspect relates to human dignity. One of Unbound's four core values is "Recognizing the God-given dignity of each person is essential to sincere, lasting, loving relationships." In other words, any loving relation is predicated upon a gift that God gives each human being; it is crucial for Unbound that US sponsors not view their monetary donations, no matter how loving, as conferring dignity upon recipients. Rather, God's love for humanity gives each individual dignity, which then opens the possibility for loving human relationships. Again, the order of love is crucial.

Mary Geiss, the Sponsor Experience team leader, was one of many staff members, including CEO Scott Wasserman, who emphasized to me that it is often a slow process as Unbound tries to move US sponsors (and the children or elders they support) toward understanding their growing relationship as a facet of God's broader love.[13] Unbound communicates this idea to donors in a variety of ways. For example, I was with Mary and her team as they discussed a recent revision of the first letter Unbound sends to each new donor. Just two paragraphs long, the letter read in part, "With time your relationship [with the child] will grow and together you will experience hope and God's love." The team noted that the wording had been carefully chosen since they viewed it as a key opportunity to begin the process of framing sponsorship for donors. Using the future tense ("you will experience..."), Unbound portrays God's love as preexisting, waiting to be experienced by sponsors as they grow to love the child they support. This type of subtle phrasing repeats throughout Unbound's materials, including its online Statement of Beliefs, which reads in part: "We provide the opportunity for the sponsor and sponsored friend to *make* a real connection… This connection… *reveals* the bonds that tie us together as one human family." I have added italics to emphasize the shift I am describing: humans "make" connections through their love-labors whereas a unifying global bond (implying God's love) is not made, but revealed.

A final point about the Sponsor Experience team's introductory letter: it uses the word "love" twice. It does so in the sentence already discussed ("you will experience hope and God's love") and at the end: "God bless you for your love and generosity." This doubling of the word "love"—"God's love" and "your love"—is typical of sponsorship media in all the Christian organizations I studied. My sense is that it relates to what I noted about duality: it recalls that love has different qualities. God's is a perfect and all-encompassing love that, according to papal encyclicals, is not "derived from anything that is" (Mayblin 2012: 247). Human love is, by contrast, a never-perfect proposition that may therefore constitute but also break social bonds—particularly if it operates outside God's blessing. Furthermore, the last sentence—"God bless you for your love and generosity"—returns to the importance of effective economic action as a manifestation of human love. When the sponsor receives this first letter she has yet to actually communicate with the child she will support; that kind of love-relation will grow over time, the letter says. The love for which Unbound is thankful therefore refers to actions the sponsor has already taken, namely sending 40 dollars. In short, by doubling love language, Unbound frames love as a future promise of relationship and a current economic action. In its theology of sponsorship, sending money manifests God's already existing love, which dwells within the donor, while also creating conditions for expansive relations with the child and, ultimately, global "bonds of lasting peace and unity."

Family and Motherhood in Unbound's Love Theology

Protestant and Catholic sponsorship programs conceptualize and deploy the word "love" similarly, as noted, but in my experience the Catholic teachings that structure Unbound's theology do reveal themselves in certain ways. I have mentioned Hentzen as an embodiment of the selfless, loving pilgrim-priest. Compare this persona to the effusive, explosive, charismatic leadership of World Vision's founder, evangelical pastor Bob Pierce. He is the most famous Christian advocate of sponsorship, thanks to his friendship with evangelist Billy Graham and because World Vision became the world's largest sponsorship organization. As a result, it and Pierce have served as the subject of a number of studies over the years (Whaites 1999; Bornstein 2005; King 2019). Though Hentzen has received no such academic attention, the two men were contemporaries.[14] Pierce also began his global work in the late 1940s and 1950s, was peripatetic, and central to his organization. However, his image revolved around new technologies, fast travel, and preaching crusades; it is hard to imagine Hentzen's pilgrim-priest being legible to World Vision's audience.

Another difference concerns how Catholicism views love as "planted by God into the heart and mind of every human person" (Muehlebach 2013a: 454). At Unbound, love talk is strongly linked to God the Father. By contrast, evangelical organizations like World Vision or Compassion link it more directly to Jesus, as the immanent person in the Trinity. Their workers and sponsors are encouraged to view themselves as Jesus's "hand and feet"—the instruments by which loving touch moves through the world and makes development work Christian (Bornstein 2005: 31, 44).

A final difference relates to motherhood. The contrast is subtle since all the sponsorship organizations I studied assumed the typical sponsor is a woman and, likely, a mother. Recall that in sponsorship's loose theology of global connection, derived from its nineteenth-century roots, Christian mothers were seen as the most responsive and capable vessels for fusing human love with God's love and sending it out into the world. Historically, sponsorship promoted the idea that there was an inherent contrast between the Christian and "pagan" mother. The latter was portrayed as unable to mediate love correctly: they could neither circulate moral (Christian) emotion *to* their children nor absorb moral inspiration *from* their children. Without this circuit of human emotion, God's love could find no entry point. Christian mothers were required to step in and charitably "adopt" a child abroad.

By the time Unbound was founded in the 1980s, this idea (at least in explicit terms) had fallen completely out of fashion in liberal Christian circles. Unbound retained the idea that mother-love was the basis from which the demographically typical sponsor—a white American woman—could magnify her love by joining it to God's. This concept was so deeply rooted in the 1980s as to be effectively inextricable from the American perception of, and attraction for, child sponsorship. Yet from the start Unbound also sought to communicate a different vision to its sponsors regarding mothers abroad. It has done so, in part, by elevating *caritatis ordo* to an unspoken organizing principle. Unbound emphasizes that it is natural, and also right, that sponsors feel more strongly about their own children than "their" sponsored children. It views correctly ordering human love in this fashion as, in fact, necessary for rejecting charitable paternalism because it also recognizes that parents abroad have primacy and agency in their children's lives. Unbound impresses upon its sponsors that they should consider the child abroad as "my sponsored friend" and not "my child," as other organizations so often put it.

What this *caritatis ordo* retains, however, are the gendered implications of nineteenth-century sentimentalism: families are still understood as the central conduit for love, with mothers as the ultimate mediators of this flow of Christian emotion. Even more than its Protestant counterparts, Unbound emphasizes how families abroad, and especially mothers, are inherently hard-working and sacrificing. Its five-point mission statement reads:

We believe in strong families.
We believe in the wisdom of mothers.
We believe in the power of friendships.
We believe in the dignity of all human beings ("to exchange and love as equals").
We believe in hope.

The mother abroad is viewed as a counterpart to the "typical" US sponsor, who statistically speaking is generally a mother too; Unbound staff call this sponsor "Patricia," "Beth," or "Susan" around the office (Figure 5.2). On both ends of the sponsorship exchange, mothers are expected to manage their feelings—suppressing some, cultivating others—to mediate love through their bodies and actions, which offers an access point to God's love that covers the world. Ideally, both sides, including the US mother, labor and sacrifice for the love they circulate.

In his work on Muslim devotional practices, Patrick Eisenlohr notes that objects and technologies designated as "media" have a "tendency to vanish in the act of mediation" (2011: 267; Gershon and Manning 2014: 540). This oscillation between the obscure and the apparent applies here too, insofar as the word "love" in sponsorship-related media alternates between designating mundane and marked feelings. Often it is barely noticed and colloquial (a sponsor loves an aspect of the program or a child loves playing a game). At other times, it designates the complex human-God love relation discussed above ("We can send our love around the world!"). In bundling these multiple qualities, love shifts its "value, utility, and relevance across contexts" (Keane 2003: 414). I believe this rhetorical capacity is important since it helps position Unbound in multiple ways: as simultaneously Catholic and not Catholic, authoritatively sacred and "secular" (lay-led, humanitarian), religious and American, divinely guided and

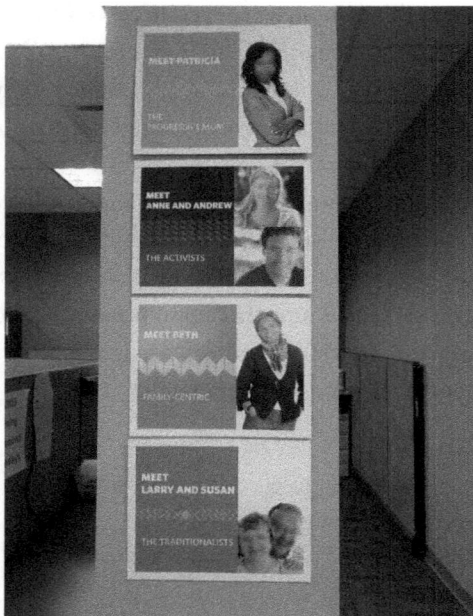

Figure 5.2 Unbound's prototypical sponsors, as displayed in its offices in 2014. Staff used these profiles as a tool to craft new policies and messaging. "Patricia" and "Anne and Andrew" represented markets they hoped to grow, while "Beth" and "Larry and Susan" typified their base supporters. Regardless, sponsorship is pictured as driven primarily by mothers (or mothers-to-be, in the case of "Anne") (photo by author).

voluntary. It therefore may be important that, apart from a couple times on Unbound's blog, I never heard anyone use the theological term *agape*, which would necessarily pull love and its global projects into a more institutionally Catholic frame. As I note below, it is essential for Unbound, and most of the sponsors I got to know, that the work is tinged with the sacred, especially the "sacred" sphere of motherhood, without being mistaken for the institutional Roman Church.

Coextensive Media: Words and the Stuff of Love

Sponsorship's love talk elides much of what is actually moving abroad, namely money and consumer objects. Rhetorically speaking, love's bundled qualities are useful in this respect too. Sponsorship organizations often use the word as a euphemism for money; for example, "God bless you for your love" in Unbound's first letter or "your love makes a difference" printed next to the box where one ticks off the amount to be debited from a bank account each month. Love sacralizes money-gifts and envelops sponsors' charitable actions within positive affective registers rather than negative ones, such as guilt.

Many of the sponsors I met hoped that giving their "love" (money) to a person faraway might disrupt the troubling cycle of materialism to which they felt that they and their families, along with all Americans, were prone. On Unbound's blog, this goal is theologized by defining love as a form of "self-emptying," or *kenosis*. It refers to the intense humbling—even debasement—that God chose to undergo through Jesus's crucifixion. In Catholicism, by filling oneself with the Eucharist a believer "self-empties" in imitation of Christ and can give in love for others. In Unbound's theology, giving up material attachments is also a form of self-emptying that creates room to be filled up with God's love. Once God is present—sufficiently inhibiting the negative impulses of guilt, greed, and materialism—Americans are able send their "love" (money) through Unbound, which provides the hope and security necessary for Catholic people elsewhere to also empty themselves to God's love (Hoopes 2015; Hornbeck 2015).

In this schema, too many material things can weigh one down and block love's flow outwards. And yet sponsors who told me that *materialism* is a problem also said that *material things* can serve the important purpose of mediating their love from afar—especially since, unlike Hentzen, their own bodies never act as mediators on the move. Sponsors' practice of sending physical gifts has been severely curtailed over the last two or so decades; all major sponsorship organizations, including Unbound, strongly discourage it, due to rising postal costs, complicated logistics, and ethical questions about buying abroad what could be gotten locally. Because sponsorship organizations know that donors want to send material stuff, they do allow flat gifts in letters, such as stickers, hair ribbons, and craft supplies.[15] Not surprisingly, Catholic sponsors also send objects like saint cards and medallions; the Catholic children they support send similar items back. At least some children did so even when they were sponsored through an evangelical organization: sorting letters in Compassion's mailroom in Colorado Springs, I came across one where a Nicaraguan boy enclosed a Blessed Virgin prayer card. I wondered what the evangelical recipients in Ohio would make of it as I resealed the envelope and sent it on.

Various anthropological studies confirm that the physical manipulation of gift-objects is one of the most powerful ways to mediate love across distances.

People who make humanitarian handcrafts may picture their global trajectory as they paste, cut, and sew, creating a particularly "evocative form of making virtual and enchanted connectivities" (Malkki 2015: 124). Anderson Blanton's study of Appalachian Pentecostals sharpens this idea of virtual/enchanted connectivities in more explicitly Christian terms. The faith healers with whom he works use objects, such as scraps of cloth, as a "point of contact" with the holy. A preacher in one location prays over it, infuses it with Spirit, and can then mail it to believers, for whom it retains efficacious power (Coleman 2000: 170–1, 177; Blanton 2015: 53–62; Coleman 2009: 420). Catholic concepts differ, of course, but at a basic level they also view objects as points of contact. In obvious terms, a priest's touch blesses objects (everyday objects or the Eucharist). But in Unbound's lay theology, the emphasis is more often on a single object that is multiply touched.

For example, in September 2015 I clicked open Unbound's biweekly e-newsletter, which was already promoting the holiday season. Titled, "Journey of a Christmas Card," it featured text and photos tracing the trajectory of the cards that sponsors receive. The journey begins with the card's creation by a child "with love," followed by the loving labor of in-country staff, postal workers, and elderly volunteers at Unbound's Kansas City headquarters: "Some are small, active hands filled with crayons and glue sticks. Some are large hands, calloused from lifting palettes filled with letters onto trucks. And some are gentle, wrinkled hands that have known many blessings and seek now to pass them on. Each hand adds its own loving touch, and the final one is that of the sponsor."[16] Organizations often downplay this chain of mediation to create a sense of one-to-one communication between child and sponsor. In this case, however, Unbound chooses to emphasize the "loving touch" of hands that have known gratitude or blessings, and that pass them on by manipulating the same object: it makes the card into a point of contact that mediates spiritual power. In more Catholic terms, it evokes a Eucharistic communion between "people of goodwill" whose embodied ritualizations (manipulating a shared object in this case, rather than ingesting a wafer) connect them in the Body of Christ. Through these "chains" of persons and objects, grace becomes partible and distributable in ways that exceed the intentionality of the discrete individuals involved (Mayblin, Norget, and Napolitano 2017: 21).

In mid-twentieth-century iterations of Catholic humanitarianism, blood was often the substance that mediated such bonds. Catholics told each other about the links between the suffering Christ, the Church's suffering missionaries bleeding as they died (in Communist places, especially), and the pennies that donors "bled" in sacrifice (Kaell 2019: 284). By contrast,

Unbound's post-conciliar love talk makes touch the mediating force and, moreover, the touch of one layperson to another. Also notable are the "active hands" abroad. Whereas its evangelical counterpart, Compassion, positions the child as a subject who self-transforms to reach his spiritual and economic "potential," Unbound usually portrays the child embedded within a community that is already moral and unflaggingly hardworking. It is an overarching vision of Catholics elsewhere—especially Catholic *mothers* elsewhere—as aspiring, active workers who, if given a chance, will become "artisans of their destiny,"[17] which Unbound interprets to mean the moral lodestar of economically secure family units.

In her work with Brazilian lay Catholics, Maya Mayblin notes (2012: 249) that mother love is at one moment viewed as "literally continuous with... divine [love]; a mother's hands are the hands of God." Then the next moment it is "merely metaphorical... mother's hands are like the hands of God." Mayblin's point is helpful in thinking about how Unbound treats human love generally (of which mother love is the exemplar) as it circulates via sponsorship's various forms. One moment love seems to be mediated *through* gift-objects and at other moments love is the gift itself. Sponsors are also reminded not to confuse their gift-objects with love, lest they fail to empty their egos (*kenosis*) to become mediating vessels for God's love: Americans may easily become paternalistic, patronizing givers, Unbound warns.

The unstable set of relations between gift-objects, loving touch, and self-emptying *kenosis* may help explain a deviation between Catholic and evangelical sponsors that Unbound staff had noticed and wanted to address. Whereas Compassion benefits from sponsors promoting the program through word-of-mouth, a significant minority of Unbound sponsors kept quiet about their charitable work. The reason, I believe, speaks to subtle differences in theologies of love. No sponsor I met told me that they wanted to benefit from sponsorship by telling others about their work. After all, US Christians define materialism, in part, as seeking personal pleasure or social status; as noted, they hope sponsorship will break the cycle of materialism, not feed it (Muehlebach 2013b: 517; Cf. Rudnyckyj and Osella 2017: 18). Yet evangelical organizations, like Compassion, have emic language for "witness" as a form of loving sacrifice: it may feel awkward to tell people about Jesus or about one's charitable giving, it tells its donors, but you must make this social sacrifice to further God's work. By contrast, Unbound's theology of loving sacrifice generally emphasizes *kenosis* (or humility) as the channel through which Americans mediate God's love. It may lead some Unbound sponsors to be more reticent to discuss their charitable activities. As one woman told me, "It would be a self-promotion. It wouldn't be right." To promote the self risks blocking the very mechanism of self-emptying through which human love can be joined with God's love to flow across the world.

Organizational, Not Institutional

An even more significant difference between Unbound and Compassion concerns unmitigated growth. The evangelical organizations I studied tended to view it as a sign of God's favor. As Simon Coleman (2000, 2009) has pointed out in other contexts, this ethic arises out of a theology that says evangelism is always on the move because God is infinite. Unbound, by contrast, tailors its growth according to needs in its field sites and, as a result, its sponsor base has remained largely stable since 2006. I believe this nongrowth (or lesser growth) model reflects a Catholic sensibility. It assumes, first, that the people it serves are already moral, hardworking, and do not need to be born again, which staves off some of the urgency of its more evangelical counterparts. Second, and importantly, growth may seem less imperative since Unbound views itself as one piece of a larger puzzle: one entity working within the framework of the global Catholic Church.

Unbound's relation to the Church is a crucial issue, for the organization and its sponsors. On the one hand, Unbound explicitly disrupts "institutional" Church by always emphasizing its local (Midwestern American) and lay character. It emphatically does not want to be mistaken for "the Church." Yet it is also unmistakably a Catholic organization. It harnesses the authority of the institutionalized sacred sphere—most notably, in how its method of publicizing the program is still almost entirely through volunteer priests who discuss the program during their homilies and encourage parishioners to sign up (Figure 5.3). It also retains former priests in its directorship, including many key positions.[18] Unbound typifies a particularly Catholic problem related to authority and power (also see chapters in this volume by Loustau and Dugan). None of the Protestant organizations I studied had to navigate comparable difficulties vis-à-vis their pastor-founders' denominations. None of the Protestant organizations were both reliant on a particular Christian institution and also made continual efforts to distance themselves from it.

In speaking with Unbound sponsors, I found significant distrust—or certainly ambivalence—about the institutional Church, especially in its dealings with children. Some sponsors made oblique references to the child abuse scandals; it had been a decade since the *Boston Globe* exposé, and the international extent

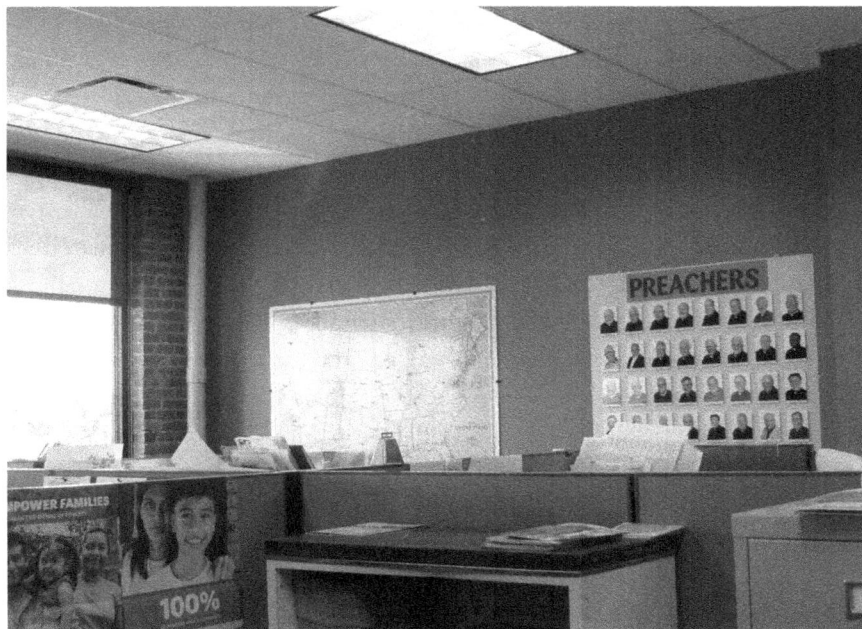

Figure 5.3 Poster of the team of priests who volunteer to promote the program, which has been Unbound's main promotional method since the 1990s. The poster, which featured in several locations around Unbound's offices, is a reminder of the continued role of "institutional" Catholic authority in the organization (photo by author).

of the problem was now common knowledge. Many more sponsors explicitly discussed what they viewed as the institutional Church's distasteful history of missionary work, including when children were removed or estranged from their families. Yet few sponsors rejected *contemporary* missionary work as such—in fact, most of them told me they supported missionary priests who raised funds in their parishes. The difference lay in how the focus was on the "humanitarian" side, which they felt was separate from what they condemned as a historically authoritarian disregard for local cultures. It was highly important to Unbound and its sponsors that its layperson-to-layperson model of development not be confused with this missionary past (though Unbound's initial spread in the 1980s and 1990s was through missionary priests and the institutions they served).

At the same time, Unbound sponsors told me that one reason they trusted the organization was precisely because a priest had come to their parish to promote it. "A priest isn't going to lie to you knowingly," one sponsor told me as we listened to a guest homilist promote the program in her parish, "He's not profiting... not trying to sell you something like you see on TV [in sponsorship advertisements]." Many Unbound sponsors told me something similar when I asked them point-blank in our interviews if they would choose a Catholic organization over a nonreligious one, if the programming, audit reports, and all other factors were equal. Over and over, they told me they would still choose the Catholic one: it was a question of *trust*. Thus by and large Unbound sponsors felt ambivalent about Catholic "institutional" power, even while they trusted Catholic "organizational" power—a delicate balance that seems rather in keeping with other facets of their lives. After all, sponsors were among those US Catholics who chose to still attend institutional churches (since that is where Unbound publicizes its program) and stay involved in parish life. Yet they also generally defined Catholicism's "real" core, for themselves and others, as rooted in their own experiences of love, security, and family. Unbound's sponsorship program put Catholic development projects into the same terms.

Media technologies play an interesting role with respect to the thin line between institutional and organizational power. The internet, and especially social media, can democratize laypeople's participation and promote their creative power and yet, as Norget (2017: 191) shows at the Guadalupan pilgrimage, Rome increasingly uses the same technologies to control and reroute messages and experiences. To some degree the same can be said of child sponsorship organizations, which have always used new media to stoke sponsors' feelings of global connectedness, while also rerouting and controlling those mechanisms. In the internet age, for example, organizations have tried to suppress contact between children and sponsors outside of their mediated systems by creating their own internal email programs and social media networks. This strategy will likely crumble as more older Americans join Facebook and other social media sites and as sponsored children have better access to the internet and cheap smartphones.

While new media technologies are therefore fraught in certain ways, they are also full of promise. Sponsorship organizations mobilize them to expand their base and, more generally, to spread their theologies of connection into places not usually occupied by Christian entities. For example, during my time at Unbound's office the team was piloting a new idea: photo exhibits in cafés with accompanying QR codes and videos. The first one, housed in a trendy café in Kansas City, featured images of musicians from Unbound field sites. A café goer could work on her laptop, surrounded by these images on the walls, and set her tablet or phone to hear relevant music recorded in situ or see the photos come "to life" through video (Figure 5.4). The idea was to attract new (and younger) sponsors. But at a larger level, Barclay Martin, Unbound's New Channels

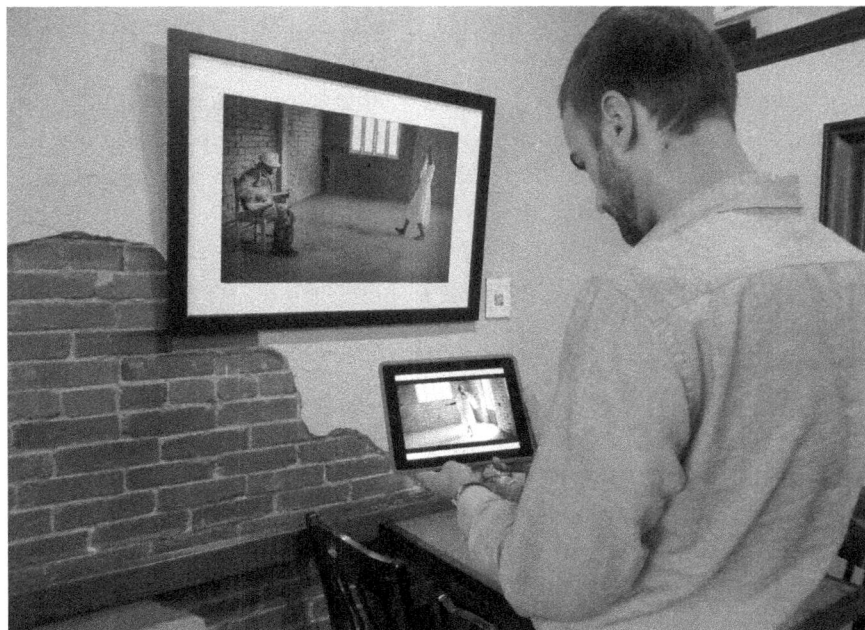

Figure 5.4 Barclay Martin, Unbound's Coordinator of New Channels in 2014, demonstrates how café goers can access interactive videos as they sit amid the photo display (photo by author).

Coordinator and the youthful curator of the exhibit, explained it as producing an ambient (Engelke 2012) experience of sacred/secular uplift through feelings of connectedness. For him, the possibility of creating a sensory connection with people faraway held its own rewards, whether it resulted in new sponsors per se.

This kind of ambient messaging promotes theologies of connection well beyond the churches that gave rise to them. In this respect, Unbound's use of participatory media in public spaces (brick-and-mortar and virtual) is similar to its Protestant counterparts. But I believe it has an added benefit too. For Catholic organizations, such media widens, and even creates, a viable space in which (lay-led) projects thrive alongside, but not exactly within, the (Roman) institution. Social media's democratic, personalized ethos can suture new "people of God" through participatory theologies and ritual-like experiences, such as circulating along the walls of a café to gaze at images of human bodies in motion and let soaring music fill the senses through one's smartphone earbuds. If one knows something about Catholicism, it is hard not to feel an echo of the Stations of the Cross. Thus new media might carve out ways of doing "Catholicism" (of the most ambient sort) that support and reinforce lay Catholic organizing.

A Note about Blockage and Concluding Thoughts

Mediation is as much about blockage as it is about transmission and connection. Indeed, the role of mediation in bridging the gaps between divine plan and human action (Tomlinson 2010: 743, 755), God's Kingdom here and to come (Haynes 2013), or what is heard and believed (Harding 2000) has long been important to anthropologists of Christianity. Such gaps—and therefore the necessity of mediation—take on particular intensity for people who do not travel but are engaged in global projects. Sponsors encounter various challenges as they try to keep love on the move.

In June 2015, for example, I spoke with Genevieve, an informatics analyst and mother of four in her early fifties. She attends Mass infrequently and views her Catholicism as best expressed through her volunteer and charitable commitments, such as sponsorship with Unbound. She was one of the first people I met who impressed upon me that love's trajectory could be blocked, even when the money was forthcoming. We were sitting in Unbound's offices surrounded by the organization's media publicity—images of happy children and Hentzen's pilgrimage—when I asked her if she thought of sponsorship as a relationship. "Not quite," she told me and paused. "And part of it [pause] is because, I kind of went through a time in my life where I was kind of depressed so it was hard for me." She could not properly love herself or those close to her, even her own family. As a result, she continued,

> I had this block about being able to write back or communicate and I even called the [Unbound] offices one time and said, I'm really bad about being able to communicate or write them letters... and I don't know what to do about it and it was around Christmas time and they were like well, we can send the Christmas gift for you... and I thought good. We'll just do that....I even went to the point where [I asked the telephone operator], do you want me to stop sponsoring? Because I'm not good at this.

Genevieve felt she could not muster the love from within herself that is the imagined wellspring for the love that travels into the world; that is, the "natural" *caritatis ordo* (order of love). Without her own capacity to love, God's love could find no way to circulate and the chain of mediation seemed to break down. Genevieve thought it might be better to give up sponsorship altogether, though she had a steady job and the regular payments were never an issue. Upon hearing Genevieve's problem, the Unbound operator responded in a way that accords with the organization's theology of connection: by sending a gift-object, Unbound could fill the gap to circulate love—or at least a semblance of it. The operator probably hoped that Genevieve would soon come to feel love again and resume her place within the chain of connection.

To create a properly robust anthropology of Catholicism, we must find ways to include the many people who populate the Church's "lapsed peripheries." How does Catholicism encircle doubt and indifference within its embrace? (Mayblin, Norget, and Napolitano 2017: 19). Genevieve gives us a sense of how Catholics on the "periphery" of Roman Catholic ritualization—she only sporadically attends Mass and ingests the Eucharist—may still trust Catholic organizations, such as Unbound, to make space for embodied forms of ritualization that create global connection. That she called Unbound and voiced her dilemma, and then repeated it to me, underscores the seriousness with which she takes the goal of meditating love between strangers (herself and the child). It reminds us that, although Unbound largely avoids formalized concepts like the Body of Christ, the organization's love-talk, and its relation to gift-objects, is an important vector for a lay-centered theology of connection that draws deeply upon Roman Catholic forms.

Hentzen's own body is one of those forms: on epic pilgrimages, his traveling body mediated love and priestly authority, which is then remediated for Unbound's sponsors through technologies like photographs and YouTube videos. In one sense, Hentzen's pilgrimages were typical of older ways the Church understood itself as corporeal and immediate. Though he was no longer a priest, it is hard not to see Hentzen's touch as imbued with the authority of his former status. One thinks of Eucharistic connection as he is shown breaking bread with laypeople on the road or grasping their hands as they approach him.

Hentzen's status as former priest and cosmopolitan traveler, read alongside Genevieve's worry about blockage, cuts to the heart of Unbound's promise that it circulates love between laypeople who never actually meet. The problem is not unrelated to what is already debated within the Catholic Church regarding older corporeal forms (notably, the Eucharist) and their possible conveyance through new media (notably, the internet). Namely, what is the relation between *communication* and *transmission*? One merely tells; the other promises to substantively *cross* divides. How is the latter possible when corporeal presence is not? How does love move?

At Unbound, I argue that part of the response rests on the entexualization of love—the circulation of this text fragment via multiple mediated forms. In fact, it links communication to transmission. Love talk circulates in Unbound's communication to sponsors: videos of Hentzen, for example, or didactic articles about *kenosis* on social media. But it is also the central mode of transmission: sponsors are encouraged to come to know their bodies, and the things they touch, as vectors through which love crosses divides. Just as importantly, love's multiple entextualizations oscillate between the mundane and the marked. The same word refers to everyday situations in nonreligious contexts, while also denoting a central theological concept in the progressive, post-Vatican II Catholicism that gave rise to Unbound. Through this oscillation, love-talk helps co-constitute "secular" and "sacred" media. As secular media multiplies love across various forms and platforms, it spreads and authenticates Unbound's interpretation of Catholic social teaching. Love-talk is thus essential to keeping Unbound a Catholic organization, able to walk a fine line between claiming authority as (lay) Catholic, yet avoiding too close an association with the institutional Roman Church.

Notes

1　I draw on fieldwork conducted at intervals from 2014 to 2016 at Unbound's Kansas City headquarters and among sponsors, including fifty-two conversational interviews with sponsors in upstate New York and Missouri. Unbound sent out letters on my behalf and sponsors self-selected by getting in touch with me. I conducted interviews during my visits to their region, with follow-up by email or phone.

2　I do not want to overstate Catholic uniqueness though. Simon Coleman (2017: 279) notes that "a key research question may be whether and how a Catholic-inspired landscape of global movement compares, interacts, interleaves, and indeed contrasts with Pentecostal and evangelical patterns." My body of work tries to accomplish this task, including in this project, which included evangelicals and Catholics. Ultimately, I found significant agreement among US sponsors. In other words, studying a shared Christian activity (e.g., one form of charity) within a local/national context may reveal significant similarities, more so than if one was to extrapolate generalized "Catholic" or "Protestant" attributes.

3　Hentzen and Tolle first set up their organizational headquarters as a quasi-retreat center for the spiritual renewal of staff and volunteers. Some staff lived on-site and everyone joined in daily meals, prayers, and volunteerism for the sponsorship program and at Christ House, the organization's former soup kitchen in Kansas City.

4　Hentzen and Tolle first founded the organization with help from Hentzen's siblings Jim, Bud, and Nadine. Jim died in 1993 and Tolle died in 1995, just as the organization was beginning to grow. Bud and Nadine became nonvoting members of the board, while Hentzen took on the Presidency, which he held until his death. His vision and leadership were utterly central.

5 The importance of these particular lyrics is evident from how they feature in Unbound publications, including Hentzen's obituaries. Here I quote from Paco Wertin, repeating the lyrics in Fincher (2013).

6 Scott Wasserman, President and CEO, July 29, 2015. Though perhaps not intentional, this language echoes the USCCB (1986: xi, 11).

7 "Bob Hentzen Remembered as Humble Servant," *Unbound website*, October 12, 2013. Available online: https://www.unbound.org/Stories/2013/October/Bob-Hentzen-remembered-as-humble-servant.

8 "Unbound," *Unbound Video*, February 17, 2014. Available online: https://www.youtube.com/watch?v=l_Vz1pDiPJA.

9 Merton (*Seven Storey Mountain*) and Day (*The Long Loneliness*) both based their memoirs on Augustine's *Confessions*, which explains the focus on love. Augustine also inspired Thomas Aquinas's writings on love's "order," mentioned below. The premise of sponsorship overlaps with Day's thought, in particular, insofar as her Worker Movement focused on loving the poor and, fostering a deep suspicion of state-led programs, viewed individual actions as the most radical form of societal intervention. While Hentzen and Tolle were likely not as pessimistic about the state, they too saw individualized giving as fundamental to reinvigorating the People of God. On Day, these insights thanks to Jeffrey Burns, *Pers. Comm.*, August 22, 2019.

10 This wording is almost certainly from Unbound's publicity team.

11 "Prophetic" from Scott Wasserman's interview, cited above. "People of good will" features on Unbound's website and I often heard the phrase in Unbound staff meetings and my conversations with employees. Multiple types of relatedness appear in the encyclical *Lumen Gentium* (1964, sec. 13) and "men of good will" prefaces the encyclicals *Pacem in Terris* (1963) and *Populorum Progressio* (1967). Most influential for Unbound, at least during my research, was Pope Francis's use of "people of good will" in *Laudato Si* (2015). I also imagine that Hentzen and Tolle may have been influenced by USCCB pronouncements in the 1980s, just as their organization was expanding. For example, the US bishops wrote (1986: 84, 89), "Communion with God, sharing God's life, involves a mutual bonding with all on this globe. Jesus taught us to love God and one another and that the concept of neighbor is without limit. We know that we are called to be members of a new covenant of love... Love implies concern for all—especially the poor—and a continued search for those social and economic structures that permit everyone to share in a [global] community that is a part of a redeemed creation."

12 I say "ideally" because fewer than half of Unbound sponsors actually exchange letters, although the organization considers it essential to the program.

13 This was a central theme in my interview with CEO Scott Wasserman and something the Sponsor Experience team also discussed on the occasions I was able to join their meetings.

14 Pierce was twenty years older than Hentzen; however, the organizational structure of Catholic ministry (i.e., Hentzen was sent to Latin America through his order) meant that both of them began their global work in the same period. Pierce was in his mid-thirties when Youth for Christfirst sent him on one of its China crusades.

15 At Unbound, sponsors can occasionally send money via the organization for particular "big ticket" items, such as a pair of glasses or a new stove. Mary Geisz, Director of Sponsor Experience, Personal Interview, July 28, 2015.

16 "The Journey of a Christmas Card," *Unbound blog*, September 28, 2015. Available online: https://www.unbound.org/Stories/2015/September/ChristmasCardJourney.

17 Pope Francis, *Evangelii Gaudium* (November 24, 2013), 190. It is a direct quote and reference to *Populorum Progressio* (1967), sec. 65. Pope Francis's apostolic exhortation *Amoris laetitia* (2016) post-dated my research but it has almost certainly become a touchstone for Unbound.

18 The first interim director after Hentzen's death was also a former priest, Paco Wertin, who remains an important figure in the organization. Furthermore, Unbound's promotional team is still almost exclusively made up of retired priests who volunteer to promote sponsorship when they give guest homilies.

6

Religious Celebrities and the Expansion of Suffering in the Philippines and Timor-Leste

Julius Bautista

In *The Body in Pain: The Making and Unmaking of the World* (1985), Elaine Scarry argued that pain and suffering are experiences that "obliterate[s] and deconstruct[s] the self," and in that respect they are the "radical opposite" of creation and agency (see also Scarry and Geddes 2000). The "characteristic Catholic position" on this issue was articulated by Pope John Paul II in his 1984 Apostolic Letter *On the Christian Meaning of Human Suffering*. Instead of centralizing the negating neurological and cognitive ramifications of the pain experience, the former pontiff's exegesis emphasized that Christ "transformed suffering into an opportunity for loving, salvific sacrifice where every man becomes the way for the church." In essence, suffering is an edifying ontological condition in that it evokes the analogy of Christ's passion as the central truth of Christian soteriology. Moreover, the world of the Christian sufferer is one that has "personal and at the same time collective meaning" (John Paul II 1984, para. 8). For while the experience of suffering is one of subjective solitude, it is simultaneously a communal condition in which "people who suffer become similar to one another through the analogy of their situation… and above all through the persistent questioning of the meaning of suffering" (John Paul II 1984, para. 8).

In this chapter I discuss how Roman Catholics constructively channel the communal-soteriological significance of their suffering toward the formation of affective communities. The protagonists of this expansion of suffering are Roman Catholic religious actors who have achieved a degree of popularity and celebrity as an unintended consequence of the media attention generated by their pursuit of ritual agency or political advocacy. In showing how religious celebrification emerges as a facet of global mediatization, I examine how the kind of suffering subjectivities described by the former Pontiff intertwine with various modes of media outlets, including print, radio and television broadcasts, and social media platforms.

My concern with "mediatization" refers to a meta-processes characteristic of late-modernity (one that is akin to globalization and commercialization) in which technologies and platforms of mass dissemination become enmeshed with and/or co-opted into the pursuit of social and political transformation[1] (Krüger 2018: 2). Mediatization in this sense involves the institutionalization of a "media logic" that "serve[s] as an interpretive schema, and guide[s] routine social interaction, and thereby become integral in creating, maintaining, and changing culture" (Altheide 2016: 1).

I refer to a celebrification in which public recognition and notoriety are *attributed* onto people who are otherwise reluctant to be so accorded. What I describe, therefore, is distinct from "celebritization," in which a person's popularity is cultivated so that she is depicted as embodying desirable attributes that can be traded and consumed in a marketplace of fans. In the specific context of Roman Catholicism, the theme of celebrification evokes the pantheon of saints and spiritual exemplars, who have been distinguished as personifications of the virtues of humility, self-sacrifice, and suffering.[2] This celebrification of modern-day religious personalities occurs in the course of their participation in events such as popular rituals and award recognition—events that may qualify as what James F. English (2005) referred to as the "economy of spectacle" in modern social life.

Pope John Paul II can be seen as part of a pantheon of spiritual exemplars who channel suffering toward ontological edification and communal solidarity. I look to demonstrate the diversity and contemporaneity of this occurrence across Christendom by examining the two predominantly Roman Catholic countries in Southeast Asia: the Philippines and Timor-Leste.[3] In the Philippines, I discuss suffering in the context of the extra-liturgical, theatrical performance of ritual nailing, particularly in the province of Pampanga, where hundreds of men undergo rituals of self-mortification. In Timor-Leste, I consider the Roman Catholic Church institution's pursuit of resistance and liberation during the period of Indonesian occupation from the mid-1970s to late 1990s, personified by religious activists who embody the suffering of the nation amidst state-sanctioned media repression.

In examining cases from these two domains, I seek to enrich the discussion of religious celebrity by considering individuals who, unlike the Pontiff, do not have at their disposal the broad spectrum of publicity apparatus or "cultural intermediaries" (ranging from agents, publicists, photographers, administrative staff, and wardrobe and personal assistants).

In channeling an ethnographic and historiographical methodology, this chapter is responsive to the call for widening the scope of empirical case studies, which can in turn effect an expanded theorizing about the nature of religious engagement with technologically mediated communicative capacities (Zeiler 2019: 9).

Mediatized Religion and Celebrification: A Review of Relevant Literature

There has been a preponderance of work in which mediatization is discussed in relation to specific twentieth-century media platforms, which have not only described the nature and manifestations of "media logic" but also discussed how the acceleration and diversification of media technologies have contributed to processes of social transformation. The field of mediatization and its specific impact on the religious domain, however, is still an emerging field. Many would draw on media studies scholar Stig Hjardvard's 2008 article "The Mediatization of Religion" as a starting point of theorization. As Oliver Krüger puts it in his recent review of the field, however, "What appeared to be a chain of arguments for the theory of the mediatization of religion turns out to be a row of shaky dominos" (Kruger 2018: 23). Similarly, the anthropologist Xenia Zeiler has observed that while a few empirically based studies that focus on media and religion have been released in a wide array of publication outlets, "more structured and systematized overview publications are still largely lacking" (Zeiler 2019: 4). In the end, the concept of mediatization and religion "lacks coherence, clarity and conclusiveness while claiming far reaching insights about religion, secularization and modernity" (Kruger 2018: 26).

An underlying assumption which posits an opposition of (modern) media and (traditional) religion has been a common theme of debates on religion in television in the social sciences since the 1970s (Krüger 2018: 11). Kerstin Radde-Antweiler, Hannah Grünenthal, and Sina Gogolok (2018) postulate that studies on this field prognosticate either the weakening of religious authority from increased mediatization, or the opposite, that a deliberate and guided use of media technologies would strengthen religious institutions as they seek to modernize (Radde-Antweiler et al. 2018: 269–71). The anthropologist Deirdre de la Cruz observes, rightly I think, that anthropologists of religion are moving productively toward seeing "similar structures of commensurability and mutual influence between religions and technological media taking place throughout the world" (de la Cruz 2009: 462). The case studies that I bring to bear on this inquiry are conducted in concert with such studies, which include (among many others) those of Hirschkind (2006), Lim K.G. (2009), Pertierra (2006), and Han and Kamaludeen (2015).

In a similar vein to the study of mediatization, the sociologist Gerry Lanuza observes that in spite of the increase in studies focusing on celebrity culture in recent decades, "there has not emerged a clear theoretical direction for studying celebrities, celebritization, and celebrification" (Lanuza 2017: 2). Although consistent analytical momentum has yet to be generated in the study of religious celebrity, a few key works define the shape of the discussion. The British sociologist Chris Rojek construes aspects of celebrity culture as having "inescapable parallels with religious worship" (Rojek 2010: 53). While he does qualify that celebrity culture is not a substitute for religion, Rojek's main contention is that celebrity culture "is the milieu in which religious recognition and belonging are now enacted. The ubiquity of the milieu is the real issue" (Rojek 2007: 181).[4] On the other hand, the French sociologist Nathalie Heinich (2014) contends that studies such as that of Rojek have an overly expansive notion of religion without regard for specificities in practice, doctrine, and text even within specific faith traditions. I agree with Heinich that one of the problems of analyses of the celebrification of religious actors is the absence of any deep reading and anthropological engagement with the substance of religious subjectivities. It is with this in mind that my analysis is deployed.

There have been a few works that engage in region-specific analyses of the nexus of religion and media. Xenia Zeiler and Radde-Antweiler (2019), for example, consider their contribution as bringing together the three crucial parameters of media, religion, and Asia in their analytical approach (Zeiler 2019). There are also a few separate works that have discussed the nexus of mediatization and Roman Catholicism in Southeast Asian contexts. Thus far, anthropological works on the Philippines dominate this field of theorization and empirical analysis. Anthropologist Claudia Liebelt (2011) demonstrates how Filipino Roman Catholic female migrant workers in Israel claim a "celebrity status" by deliberately positioning themselves at the center of media events where "they 'rub shoulders' with and become a part of the people who allegedly make world history" (Liebelt 2011: 231).[5] Meanwhile, the capacity of Filipino Catholic charismatic personalities to draw a massive audience has also been analyzed, most notably by Katherine Wiegele (2005) whose analysis of the organization *El Shaddai* exemplifies the capacity of religious institutions to harness the powerful reach of telecommunications, radio, and other media networks.

Complementing Wiegele's (2005) analysis of the "production side" of religious mediatization, the communications studies scholar Jonathan Corpus Ong (2015a) discusses the "receiving side" in analyzing how viewing audiences respond to the distant and proximal suffering of vulnerable others in Philippine television. With due sensitivity to how considerations of class in Philippine society shape people's moral judgments about media (Ong 2014), Ong's work considers how "media audiences in the global South are implicated in moral dilemmas of bearing witness" (2015b: 1). In the context of Timor-Leste, analyses of mediatization and religion are typically implicated within broader studies of post-colonial, post-conflict state formation and the pivotal role played by the Roman Catholic Church in resistance and liberation movements. Key works that analyze this topic from various disciplines include that of Carey (1999), Lundry (2002), Smythe (2004), Lyon (2013), and Hodge (2013, 2017).

Hesukristo Superstar

In this first section, I consider the extra-liturgical enactment of ritual nailing as it is performed within the frame of vernacular public theatre during Holy Week. The elevation of the event as "media spectacle" engenders the celebrification of its main protagonist, a man known as Hesukristo superstar (Bautista 2017).

When I first met Ruben Enaje, a sign painter from the small town of San Pedro Cutud, he told me that he found it odd that I did not have a film crew and entourage with me. It would not be difficult to surmise that he must be the most popular man in the Philippines in the days leading to Holy Week. Ruben is sought after by scores of foreign and local cultural intermediaries, including news crews, photographers, documentary filmmakers, novelists, and researchers. From his hectic media schedule to the frequent request for selfies from passersby, it seems like everyone wants a piece of the only man in the world who has willingly submitted himself to be ritually nailed to a cross in front of thousands of spectators for the better part of three decades. It would not be far-fetched to say it: Ruben, the "Kristo," is a religious superstar.

In the presence of reporters and spectators, Ruben has become quite adept at explaining the motivation and rationale for his continued ritual nailing. It is, as he puts it, a *panata* (a vow) to reciprocate an act of God's salvation when, in 1985, he miraculously survived an accident that should have killed him. Ritual nailing, particularly in the way that dramatizes the suffering of Christ, was the only commensurate response that would go some way toward addressing the imbalance between God's compassion and his own status as an "ordinary man" who is undeserving of such divine magnanimity. Ruben's panata is a deeply felt, interiorized expression of gratitude that is motivated by the perpetual deferment of its consummation. "It doesn't end until I feel God has told me so. That's why I continue to give thanks to the Lord through the example of Jesus."

Although as many as twenty other men perform ritual nailing as panata at any given year, Ruben is the only one who performs it as the main protagonist in a street play called the *Via Crucis o Pasion y Muerte*. This is a dramatization of the Stations of the Cross depicting the various ordeals Jesus Christ underwent leading up to his crucifixion. The performance takes place along a 5-kilometer route, along which about forty local, nonprofessional actors deliver lines from a script written by an amateur dramatist, the current director's grandfather, in 1955. The play concludes in a purpose-built hill on the outskirts of town where a huge crowd would amass to witness the dramatic climax of Ruben nailed to the cross where he remains for a good ten to fifteen minutes.

These days the Via Crucis attracts audiences of as many as 20,000 to 25,000, a figure estimated as far back as the mid-1980s, with tens of thousands more tuning in to broadcasts and live streams of its performance. This mediatization has affected the practical enactment of the passion play itself, which is an observation made by anthropologists Nicholas Barker (1998) in the 1980s and Peter Bräunlein (2009) in the 1990s. The actors have been encouraged by the city government to wear lapel microphones so that their voices can be transmitted wirelessly to several large speakers loaded on to a slow-moving lorry that follows the entire street play. Professionally made costumes and props have been provided to enhance the aesthetic appeal of the play for the viewing audience. The Roman centurions have been designated to act as crowd control, using their spears to form a cordon to manage the throng of cameramen, photographers, reporters, and others who cram the streets in their relentless attempts to get a clear shot of the spectacle, or even interview the actors in the midst of their performances[6] (Bräunlein 2009: 908).

Anthropologists have analyzed the various forms of mediatization that have become part and parcel of crucifixion rituals in the Philippines (Zialcita 1986; Barker 1998; Bräunlein 2009). They point to how the revival of rituals of self-mortification, a legacy of Spanish missionization since the sixteenth century, "was itself clearly fostered by the Philippine media with sensational front-page headlines, news reports and photographs" (Bräunlein 2009: 897). The Via Crucis as a mediatized spectacle has become so entrenched to the town's identity that journalists have dubbed it "the Calvary of the Philippines" (Orejas 2005). The municipal government—more than complicit in the management and mediatization of the spectacle—has also caught on, listing the official motto of the town as "*Lakbayan taya ing Pagkasakit Ning Bie ng Hesu Cristo*" (Let us Journey with Christ in his suffering).

Spectacles of Fanaticism

A common genre in the news reportage of Ruben as sufferer is one that has a visual and thematic focus on the gruesomeness of his pain experience. Close shots of the nails on his hands and feet, blood gushing from his wounds, face writhing in pain, are common features of this particular genre. Anthropologists Peter Bräunlein (2009) and Fernando Zialcita (1986) have described how witnessing the bloody rituals had "resembled a funfair more than a solemn Christian celebration" (Bautista and Bräunlein 2014: 478), evoking in its viewing audience an interwoven spectrum of emotions from revulsion and aversion, to intrigue and even enjoyment. This complex aesthetic evokes what the philosopher Maurice Pascale has called the macabre fascination: "an intrinsic desire in the imaginative exploration of the phenomenology of death, dying, or preceding states of fright, pain, and suffering" (Pascale 2016). Moreover, news reports and bulletins that highlight Ruben's crucifixion would typically include a reiteration of the institutional Roman Catholic Church's prohibition of such practices, typically through an interview with a Roman Catholic priest who would indicate the extra-liturgical (and therefore, illicit) nature of the rituals.[7]

Mediatized images of suffering through passion rituals resonate with a TV audience who extend what media studies scholar Jonathan Ong has called "lay moralities" in relation to media conventions of representing suffering (Ong 2015b: 2). Unlike pure entertainment, the news landscape in the Philippines "is a moral context that is more likely to provoke moral reflection about obligation and action toward suffering others" (Ong 2015a). In effect, this kind of reporting is akin to what Lilie Chouliaraki in *The Spectatorship of Suffering* (2006) described as "adventure news" which "maximize[s] the distance between spectator and the scene of suffering, and a void of agency," thereby rendering the subject of the news as a capital-O Other (Chouliaraki 2016: 10).

Taken together, the combination of macabre fascination, institutional denouncement, and lay moralities of viewing audiences produces depictions of the Via Crucis as a mediatized "spectacle of fanaticism." In highlighting the gruesomeness of Ruben's suffering selfhood, news reports magnify the extent of his religious transgression, effectively depicting him as a stereotypical religious fanatic driven by uncritical zeal and obsessive enthusiasm. Rarely is there any sustained depiction or explanation of the complexity of Ruben's ideas about trust and panata, which are not taken as serious or authentic motivations for ritual agency. There is virtually no effort to distinguish between pain as a sensation and suffering as a positively edifying ontological condition. Rather, the spectacle of his pain is the message itself. Depictions such as this effectively dispossess him of forms of rational agency, and do not contain any moral encouragement for audiences to "care" for the ontological and edifying aspects of his suffering. In fact, the main message of these depictions is that Ruben's act of embodied identification with Christ should not be emulated, not only because it goes against official Catholic doctrine, but because it poses a danger to oneself and others.

While a common effect of the mediatization of Ruben's suffering as a spectacle of fanaticism is the production of social, emotional, and moral distance, it can also elicit a ritually embodied identification. Ong (2015a) argues, further, that "sympathy with or denial strategies towards suffering others are shaped not only by audiences' geographical distance to tragedy, but crucially by classed moralities that profoundly shape judgments to sufferers and the media that represent them" (Ong 2015a: 1). It is to how Ruben appropriates his own celebrification, and to how this appropriation resonates with the socially and emotionally disempowered TV audience that we shall now turn.

Ruben's Expansion of Suffering

For all his popularity, Ruben depicts himself as just an ordinary man undeserving of God's favor. His reticence at being given star treatment is akin to the "spiritual star" described by media studies scholar Simone Natale (2013). Like the spiritualist mediums that are the subject of Natale's analysis, Ruben distinguishes his media profile from those who are "*nagpapasikat lang*" (just in it for the fame)—a subjectivity he associates with the commodified industry driven by managers and publicity agents. Ruben in fact considers the commodifying nature of showbiz as undesirable and counter to the essence of his suffering selfhood. As Natale puts it, Ruben's celebrification likens him to "marketed commodities who struggled to demonstrate that they did not pertain to the market. Paradoxically, their denial of the market, given as a testimony of their honesty, was also one of the foundations of their success as mediums and of their celebrity status... the medium needed to deny the market in order to become the market's hero" (Natale 2013: 96).

This does not mean, however, that Ruben rejects his celebrity status, or even shies away from the spotlight. He is fully aware of the telecommunicative reach of his celebrification, and of the potential for his media profile to encourage a broader awareness of panata. "With ongoing mediatization," argues Zeiler, "actors from outside institutionalized structures also have increasing opportunities to contribute their opinions and thus to shape religion and religious practice on diverse levels" (Zeiler 2018: 9). What the news reporters often neglect, or perhaps underestimate, is Ruben's acts of deliberately extending (that is to say, communicating precisely) the foundations of his suffering agency into mediatized domains as a way of co-opting and taking more control of the many years in which he has been depicted as a fanatic. Over the years, Ruben has mastered a carefully choreographed way of speaking with the dozens of reporters who come to see him. A constant message that he emphasizes time and again during TV interviews is that only those with a genuine panata should consider crucifixion or other forms of self-mortification. "Crucifixion is not those who just want to get famous," he would tell me, "only to those whose suffering is pure."

The impact of Ruben's own "telecommunicated agency" is evident in the centripetal force of his celebrification. The case of Dodong, a welder in his forties who I met in the course of fieldwork, serves to exemplify how Ruben's celebrification conveys Roman Catholic suffering in ways not intended by media outlets. Using his entire savings, Dodong made the 700-kilometer journey to Pampanga after seeing Ruben on television on several occasions. He said he wanted to be nailed on the cross because he had promised Jesus that he would do so, and that he had his own "true" panata. In his television appearances, made possible by the mediatization of the Via Crucis, Ruben became seen as the facilitator of crucifixion. In the mediatized telecommunicative reach that expanded his suffering, it is not Ruben's "fanaticism" that shines through but the logic of panata, one that Ruben himself deliberately cultivated in his media appearances.

The facilitators of the nailing rituals were initially skeptical about Dodong's desire to undergo nailing because they have seen many who simply used the ritual to achieve fame and even monetary gain (*nagpapasikat lang*). The following day, I encountered Dodong again at the house of Ruben, where he told me that after some persistent pleading, he had finally been granted permission to be crucified from the secretary at the city hall. Although Ruben was never forceful or even vocal in his support for Dodong, he took him into his own household, offered him food and lodging, for which Dodong was immensely grateful: "That Ruben... he really is Jesus."

What we learn from Dodong's story is the efficacy of Ruben's deliberate efforts at appropriating his own celebrification, which he sees as a positive act of projecting his (and by extension, Christ's) suffering onto mediatized domain. Dodong's attitude to Ruben exemplifies what Ong observed regarding how socially disempowered viewers respond to televised images of suffering, that "viewing suffering may not carry the impact of shock or trauma, but instead serve as an opportunity for personal reflection, catharsis and therapy" (Ong 2015b: 4). In effect, Dodong's response to mediatized images of Ruben does not accord with the spectacle of fanaticism, one that fetishizes pain and reduces panata to an "obliteration of the self." Ruben's suffering, rather, is received as the act of an exemplary "holy man" who has, through panata, facilitated a mediation between God and humanity. Peter Brown (1971) had called the holy man "one who brought the holy into the domain of the world, mediating between God and man, serving as well to flatten the distinction of greater and lesser patrons" (Brown 1971; Howe 2000: 641). Ruben's holy man celebrity, to be sure, is a modern construct that is predicated by his deliberate appropriation of technologies of mass-circulation. The anthropologist Dierdre de la Cruz discusses this agentive convergence of divine mediation and media, wherein "religious mediation is fantasized to bring about a certain influence or communication in a way compatible with those imagined to be the charge of the government and the mass media" (de la Cruz 2009: 458).

The Suffering Shepherd of Timor-Leste

In the following section, I inquire into how the agentive appropriation of mediatization shapes agendas of social and political liberation. By considering the social and political impact of Bishop Carlos Felipe Ximenes Belo, I seek to demonstrate how the personification and extension of Timor-Leste's suffering serve to "enable (Western) audiences to effectively relate or identify with the situation of distant sufferers" (Ong 2014: 181).

The citation for the 1996 Nobel Peace Prize recognized Bishop Belo's role in bringing the world's attention to the atrocities committed by the Indonesian military during their twenty-four-year occupation of Timor-Leste. Belo and his Nobel co-laureate, East Timorese President Jose Ramos-Horta, were lauded for their efforts in speaking up for the cause of nonviolent resistance in spite of direct threats to their lives. Specifically recognized was Belo's resolve amidst a biased and heavily censored Indonesian media. Belo's campaign was challenging in light of a largely reticent, if not complicit, Indonesian Roman Catholic Church which, in being mindful of their own tenuous position as a minority faith in a Muslim majority nation, chose not to offer substantive support to the resistance in Timor-Leste.[8] One could say that the essence of his political advocacy was not just his direct response to military brutality, but his extending the suffering of the people by harnessing the force of mediatization against seemingly insurmountable odds

The Indonesian occupation of Timor-Leste in 1975 followed shortly after the withdrawal of Portuguese colonial control and an ensuing civil war from which the Frente Revolucionária de Timor-Leste Independente (FRETILIN) declared the nation's post-colonial independence. The Indonesian incursion was motivated by fears that communist groups in an independent Timor-Leste could inspire separatist movements in other Indonesian provinces. The Indonesian military's (TNI) campaigns to subdue a steadily growing East Timorese resistance were devastating for the local population. Air and naval bombardments were followed by a destructive ground operation characterized as one of "encirclement and annihilation" (Taylor 2003: 166–7). In 1976, an East Timorese Church report estimated the casualties as between 60,000 and 100,000 (Dunn 1983: 310). The final report by the UN Commission for Reception, Truth and Reconciliation in East Timor estimated that as many as 183,000 people were killed by 1999—close to a third of the population at the time (UNTAET 2005).

The Indonesian occupying force had complete control of the media at that time. Indonesia's public infrastructure projects were frequently highlighted in the reportage of the situation in the country, citing in particular how paved roads had made travel across the landscape far more efficient than during the Portuguese colonial period. There was no acknowledgment of the fact that the new roads had all but served the interests of the Indonesian military who were advancing deep into resistance movement territory. Biased reporting such as this had served to mask the violence that typified the occupation. Far from even stating that a "war" was actually taking place, there was virtually no coverage of the number of casualties. This kind of selectivity in the news, according to Bishop Belo's biographer Arnold Kohen, "made many Indonesians believe the East Timorese were fairly treated, even pampered. It vexed Bishop Belo to hear this, as though East Timor was merely a construction project" (Kohen 1997: Loc. 515). The fact remained that the Indonesian state had a far better capacity to influence the world media than anyone in the resistance. Western governments and Japan "were inclined to echo whatever Indonesia said, whether they believed it or not" (Kohen 1997: 1702). As such, the Indonesian occupation received the tacit support of the international community, particularly those countries whose foreign policies were influenced by a fear of Timor-Leste turning into an "Asian Cuba" (Philpott 2006: 137).

Apart from this, there were simply no significant or sustained challenges to Indonesia's control of the media, even by religious institutions. Crucially, the Indonesian Bishops Conference (IBC), whose clerics were working on the ground, did not encourage vocal forms of protest or any kind of practical advocacy against the occupation (Smythe 2004: 79). This led to a sense of isolation on the part of East Timorese clerics, many of whom were witnesses to the military atrocities committed in their parish communities. This isolation was compounded by the fact that the Vatican "failed to state openly and officially their solidarity with the [East Timorese] Church, people and religious of Timor-Leste" (Carey 1999: 82). To be sure, the Vatican had offered indirect support for the East Timorese cause by eventually facilitating an institutional separation between the East Timorese Catholic Church and the IBC, effectively empowering the former to circumvent the latter's reluctance to engage. Nevertheless, the lack of explicit support and strong denouncement of the occupation from both the Indonesian Church and Vatican—this in spite of a visit to East Timor by Pope John Paul II in 1989—did constitute what members of the various religious orders in East Timor clerics have famously called "the heaviest blow" to their struggle for independence (Smythe 2004: 1).

Bishop Belo and other East Timorese priests played a key role during this period of upheaval and censorship, primarily in trying to limit loss of life and property. Unlike their Portuguese predecessors and Indonesian counterparts, Bishop Martinho da Costa Lopes and his eventual replacement, Bishop Belo, were vociferous in their criticism of the Indonesian occupation by speaking out in whatever media platform they could access. As Lundry observed, from 1975 the East Timorese Church became among the very few institutions that had the wherewithal to keep in check the excesses of the Indonesian occupation such that it became "the only tolerated public representation of civil society" (Lundry 2002: 2).

With the reticent attitude of both the Indonesian Church and the Vatican during the early years of the occupation, it was left largely to the East Timorese priests to take on an increasingly active role in being more socially and politically engaged with the East Timorese resistance (Lundry 2002: 8). Bishop Belo, since ascending to the role of Bishop of Dili in 1983 and later Apostolic Administrator in 1989, played an instrumental role in raising international awareness about the situation in Timor-Leste, in spite of being placed under close surveillance by the Indonesian military. His political advocacy resonated strongly with the spirit of Vatican II reforms, in which the positive social role of the clergy was greatly emphasized.

Two mediatized events turned the tide of media repression in East Timor. The 1991 Santa Cruz Massacre, in which 250 East Timorese independence activists were shot by Indonesian troops, was the largest demonstration against the Indonesian occupation since 1975. The massacre was witnessed by three foreign investigative journalists, whose testimony and smuggled video footage became the basis for an award-winning documentary, *Cold Blood: The Massacre of East Timor* (1992). The Santa Cruz massacre was a turning point in galvanizing the mediatization of the suffering of the people of East Timor. TV news bulletins around the world broadcast the horrific images of the massacre sparking great interest in the plight of the East Timorese people (Kohen 1997: Loc. 3516). Although the Santa Cruz massacre was not the first or the last atrocity committed under the occupation, " for the first time," observed Kohen, "there was a great deal of critical reporting on East Timor in the Indonesian news media, provoking unprecedented domestic debate on the issue, and encouraging the Timorese resistance movement" (Kohen 1997: Loc. 3465).

In 1994, a group of East Timorese students scaled the walls of the US Embassy in Jakarta just as the Indonesian president was welcoming then US President Clinton to the APEC Summit. Major news networks like CNN ran half-hour updates for the duration of Clinton's attendance at the Summit. Editorials in the major American, British, and Canadian broadsheets gave serious attention to East Timor, providing the background into the history of violence perpetrated by the Indonesian occupation. As Kohen described it: "the fence-jumping initiative of the young people had struck a chord in the American psyche, and their point had been made forcefully, well beyond the United States" (Kohen 1997: Loc. 3846).

The international media coverage of these two events exemplified how mediatization had made Indonesian control and suppression of information an increasingly difficult challenge. Scholars have cited Church sources as saying that "there was a direct connection between occasions when the Indonesians relented in their repression and actions by the American Congress, editorials in the mass media, and statements by the American government" (Kohen 1997: Loc. 3516). It is under these circumstances that Bishop Belo had come to recognize the power of mediatization as a means toward conveying the suffering of the East Timorese to a much broader audience.

The conferment of the Nobel Peace Prize would be a catalyst for this endeavor. Belo recognized that the notoriety that the prize afforded would also constitute an appeal for responsible news reporting on the part of "all professionals of the information media, charged with this great mission, that they regulate communication between all latitudes of the globe, doing it with a sense of truth and immunity for building up a society more humane and more just, without tendentious manipulation" (Belo 1996).

Belo's "enNobeling"

As a media event, the Nobel Peace Prize award ceremony established Belo's activist celebrification. Swiatek (2019) depicts the potency of the activist celebrity as a wielder of soft power—that capacity to attract other individuals and groups to empathize and act to ameliorate suffering. Suffering was a central motif in Belo's Nobel Peace Prize acceptance lecture. He likened the situation in Timor-Leste to those in South Africa, Afghanistan, Rwanda, and Burma— places where ordinary citizens had persevered through and triumphed over great violence and turmoil. His gratitude to the King and Queen of Norway (for being "susceptible to the suffering of the people of East Timor...") and to the Pope (for "following the situation and the suffering of the people and the Church in East Timor") was made in the spirit of the Vatican II document *Gadium et Spes*, which called for the protection of human dignity in the midst of suffering.

Significantly, Belo emphasized the role of the international media industry "who have lent their voices in making known to the world the anguish and the suffering of the Timorese." Journalists, photographers, and filmmakers were singled out as not only depicting suffering, but embodying it themselves in their reportage amidst the repression of the Indonesian state. Indeed, his speech culminated in a "tribute to those who provide information about Timor, who risk their lives, some of them falling in East Timor's soil."

Literary scholar Sandra Mayer characterizes awards such as the Nobel Prize as a media spectacle that "apotheosises the [awardee] as a fetishised object in a 'star-centred economy'" (Mayer 2013: 8). The Nobel laureate in literature, for example, has an "enNobeling" quality that catapults the winner to the heights of mediatized literary stardom: "the defining epithet 'Nobel Prize-winning' persistently makes catchy media headlines and has come to signify well-nigh universal renown and cultural authority as an ostensibly reliable marker of artistic merit and distinction" (Mayer 2013: 3–4). Mayer discusses how intense publicity and mediatization of the Nobel Prize empower its awardees to utilize "an actively engineered stunt of authorial self-fashioning in which the message was underscored by the choreography of its delivery" (Mayer 2013: 8).

In contrast, the Nobel laureate typified Belo's own mode of celebrification, which to an extent defies its enNobeling. Belo's expansion of suffering was predicated upon him framing his celebrification against Christ's passion. For example, shortly after his arrival in Timor-Leste following his award, Belo addressed a public gathering: "People were at the airport to meet me. Nobody beat them. Nobody maltreated them. God was protecting them. But people with our Lord Jesus Christ, they crucified him on the cross. Nobody crucified [me] on the cross" (Stahl 1997). Consistent with the motif of suffering, Belo had confronted his surge in international popularity in a way that was always tempered by deflection and declarations of self-effacement. In a speech at the ceremony awarding him the collar of the "order of Timor-Leste" in Dili in August 2016, Belo recalled: "In fact, when I received the Nobel Peace Prize in 1996, alongside His Excellency Mr Ramos-Horta, I always said that this prize was for the people. For the people who struggle, the people who suffer, the people who cry, the people who die. We are only their servants" (Belo 2016). Consistent evocations of suffering underscore Belo's deliberate channeling of the symbolic power of the award to deflect attention away from himself in favor of "mak[ing] visible the suffering of others and thus offer claims for compassion from audiences" (Ong 2014: 181).

Communication studies scholar Kaarina Nikunen (2019) argues a position consistent with most research on celebrity humanism: that "instead of alleviating suffering, celebrity humanism advances consumerism and promotes the star brand." Bruno Campanella (2019) corroborates this by arguing that humanitarian aid work generates solidarity capital for the celebrity herself rather than the cause being campaigned for. What Belo achieves in the expansion of Timor-Leste's suffering, rather, is a movement away from the conventional telos of celebrity humanism, thereby subverting the very enNobeling process that facilitated his notoriety to begin with.

Conclusion

Whereas Pope John Paull II had been the most articulate about the meaning of suffering in the Roman Catholic context, it is Pope Francis who has personified the paradoxically complex, even ironic nature of Roman Catholic mediatized religious celebrification. Depictions of suffering underscore the "Francis effect,"[9] which may well be attributed to his embodiment of values rooted in the long tradition of the Church—such as humility and an unwavering concern for the downtrodden and vulnerable. His celebrity stock is seen to rise, for example, when he kisses and embraces a man afflicted with neurofibromatosis, when he visits prisoners and convicted criminals, takes a selfie with a girl with kidney disease, prioritizes disaster survivors over dignitaries, or when he sneaks out of his Vatican apartment to secretly feed the poor. On the one hand, a Papal persona that emphasizes suffering and self-effacing humility would seem to contradict the celebrity culture that fetishizes as a spectacle the aspirational value of individual notoriety. By the same token, Pope Francis's advocacy for the poor and suffering corresponds with his critique of neoliberal capital and, by extension, of the very ideological value-system that made the attribution of his celebrity possible in the first place.

Seminal texts on the field of religion and mediatization have been criticized as downplaying the role of "ordinary" religious actors—that is, those who do not have the public profile of the Pope—as agents of mediatization capable of purposefully channeling and even manipulating its sensationalist rationale (Kruger 2018). Similarly, scholarly understandings of celebrification underestimate the agency of religious actors in appropriating, and to some extent subverting the logic of the media. The two case studies that I have considered remind us that agency is a central feature in the dynamics of mediatized attributed celebrity, particularly in religious domains. The expansion of suffering is coterminous with their pursuit of agendas of personal ritual edification and social and political liberation. A comparative overview of the situations of Ruben and Belo sheds some light into the empirical nuances of this notion. In that regard, I make four observations by way of conclusion.

First, Ruben and Belo are religious actors whose experience and expansion of suffering emerge in vastly different, perhaps even opposing, contexts of mediatization. Ruben's notoriety had become elevated as a result of heavy news coverage of the Via Crucis, and the concomitant spectacularization of fanaticism. Belo's celebrification, on the other hand, comes in the context of deliberate and oppressive media repression by the Indonesian state, one which is exacerbated by the reticence of international religious institutions. In both cases, as nonmedia producers, both have had to appropriate the "media logic" of their respective contexts as a prerequisite for channeling the technologies of their dissemination as a platform for extending suffering to both proximal and distant others.

Second, Ruben and Belo's cases offer conceptual variation on what Graeme Turner (2010) described as the "demotic turn," the phenomenon in which modes of mass-oriented media (such as reality TV and internet) create the potential for "anyone" to be a celebrity for long as there is a demand for them. Both Ruben and Belo have achieved *attributed* celebrity—that is, their popularity in the public sphere is "largely the result of the concentrated representation of an individual as noteworthy or exceptional by cultural intermediaries" (Rojek 2010: 18). Ruben is not subjected to constant media surveillance and scrutiny such that his celebrification is based primarily on specific media events. Since Belo occupies a position of clerical authority in the local Church, however, his celebrification takes on a more sustained character. It cannot be said that their celebrity is merely "sensationalized"— that is, deliberately generated by publicists or media agents for the sole purpose of generating public attention—and the events which they participate in are orchestrated "pseudoevents." The nature of their celebrification, rather, is ironic in that the basis of their popularity lies precisely in their reluctance to fully accept their celebrity status.

Third, the respective audiences of the expansion of suffering are significant. Ruben's live audiences—that is, those who are physically present in Pampanga to witness the Via Crucis—identify with his proximal suffering, one in which the spatial *liveness* of his suffering is the primary aspect that triggers a vicarious identification. In addition, the participation of Dodong exemplifies an expression of affinity on the part of distant sufferers—those who watch on TV—who, like Ruben, appeal to divine intervention for their well-being. This corroborates Ong's analysis, which concludes that "the encounter of distant sufferers in the Filipino news involves reflections about suffering as a shared affliction that can engender solidarity with distant others and facilitate a spiritual connection with the divine" (Ong 2015b: 13–14). Belo as transnational political activist, on the other hand, appeals to an audience who are estranged from the experience of suffering itself, and can only seek to add material substance (perhaps by way of donation to the cause or other means) to an imaginary solidarity with distant sufferers.

Finally, the two contexts of mediatization demonstrate how celebrification can, to an extent, erode the deliberate attempts at expanding suffering. Lanuza observed, "The celebritized spectacle of Pope Francis overshadowed the prophetic message of the 'Pope of the poor.' He was merely the 'people's Pope' with a charismatic smile" (Lanuza 2017: 30).

In a similar fashion, the mediatized spectacle of fanaticism of the Via Crucis had resulted in a "flattening" of the ontological and intersubjective complexity of Ruben's suffering panata, reducing it to stereotypical depictions of religious fanaticism. Ruben does indeed emphasize the distinction between "regular folks" and those who are merely seeking publicity by performing crucifixion rituals. Belo's agenda of bringing the world's attention to the suffering of Timor-Leste, on the other hand, was largely achieved through the platform of the Nobel Peace Prize. He had deliberately sought to appeal to a wider global audience, particularly professional media producers who can direct as much publicity onto the Timor-Leste case. However, while journalistic reports depicting the atrocities of the Indonesian military have increased, the suffering of East Timorese is viewed largely from the "zone of safety"—that is, in the secure zone of Western domesticity (Chouliaraki 2006: 83; Ong 2015b: 2). This awareness of Belo's activism did not engender a full acknowledgment of the agency of East Timorese themselves, who largely remain distant sufferers.

Notes

1   I refer here to mediatization, as opposed to mediation. These two concepts are commonly used interchangeably. The concept of "mediation" has a fairly robust discourse (see Morgan 2011; Hovland 2018; Meyer 2020; and Reinhardt 2020) in the anthropology of religion. Anthropologists such as Birgit Meyer place mediation as a definitive principle of "religion" itself in describing the latter "as a practice of mediation between humans and the professed transcendent that necessarily requires specific material media, that is, authorized forms through which the transcendent is being generated and becomes somehow tangible" (Meyer 2020: 8).

2   My focus on the virtuous externalization of suffering evokes a well-established theme in Roman Catholicism. See, for example, Robert Orsi's *Thank You, St. Jude* (1998) and *Between Heaven and Earth* (2005) that discuss how people orient their lives according to the example of exemplary individuals and sacred figures.

3   These two Southeast Asian countries have both experienced centuries of European Roman Catholic missionization—the longest in Southeast Asia. The Philippines, with over 80 million Catholics, is already the largest Christian country in Asia. The most recent data project that it will be among the world's fastest-growing Catholic populations by 2050 (Pew Research Center 2011). Meanwhile, Timor-Leste—Asia's youngest nation—has a Catholic population that grew by about 400 percent over the past forty years, with the highest proportion of Catholics at 97 percent (Carey 1999).

4   A study that might exemplify this is by Kim and Chen (2020), who argue that
     religious celebrities have affected the public perception and experience of religious
     pilgrimage, with an emphasis on "celebrity effectiveness" as measured by how
     religious endorsers condition consumer decision making.

5   Another anthropologist, Dierdre De la Cruz (2009) has analyzed Filipino
     Marianism as a rubric through which we might understand the intersectionality
     between religious and technological mediation. Like Liebelt, she examines how
     religion and the mass media are "heavily imbricated" with the configurations of
     transnational labor, mobility, and geopolitical conflict. De la Cruz examines the
     affinities between religion and media, which can variously intensify one another's
     capacities for signification, while at times be "rescuing one from the consequences
     of a breakdown in mediation" (2009: 476).

6   Like Ruben, the cast of the Via Crucis—most of whom are from a lower socio-
     economic background—are aware and receptive to the intense mediatization of
     their ritual. The anthropologist Claudia Liebelt (2011) has described the effect of
     mediatization on Filipino Roman Catholic subjectivity, particularly in the case
     of migrant women in Israel. Like the Roman Catholics in transnational domains,
     stepping into the spotlight as a cast member in a heavily mediatized performance
     provides an opportunity to transcend social marginality, "creat[ing] possibilities
     for dressing up, being part of a happening 'in the name of Jesus', rubbing shoulders
     with 'VIPs' and acquiring tokens as pieces of the sacred" (Liebelt 2011: 244). The Via
     Crucis cast came to "perceive themselves no longer as the peripheral performers,
     but, encouraged by charismatic narratives of healing and empowerment, at centre
     stage of mass mediated, global happenings" (Liebelt 2011: 246).

7   In previous works (Bautista 2018, 2019), I have reviewed and categorized the
     Church's institutional denouncement of passion rituals as based on notions of
     redundancy (that there is no need for painful rituals given Christ's sacrifice) and
     misguided emphasis (that the painful rituals focus too much on Christ's death at
     the expense of appreciating the significance of his resurrection).

8   While Indonesian clergy and personnel observed the injustices perpetrated by
     the Indonesian military, such observations were tempered with calls for prudence
     and restraint in openly criticizing the occupation (Smythe 2004: 78). In effect, the
     dioceses in Indonesia were "for the most part agents of their government's policy
     (albeit generally with good will and intentions)" (Smythe 2004: 78).

9   In 2013, the Pontiff was named *Time* magazine's "Person of the Year." Following
     suit, *Fortune* magazine ranked him first among the "World's 50 Greatest Leaders"
     in 2014. One might say that the Pope's "rock star" status is evidenced by his
     18.7 million Twitter followers and a highly subscribed Vatican YouTube channel.
     Demonstrations of the Pope's direct confrontation of suffering are deliberately
     processed for media saturation by a dedicated publicity apparatus that cultivates

a sense of intimacy between the Pope and a global market of media consumers. Greg Burke, the former senior communications adviser to the Vatican's secretariat of state (variously referred to as the "Holy See handler" or "Papal spin doctor"), has described his job as "to formulate THE message and try to make sure everyone remains on message" through means that Vatican observers have described as "[combining] doctrine with Buzzfeed-like spin" (Englehart 2013).

7

Exorcism in the Media

Thomas J. Csordas

The presence of religion in media is increasingly consequential and increasingly often observed by analysts of contemporary culture. Noomen, Aupers, and Houtman (2012) examine the internet presence of Catholic, Protestant, and holistic spiritualities specifically in the form of websites by interviewing designers of religious websites. In an analysis of how religion is mediated by television that focuses on a popular religiously themed TV series, Angela Zito observes that "Religion, like the media and mediations of all sorts, functions best when no one notices it, when people appropriate it as an always-already present aspect of social life" (Zito 2008: 728). When we pose the question of exorcism in the media, we are talking about a specific Catholic religious practice the legacy of which begins long before the age of media, and that has undergone periods of waxing and waning influence in Church history. Yet its contemporary media presence as a recurring theme at least approximates an understanding of exorcism as precisely this kind of always-already present aspect of social life.

The first thing that comes to mind regarding exorcism in the media is what is usually considered a subgenre of Hollywood horror films dramatizing demonic possession and the priest's struggle against the dark forces. Most important for our purposes is that some of these films are based on actual cases. *The Exorcist* which inaugurated this subgenre in 1973 was based on a 1949 case in Maryland. *The Exorcism of Emily Rose* in 2005 was based on the 1985 case of Anneliese Michel, documented in monograph form by the anthropologist Felicitas Goodman. *The Rite* in 2011 was based on the experience of an exorcist still active and prominent in exorcism circles in the United States. A practicing exorcist commented that the demonic manifestations that occur in some sessions of exorcism could be "almost Hollywoodesque." Yet fictional or fictionalized Hollywood movies, entwined as they are with the actual practice of exorcism, represent only a part of how this mode of ritual healing appears in the media.

Journalistic accounts that invoke exorcism or exorcists are not infrequent. In the summer of 2018 the American news media reported that a group of witches opposed to the appointment of Brett Kavanaugh to the Supreme Court had placed a hex on the nominee, followed by the response of a prominent Catholic exorcist who publicly announced that he was offering prayers at Mass to counter the witches' hex. In 2019 the media reported that the leader of the Jesuit order had opined that the devil was a symbolic reality, whence the International Association of Exorcists responded that the devil is an ontological reality. In 2020 a Trumpist priest performed exorcisms against "election fraud" in the midst of an exceedingly partisan election season that exacerbated political division in the United States. Exorcism also has online presence in the form of lecture videos by exorcists on topics ranging from the cosmological "spiritual warfare" to the interplay of psychology and spirituality in the understanding of demonic affliction. Finally, periodic documentaries appear about exorcism as an ongoing practice, with varying degrees of acceptance or skepticism.

In this chapter I focus on two such documentaries that feature exorcists who at the time of their production had the highest profile in the United States and Italy—one a country with a highly influential Catholic population and the other where Catholicism is highly influential. The first is a 1991 episode of the ABC News show *20/20* with Hugh Downs, Barbara Walters, and Tom Jelton that features Father James LeBar, who was the official exorcist of the Archdiocese of New York. The second is a 2018 documentary by William Friedkin (not coincidentally the director of *The Exorcist* in 1973) featuring Father Gabriele Amorth, the official exorcist of the Diocese of Rome. My intent is to provide a specific example of how contemporary Catholic exorcism articulates a discourse of evil at large in the world and at the same time addresses the suffering of particular individuals, and does so via the conventions of television journalism and documentary film.

ABC *20/20* Television Documentary on Exorcism

The ABC News report was prompted by a public statement at St. Patrick's Cathedral on March 4, 1990, by the prominent John Cardinal O'Connor, Archbishop of New York. In the words of the television journalists, O'Connor delivered a "provocative message" in which "an incredible secret was revealed" and "exorcism came out of the dark of the past and returned to the world of the present." They reported that the message was a "warning that the devil was real, his evil spreading, and exorcisms approved by the Church were being used to rid some people of their demons." The Cardinal revealed that two exorcisms had been performed recently, which according to the reporters had the effect of "rekindling controversy between the Church and modern psychiatry, between religious beliefs and medical science."

The television journalists frame their report by asking "Heaven and Hell, are they real? Does the Devil exist? People have anguished over these questions for centuries." They say that social ills like pornography, drugs, and violence may be evidence of his evidence of his handiwork but that there is "nothing more provocative, more terrifying, more fascinating than the ritual of exorcism." They describe their report as an opportunity to witness "an extraordinary event never before seen on American television" noting that "some sights and sounds may be disturbing, particularly for children." Part of this is presented against the background of historical paintings and drawings of the Devil, Beelzebub, Satan, or Lucifer, who is "capable of possessing the minds of innocent victims and turning them evil," but that "when these ancient prayers are spoken the believers say the demons must leave." They observe that exorcism is controversial insofar as:

> Years ago mental disorders like schizophrenia, tourette's disorder, multiple personality disorder, even problems like epilepsy were misdiagnosed as cases of demonic possession. As modern science showed that those were medical problems, the practice of exorcism sharply declined. But interest was rekindled in 1973 after release of the film *The Exorcist*, which was based on an actual, well-documented case of suspected possession. The highly dramatized film seemed so far-fetched that exorcism was still largely dismissed as the stuff of horror movies. But then last year in New York an incredible secret was revealed. At St. Patrtick's Cathedral in Manhattan, exorcism came out of the dark of the past and returned to the world of the present.

The exorcisms were performed by a priest calling himself "Father A for Anonymous," assisted by Father James LeBar. At the time the journalists referred to Father A as "one of the few exorcists in the Catholic Church." Immediately following the Cardinal's announcement, Father LeBar received over seventy-five cases from all across the country to investigate. ABC News, after considerable negotiation, gained permission to follow one of the cases for twelve months and to film an exorcism session. This was the case of sixteen-year-old Gina, who lived with her family in Florida.

In her own words, sixteen-year-old Gina "saw demons and stuff." The journalists report that for years she had "violent seizures in which she would spit, vomit, scream in strange voices and have visions of demons. She had not attended school in several months." Her mother took Gina to a spiritist healer who scratched her with a pair of scissors on the back and on chest as part of what they thought was an exorcism. Gina did not want to go but her mother prevailed, yet the behavior only worsened, and she would make noises in the night. Gina had already spent two months in the Miami Children's Hospital psychiatric ward, diagnosed as having "recurring psychotic episodes." They turned to the Church and after six months of investigation the priests obtained permission from the bishop to perform an exorcism. Father A says Gina exhibited one of the classic signs of possession, knowledge of things and people that there was no way she could have known, in particular knowing where he had been the previous week dealing with another case and mentioning the person by name, which to the priest was "very astounding, very revealing."

They assembled an exorcism team composed of a psychotherapist, a nurse, a Spanish translator, women to restrain Gina when she (as the demon) struggled to resist the rite, a doctor, and additional priests. Father A instructed the team in advance, emphasizing that this is not a game. Referring to Gina, he said "don't address her or anything that comes from her. It's looking for an out and if anyone falls victim to that then now we have two people to deal with." The session begins with mass and the Eucharist, in which Gina participates without knowing why she is there. Father A says secrecy ensures the demons can't prepare for the surprise encounter with an exorcist. There is a crucifix and several other religious objects and pictures on a table in the room. Gina kneels in front of the standing priest surrounded by team members, with several touching her shoulders. He asks "How are you feeling, honey?" and she asks "What did I do to deserve this?" "You did nothing to deserve this, Gina. Do you want to be free of this?" "Yes," she replies. "Are you going to help us to free you?" "Yes."

Father A tries to draw the demons out by giving Gina a glass of holy water to drink, a technique intended to provoke a demonic response. Before making a final determination to proceed he "probes her psyche," identifying exactly what demons he is confronting. "You can tell me what you're feeling." The report cuts in a later comment from Father LeBar who says "At this point things are moving quite slowly. The devil plays a game of deception and won't reveal himself or themselves for quite a period of time." Then something does happen: Gina begins retching into a plastic bin kept at the ready. As the pre-exorcism examination intensifies, unexpectedly low and unfamiliar voices begin to emerge. "Gina says I have to go. I don't want to go. Do you understand?" Father A retorts "Do *you* understand?" and the demon angrily rejoins "No, do you understand?!" Father

LeBar's post-session comment again appears onscreen: "The first time I heard the voice I hadn't expected it at all, then it was 'here we go fast and furious.'"

Gina becomes violent, and the priest goes to her while one woman holds her in restraint as she sits in a chair. "In the name of Jesus Christ I command you to leave" he says, holding a crucifix to her cheek while she growls "Me don't want to leave!" He stresses to Gina that she has to help in the process. A change in the expression on her face indicated that Gina was no longer herself and that the entity started to manifest itself, speaking and revealing who he was, "My name is Minga" in a doll-like voice. The demon says "Ouch" and the priest responds "You want pain, I'll give you pain." He informs participants that it is necessary to make sure the entity is not masking itself. "Why aren't you praying, Gina?" She whispers "I'm here." The journalist narrator says that just as soon as it began the episode is over and she becomes more composed, identifying in her own persona Zion and Minga as two of ten entities controlling her. Zion is African. The exorcist asks, "An African of today's age or in the jungle?" "In the jungle." "Who else?" "Minga. Minga is a very short woman."

All of this has been preliminary to the rite itself, to gather final proof of the need to proceed. Considering what they have seen to this point, the priests decide to go ahead with exorcism. It begins with Father A standing in front of Gina, seated on a chair with others seated around her, one shown raising his hands in the Charismatic prayer posture. As the priest prays he presses the crucifix to her forehead and she recoils, saying in high baby doll voice, "It's too hot." Gina reaches to her forehead, and he removes her hand which is then grasped by a team member. He exhorts the spirit not to do damage to anyone in this house. "Stay away!" "I now exorcise you." The team's prayers and Gina's reactions intensify. The team's doctor ties her arms and legs to the chair. The priest refers to "extreme hate" as he touches her head. She prophecies there are more wars coming. She appears to switch between personalities while the rite is read. The rite continues for several hours and Father LeBar says the prayers word for word along with Father A, watching him for signs of weakening. Later he said "I felt the power of God and also felt the power of Evil" adding that he always has to confront fear. In the final stage Father A says that Zion, Minga, and the other diabolical spirits must leave, and includes the spirit of Lust. Gina becomes complacent as the priest wraps up in the name of the Trinity. He has her kiss the cross, and tells her that "Mama's going to take you home now."

That night she reported that some of the troubling voices had returned to haunt her in her bedroom. Father A went to the home and performed an exorcism on the house to drive spirits out. But more help was needed and within a few days all involved, priests and mother, decided to bring Gina to Children's Hospital for further analysis and treatment with what the narrator called "a more conventional approach to mental problems." After two weeks' confinement and compared to previously she was determined still to be distorting reality but not to the same degree; and although she remained agitated it was not as extreme as during her previous hospitalization. She gradually responded to a combination of medication and various psychotherapies. By the time the journalists followed up two months later, she was still on haloperidol, a strong tranquilizer that she continued on after discharge.

I have described the proceedings as they are portrayed in the video recorded by the ABC News team. In the *20/20* report, the presentation of the videotaped exorcism was intercut with clips of commentary by several people who were either present or who had been shown the video subsequently, but for our purposes we abstract and juxtapose them in order to get a sense of the different standpoints represented. These include Gina and her mother; the priests Father LeBar and Father A; Carol Razza, a psychotherapist and exorcism team member; James Gill, a psychiatrist and Jesuit priest; and Warren Schlanger, a psychiatrist who treated Gina in the hospital. Gina's mother is present in the film as a caring and religious Hispanic parent without too much of note to say. Gina herself has a faint but engaged voice, early in the documentary saying, "I'm sick with these evil things, and every time I was coming out with voices." In a two-month follow-up with ABC journalist Tom Jelton she was on psychopharmaceutical medication and had just completed her first days back at school, reporting that "I feel much better, thanks to God that he delivered me from Evil but I'm much better now and I'm very happy now I feel free." When Jelton asked if she was frightened with Father A, she replied "After I got to know him and he prayed for me I was not frightened." "Do you remember pain?" "Oh he was praying for me and he just pressed the cross a little too hard on the top of my head, because it hurt, you know it was too tight. It was pain in other ways because those evil spirits were there and they had to leave that day." This is an intriguing phenomenological juxtaposition of the mundane physical pain of an object pressed on her head and the cosmologically salient emotional pain caused by spirits being forced to relinquish their domination.

The priests are truly the principal figures of the journalistic narrative, and it cannot go unremarked that the partnership between the public Father LeBar and the reserved Father Anonymous is reminiscent of that between Moses and Aaron, Peter and Paul, or Luther and Melancthon. Anonymity is a significant theme both with respect to self-protectiveness and the desire to avoid sensationalism, and with respect to the implicit power of secrecy and the aura of mystery endowed by operating in the shadows. The early scene of a tranquil mass in a small parish church emphasizes that Father LeBar "draws strength from its celebration, willpower that's essential when LeBar participates in another ancient church ritual, the rite of exorcism." The rite is understood as dangerous and taxing to priests, hence reference to fear and the observation that Father LeBar was monitoring his colleague for signs of weakening during the exorcism with Gina. Father A says a priest is supposed to pray and fast in preparation, and that he started fasting the previous week. "I could die tomorrow, I could be attacked, I could be taken over. And there has to be that willingness to suffer as well as to sacrifice. It's a terrifying experience at times. A very frightening experience. There's times you want to run away, just as soon pass it up and go away. Once you walk down this road you can't go back." Moreover, "an exorcism can go wrong if a priest becomes overcompassionate or overcaring and decides maybe the devil should bother him instead of the person. Then the whole thing could collapse. It started to happen and I caught myself and started all over." The devil "Sows the spirit of confusion, fear, makes you think things are happening to your body." Father A believes that with each ritual something dies inside him. He spends lonely days and sleepless nights, tormented from having incurred the direct displeasure of pure hatred. This is the price the exorcist pays "as the devil himself tries to weaken and destroy me." Then "Why do this?" asks the reporter. "She has a right to a normal life like you and I, and she's turned to the church asking for help. If you heard the cry that she and her mother have made, you would respond in the same way." In representing this aspect of exorcism the journalists capture a major theme, which from the standpoint of religion emphasizes the high stakes of spiritual struggle, and from a media standpoint captures a narrative of simultaneous vulnerability and heroism. Here the religious and media approaches serve one another quite well.

The priests also are invited to represent various technical aspects of their ministry. Through the journalists they emphasize that the painstaking screening of a candidate for exorcism can take as much as six months, and that the first thing is to make sure there are no medical problems they are attributing to possession. Father A will "sit down with a couple psychologists and psychiatrists I know and we'll go over the cases and talk about them." Father LeBar cites four major signs of possession including great strength, levitation, clairvoyance, and speaking in languages they never studied—interestingly, though exorcists do mention the occurrence of levitation, it is more common for them to cite aversion to anything sacred as one of the primary signs. Father A says that a person may react "just by the fact that I've come, and as a result we have an indication that there is something there." Father LeBar says, "It's like a surgeon going in trying to lay bare what's there until you get to the core of what you're looking for." Father A says, "A demon's screaming to be let go could also be a prelude to a levitation where she could go up to the ceiling where no one could touch her." Responding to the journalist's query of "Can a person undergoing this say stop, halt, I've had enough?" the answer is that "We have to make sure it's the person speaking" instead of the devil. Responding to the journalist's observation that the psychiatrist who worked with Gina was convinced she was psychotic not possessed, Father LeBar says, "First you have to ask if the psychiatrist believes possession is possible. Merely because its psychotic doesn't exclude the possibility of possession. I always ask them, 'All right you've explained it this far, but now what? What's after that because it's still happening,' and they can't answer it." The journalist follows up by asking whether Gina's exorcism was a success or failure, and as far as exorcism whether drugs are part of the treatment. Father LeBar says, "Actually it has nothing to do with it. Drugs treat the natural aspect of things which held control of her basic physical characteristics to allow her to learn and such, but the one thing she has said consistently those voices, those animals don't bother me any more, and that's whether or not she's had any drugs." The journalists do not fail to ask a most critical question: Why is the Church allowing this film to be made and shown? Father LeBar says, "Many people don't share the Church's belief that the devil is real. The Church hopes this exposure will help change some minds. It can also show the Church can help those who feel need for relief from evil spirits."

A final theme is the journalists' engagement with mental health professionals. Carol Razza is a psychotherapist who was part of the evaluation team and of the exorcism team that worked with Gina. In this capacity she says that "there's something more going on" than mental illness and that she has "seen it several times." She observed a difference after Gina's exorcism, saying she "saw a kid more relaxed and at peace, maybe because it was over." Commenting on the two-month follow-up interview with Gina, she says "As you can see she is now very lucid, you could say she stays in the here and now, we can talk to her, we can reason with her, you can start to impose some behavioral techniques on her. Now she's on the road to leading a normal life whereas before she didn't have a chance." James Gill, a Jesuit priest and psychiatrist interviewed for the *20/20* documentary, says with reference to the exorcists that there is a "tendency to interpret what you see in terms of your background, so if you have a background in theology you'll tend to think theologically, maybe evil vs. good, and quickly rush in with that interpretation." With reference to the afflicted he says that

"Often an adolescent will have hallucinations, see things, hear things, smell things, and believe things, or have delusions as we call them. These look like behaviors and thinking patterns and imagination of the possessed person. Schizophrenics especially if paranoid will burst forth with fierce expressions of anger, hostility, rage." He concludes that "the good thing would be if she were possessed that the possession would be terminated. But even if not possessed, if she believes exorcism will be helpful, it probably will." Warren Schlanger is a hospital psychiatrist who treated Gina during two years she had spent in the Miami Children's Hospital psychiatric ward, diagnosed as having "recurring psychotic episodes." In response to the journalist's question, he says "No, I never have seen anyone who was possessed, and personally would doubt it." When asked whether the exorcism could have contributed to Gina's well-being, he says, "I would doubt it." My principal observation about this theme is that the journalists succeeded in showing precisely the three relevant categories of mental health professional: the believing and participating therapist, the skeptical and equivocal Catholic psychiatrist, and the secular psychiatrist who uses the word "doubt" as a gesture of minimal politeness.

Finally, the journalists extricate themselves from this sensitive report. Barbara Walters thanks the Catholic Church, Gina, and her family. She notes the conflict for centuries between science and religion, noting that Gina was spiritually feeling better, while scientists would say yes but she's on strong tranquilizers and psychotherapy. She follows with "But it seems they can go together." Co-host Hugh Downs agrees, saying "I think they can. I tend to be skeptical but we're dealing with mature and responsible people who have a tradition that goes back a long ways and a ritual they have used to their advantage. The psychological aspect does have to be cranked in because belief is part of the mix on the part of the girl and the priests. The bottom line is that she's better for whatever reason." Barbara says, "This certainly isn't for everyone." Hugh responds, "No, it certainly isn't for everyone."

The Devil and Father Amorth

The second film, *The Devil and Father Amorth*, is as much a history of William Friedkin's career as it is an account of Father Amorth's work or the case study of an afflicted person, beginning with his making of the fictionalized *The Exorcist* in 1973 and concluding with this documentary account of contemporary exorcism. Whereas in the ABC account the priests themselves were not the focus of the account, here Father Amorth is lionized with a biography beginning with his role as an anti-Fascist resistance fighter in the Second World War to his work as chief exorcist of Rome and ending with the widespread adulation shown at his very public funeral. The presentation centers on Amorth's work with a possessed woman named Christina and the filming of her ninth session of the rite, a case which plays a parallel narrative role to that of Gina in the ABC News report.

Friedkin begins by pondering why an old man advised him to not make any more films about exorcism after *The Exorcist*, observing that when he made that film he had never seen an exorcism and it was more than four decades later when he had the opportunity to witness the one in this film—this over a shot of a room with table and chair covered with red cloth, then spooky smoky wisps. He answers his own question by interviewing Jeffrey Burton Russell (author of *The Prince of Darkness*), who says "People ought to stay away from the subject as much as possible. The more you open yourself up to thinking about this stuff, and you start feeling about this stuff, the more room you allow for the supernatural power of evil to come in." Having invoked a sense of apprehension he introduces today's scenario, telling us there are more than 60 million people in Italy, showing a scene of exorcistic shrieking in a church, and citing two leading newspapers and a major TV channel to the effect that 500,000 Italians see an exorcist every year. Christina, he says, is a 46-year-old woman who lives 200 miles southeast of Rome, and is an architect who can't work because she's possessed by the devil. Father Gabriel Amorth, the dean of Italian exorcists, performed the rite for her eight times without success, and we are about to see her ninth.

Friedkin loops back to his own story, from 1972 when he came to Georgetown University to film *The Exorcist*, based on the novel by William Peter Blatty that was inspired by a 1949 event when he was an undergraduate here. Blatty recounts listening to a Jesuit priest, Father Eugene Gallagher, who started talking about exorcism in a class on New Testament theology. Friedkin shows the house in Cottage City, Maryland, where the 1949 case began in a Lutheran family whose fourteen-year-old son was said to be possessed. Doctors and psychiatrists could not determine the source of his disturbing afflictions, and priests from the Catholic archdiocese of Washington, DC, were brought in to perform a series of exorcisms. The boy was transferred to Alexian Brothers Hospital in St. Louis where Friedkin reports he was eventually liberated. Blatty believed in the veracity of the case when he wrote the novel and screenplay, and Friedkin says he did as well when he directed the film. Friedkin cuts to the house in Georgetown showing how they built a false front to bring the window of the possessed girl's bedroom closer to steps so the afflicted exorcist could make his final leap to death onto the steep steps that were only a few feet from house and are now known as "The Exorcist Steps."

In 1998 Blatty gave Friedken the idea of making a nonfiction account of an exorcism, and he unsuccessfully attempted to arrange an interview, through the exorcist involved, with another family whose son had undergone exorcism but who wanted to remain private and avoid publicity. Now, forty-five years after the original film and completely by accident—"or was it Providence?"—the opportunity to film an actual exorcism had presented itself. The Italian exorcist Amorth in his first memoir had written about *The Exorcist* and said it was his favorite movie, though commenting that the special effects were a little over the top. When Friedken wrote to ask for a meeting, he agreed. Friedkin then interpolates a heroic biographical sketch of Amorth, who at age eighteen fought his first battle against evil, joining the Italian resistance against fascism. He received the Medal of Liberation from the government, but it was ten years later when he found his calling and was ordained in Society of St. Paul, thirty years later in 1986 becoming chief exorcist of Rome. Each morning he would respond to hundreds of letters from around the world from those with "spiritual diseases" and became one of the most beloved figures in his native country. In April 2016 Friedken interviewed Father Amorth for a magazine and asked if he could ever witness and film an exorcism. He says that such permission had never been granted by the Vatican, but that after a few days Amorth affirmed that he could film Christina's ninth exorcism session as long as he brought no crew or lights, and used only a small video camera.

Friedken prefaces his main account with another, that of a woman who had been successfully exorcised by Father Amorth. Paulo Vizzachero met Amorth ten years previously when his sister needed help, having realized something was wrong when she went to mass with a friend and started having unusual symptoms. She cried, her body shook, and she fell into trance. She called her brother to come to her home, she was out of control. It was her brother who connected her with Father Amorth, who she said "was funny and ironic. He didn't frighten me, helped me understand what was happening her liberation." Her brother noted that "because sometimes the evil spirit passes from one person to another," Amorth performed a brief exorcism prayer for him as well. In addition to providing a successful healing narrative to balance what was to be an unsuccessful case, this story describes how Paulo became an assistant to Amorth and was the one who recognized Christina's symptoms in a church in a small Italian town, which becomes the setting for this episode of the film.

To frame the exorcism, Friedken shows interview clips with both the possessed Christina and the exorcist Amorth. She says, "The psychiatrists couldn't help me, I had a spiritual disease. Demonic possession can hide behind other diseases. I would have attacks often on days related to Jesus. A life of pain and suffering." Father Amorth explains that Christina is possessed by the devil, who speaks and acts through her, the person, via supernatural power. Asked how he can be sure that Christina is possessed, he says, "I can only be sure when I perform an exorcism and provoke reactions that are unique to a possessed person." Cutting to the exorcism of May 1, 2016, we hear eerie Hitchcockian music as Friedken shows Father Amorth walking through ominous corridors to the exorcism room. A number of people are there, with sacred objects on a table and Christina seated on a cushioned chair covered by bright red cloth. Amorth sits perpendicular on a bench beside her. The exorcist begins with prayer and sprinkling holy water, and as Friedken's voiceover points out, he also begins every exorcism by thumbing his nose at the devil. Christina's family are seated along the back wall, and other priests are there to assist Amorth. As the exorcist prays, Christina starts nodding her head (or, her head starts to nod—one is tempted to use the passive voice) then recoils and writhes starting to shriek/scream. "Stop it! No! No!" Amorth grabs her left forearm and tells others to hold her right, in which she is holding a crucifix. He instructs them to stop holding her as she settles down and he begins praying again, right hand on top of her head and left holding her wrist. He moves his hand to the front of her knee, whence she nods again and gets a big toothy grimacing smile, then shriek-roars. She cycles through periodic outbursts as the priest and demon struggle over control of her body and soul, the exorcist by turns praying and talking to the afflicted women and participants, or commanding and interrogating the demon. As Christina screams "I am Satan! Stop this!," an added audio effect makes it sound as if her voice was tripled or quadrupled. "Christina, return to the church to which you belong. Surrender!" Finally he stops praying more or less abruptly and asks if she needs water, and Christina with eyes open nods yes. Father Amorth takes back his clerical stole which he had draped over her shoulder, an assistant hands him the crucifix which he kisses and puts it on the table next to him, and he says "Let us all thank God. How are you feeling?"

The documentary then shifts to a series of interviews with neurologists, beginning as Friedken shows a tape rewinding with squeaky tape sounds leading to an interview with Neil Martin, Chief of Neurosurgery at UCLA Medical Center, who has just watched the exorcism tape. "It's absolutely amazing. There is a major force at work within her somehow. I don't know the underlying origin of it. But there's a major force. It's interesting to see that she is not separated from the environment, she's not in a catatonic state, she appears to be responding to the priest. She's not having hallucinations, she appeared to be engaged in the process but resisting." He follows with interviews with Itzhak Fried, Professor of Neurosurgery at Tel Aviv Medical Center, and John Mazziota, also a neurologist and Vice-Chancellor of UCLA Medical Center. The physicians talk about temporal lobe function and delirium, while Friedken probes as to whether they give credence to the premises of exorcism and whether other treatments like brain surgery would work better.

In the midst of these interviews, Friedken cuts to his post-exorcism interview with Father Amorth, who says that when you ask her she says "That wasn't me. She doesn't even remember it. The devil's assaults are not constant, they can be brief and not recur for weeks or months. At other times there can be assaults on a daily basis. When this happens the person goes into a trance, and the rest of the day she lives and acts normally. But she has constant mental or physical suffering because she's still in a frail state. Even when assaults are absent, her nervous system remembers everything and therefore she's in constant suffering." He shows the exorcism team singing happy birthday after the session because it happened to be Amorth's ninety-first birthday. "He was happy and so was I" because it looked like Christina was cured, as we see her laughing and smiling, both she and Amorth still seated in the same spots they were during the session. Amorth says "Thank you and bless you, now you can all go and bless yourselves," and people laugh since apparently this was a joke.

Friedken's next interviews are with psychiatrists rather than neurologists, at Columbia University's Department of Psychiatry, where he shows his film to a group. Jeffrey Lieberman, the department chair, asks "Do we countenance the possibility of there being something spiritual or supernatural in nature that takes the form of disturbed behavior?" Among the participants are Michael First, Clinical Psychiatrist and an Editor of *DSM-IV*; Roberto Lewis-Fernandez, a cultural psychiatrist and contributor to *DSM-V*; and Ryan Lawrence, Associate Professor of Clinical Psychiatry. This group recognizes the possibility of culturally defined therapeutic value without committing to a theological or ontological position. Lewis-Fernandez observes that "The question is what kind of psychotherapy or intervention does she need, and they have a certain idea that the way you deal with this is by getting rid of that completely negative side of her experience. Perhaps in the case of some people, getting rid of it in this ritualistic way is quite good." They discuss possible description of the affliction as "dissociative reaction," which is "a recognized disorder worldwide." Lawrence describes a current inpatient from a Protestant background who behaves similarly to Christina and says "she's possessed by the devil... she has a history of trauma, and I can say what we're doing for her on the unit, is we're treating it with medication and we're giving her psychotherapy creating a safe environment. We've seen this before, it runs its course and she gets better. We don't take a position during the treatment on is this really Satan bothering you or is this you really being tormented by your illness?" Lewis-Fernandez speaks again, saying "The person is expressing a pathology that is understood as possession. She understands it as possession, the group understands it as possession. Our field of psychiatry can understand it as possession just on the virtue of what she is presenting, the phenomenon, without having to take any kind of stance on whether there actually are demons."

Friedken shifts to a third group composed of two religious figures including Robert Barron, an auxiliary bishop in the Los Angeles diocese, and Jeffrey Burton Russell, author of *The Prince of Darkness* who was introduced earlier in the film. The camera shifts several times back and forth between the two, with Friedken apparently trying to emphasize a contrast between the circumspection of the Catholic clergyman and the unhesitating acceptance of demonic evil by the Protestant author. The bishop says, "I think that phenomenon [possession] exists. I think it is extremely rare but I think it exists. And I'll say this as auxiliary bishop of this region. I get people writing to me concerned about a loved one, a son or daughter. Somebody concerned about himself—I've got these strange things going on, what should I do? So I acknowledge the reality of it." To Friedken's question about whether he would refer to an exorcist or psychiatrist, he responds that all aspects must be taken into account, and that "The natural has to be eliminated before we get to the supernatural." He also indicates that an exorcist must be extremely holy and a high level of spirituality, saying that he would not be able to fill the role himself. Jeffrey Russell says unequivocally that "a transhuman power of evil exists," and that after his most recent book he "had an attack of serious depression" because of working with evil all the time.

Nearing the end of the film, Friedken cuts back to Father Amorth in the aftermath of Christina's exorcism session. Christina's family asked for her father to be blessed by Amorth. An assistant wraps his arms around Christina from behind, anticipating a reaction. As the priest blesses her father, Christina snarls again and is restrained by an assistant. Friedken's voiceover described this as a "Shocking moment. Christina was not cured." She was once again in trance state, nodding and writhing and snarling. When her mother sat for blessing it got worse. Friedken narrates, "This is an actual exorcism. It's different from all the movies. It's not fiction. It was harrowing to witness. There are many people who suffer like Christina from what they believe is the same affliction. But where does this come from? Is this really the random invasion of an external evil force?"

The final episode begins with a shot of a pyramid in Rome. Father Amorth had become sick and was in the hospital. Friedken had scheduled a more in-depth interview with Christina in Rome, but she rescheduled to the small hilltop town of Alatri, "a religious town in an old world way." The camera showed the scenic village and its surroundings, including the Cathedral that is considered sacred and where the film crew were to meet Christina. When she did not join them Friedken called her and she was furious that they were at the wrong church, a rupture in communication narrated to the accompaniment of squeaky, scary background music. Friedken reports that when they arrived he did not take his camera inside and so is narrating based on his memory of what happened July 4, 2016. We see shots of a dark church inside and close-ups of Christina with audio of her screams and narration by Friedken. "When my assistant and I entered the church [we hear snarling, roaring] it was freezing cold inside and we were trapped in a living nightmare. Christina was screaming, she slithered on the floor in a cheap plastic chair pulling her boyfriend Davide with her. He tried to hold her around the waist and throat. 'Give us back your film' he shouted. 'No, I want it shown' she screamed in the voice of the demon. I was terrified. Davide stared at me. 'If you don't give it back to us, we'll kill you. We'll find your family and we'll kill you all.' It was the first time anyone had threatened my life. We left the church, left Alatri. For a half hour neither of us said a word. The sweat and the fear were clinging to us all the way back to Rome."

At end of July 2016 before he could perform Christina's tenth exorcism, Amorth contracted pneumonia in the hospital, and two months later he died. Thousands from all over Italy came to the funeral, and Friedken shows people thronged at his casket. Amorth's assistant from earlier in film says "He once told me he could not wait to reach heaven so he could beat the devil with a cane." Cut to a clip of Amorth using a walker, probably in the hospital. He presses the elevator button and turns to the camera. Friedken says "I hope to see you on the 30th" (for Christina's tenth exorcism session). Amorth nods slightly as Friedken says: "He was the most spiritual man I've ever met. Like everyone who knew him, I'll never forget him. He enriched my life." Amorth enters the elevator and the door closes, a metaphor of ascending to heaven. "But what about Christina?" asks Friedken as we see him face the camera. "As of this moment Christina's suffering continues. I've reached out to her without success. Friends in Italy tell me she's continued to pursue exorcism with local priests. But Amorth was in a class by himself. Like the doctors, I can't tell you what's wrong with Christina. My own belief is that there is a far deeper dimension to the universe. We know there is evil. There is also good. And if there are demons there must be angels." Closing credits run, with scary typeface and ominous music. We see the film is dedicated to William Peter Blatty (1928–2017), author of *The Exorcist*, returning Friedken's narrative full circle to its beginning.

Mediating Exorcism, Exorcism as Mediation

The *20/20* team of Downs, Walters, and Jelton adopts a stance of open-minded journalistic skepticism about exorcism, recognizing it as an element of religion in the public sphere starting from an incident reported in the press. Friedken's account documents his own journey as a director since *The Exorcist*, and includes elements of Hollywood dramatization such as long shots down dark corridors and in cavernous churches, combined with eerily squeaky music characteristic of the horror genre. Both films center on high-profile exorcists who were public figures in their respective countries of the United States and Italy. Both present images of patriarchy in which the authoritative male priest exorcizes an afflicted female, in a performance during which the cosmological struggle is between the priest and demon. Both consult experts in the form of mental health professionals, though the believing Friedken goes farther in systematically soliciting the views of neurologists and psychiatrists.

These films show how exorcism is mediatized in documentary accounts. Along with periodic news reports and Hollywood movies, they create just enough media presence, just enough public profile for exorcism and exorcists, to keep the practice periodically in the public eye and the devil at a slow burn in the public sphere. This media profile is of increasing consequence in the face of a resurgence in the practice of exorcism that has taken place largely in the past decade, and which I have been working to understand in a comparative ethnographic study of exorcism in Italy and the United States (Csordas 2014, 2017, 2019a, b). The dual premise that guides this work is that on an ideological/ cultural level exorcism articulates a discourse of evil at large in the world, and that on an interpersonal/social level it enacts a therapeutic process intended to relieve suffering and remove the cause of that suffering. What I want to emphasize in closing, however, is not how exorcism is taken up in the media, but how these films allow us to see exorcism as mediating issues in contemporary culture.

The constant low-level presence of exorcism reiterates the nagging existential ambiguity that inhabits the threshold between good and evil, reality and unreality, science and religion, oppression and liberation, man and woman, faith and reason, rationality and irrationality, fact and fiction. Like many Americans, I presumed *The Exorcist* was fiction in the genre of horror film until at the fortieth anniversary I learned that Friedken and Blatty intended to portray reality, in a kind of fact-based theological fiction that corresponds to historical fiction. Like many academics, I presumed that the Enlightenment was a movement that triumphantly and permanently transformed the intellectual landscape three centuries ago, but upon patiently listening to the rationale of my ethnographic study, one exorcist responded by saying, "So, you're a man of the Enlightenment"—evidently for him an issue still very much in question. In fact, exorcism represents, constitutes, and mediates an ontological fissure: it is not simply the question that demons either exist or they don't, but that some people live in a world where they do and some in a world where they do not. There is more at stake here than religion per se, because even some religious believers draw the line at belief in demons. Thus the ontological fissure opened by the insistent problematic of possession and exorcism is a fissure in contemporary civilization. I use the term "civilization" instead of society because exorcism raises the possibility of something anachronistically and cosmologically wild and dangerous among us—something that is the opposite of civilized.

8

Abundance and the Late Capitalist Imagination: Catholicism and Fashion at the Metropolitan Museum

Elayne Oliphant

Introduction

It was an abundant affair. Between May 10 and October 8, 2018, 1,659,647 visitors made their way through *Heavenly Bodies: Fashion and the Catholic Imagination*, an exhibition of the Costume Institute at New York City's Metropolitan Museum, making it the most well-attended event ever held at the famed cultural site. *Heavenly Bodies*, furthermore, was the largest exhibit ever mounted in the space. It exceeded the basement level to which previous exhibitions associated with the Costume Institute had been confined, extending up into more than 60,000 square feet throughout twenty-five medieval and Byzantine galleries at both the Fifth Avenue and Cloisters Met locations. *Heavenly Bodies*, along with an earlier show entitled *Michelangelo: Divine Draftsman and Designer*, made attendance in the fiscal year ending in 2018 the highest the museum had ever seen.[1]

For the first time, the Met Store worked with a cosmetics company (Pat McGrath Labs) to launch "an exclusive retail collaboration." In addition to a lip-gloss and eye shadow palette featuring artwork from the Met on the packaging, the Met Store also offered "a special edition T-shirt by Versace as well as a range of fine jewelry designed by Donna Distefano. Distefano's designs [we]re inspired by a Renaissance papal ring, momento mori, and a Virgin and Child pendant in the Met collection, as well as her own signature rosary beads." In describing the cosmetics collaboration, Pat McGrath explained that "religious history and artifacts have always been vital influences on my work, and it is an extraordinary honor for me to be unveiling these new pieces alongside this breathtaking exhibition as the first-ever beauty brand at New York's iconic Met Store."[2]

In this chapter, I argue that the abundance of *Heavenly Bodies* needs to be understood in light of potentially uncomfortable overlaps between Catholic media and the neoliberal or late capitalist imagination.[3] Scholars of religious mediation have vastly expanded our appreciation of the richness of religious life by encouraging us to focus on the varied sensoria, embodied encounters, and material forms that shape the practices found in different religious traditions. Scholars have produced a great deal of insightful critique of the supposed Protestant anxieties surrounding materiality and its preference for immediacy.[4] Generally speaking, however, in contrasts to this stated preference for an imagined immediacy, Catholic practices make ample space for objects, images, spaces, and figures in mediating connections between humans and God. Scholarly analyses of these Catholic modes of mediation—whether analyzing these complex forms as incarnational (Orsi 1998, 2010, 2016), sacramental (Schwartz 2008), analogical (Tracy 1998), or enchanted (Greely 2001)—have tended to occur in a far more celebratory tone.[5]

The historian Robert Orsi has been key to dismantling the notion that such abundance is only expressed through the wealth and majesty associated with the splendor of European cathedrals and the Vatican's treasures. He has described how many observers may be shocked by "the excess" one encounters at popular Catholic shrines: "the proliferation of souvenir shops overflowing with great heaps of rosaries and statues of the Blessed Mother and other holy figures; the great piles of wax or tin images of body parts... the stacks of holy cards, alongside umbrellas, paying cards, toys, and crockery ashtrays imprinted with images of Mary" (2016: 57). Those made uncomfortable by this abundance, Orsi says, fail to understand that "excess itself is the meaning," as the event of the infinite finding expression in the finite necessarily produces an overflow.

And yet, such abundance is also, undeniably, an expression of capitalism.[6] The abundance displayed in *Heavenly Bodies* offered the powerful mix of the luxurious and the popular that has made the fashion industry so powerful in the early twenty-first century. What was it about Catholic media that made the linkage between it and the late capitalist fashion industry appear, in the words of a review in the *Wall Street Journal*, "a gift from the Sartorial Gods... an idea so right, so inevitably majestic, that it's amazing it never happened here before" (Jacobs 2018)? In thinking through the effects of Catholic modes of mediation here, I want to encourage a return to a point well established, but too often overlooked. Abundance can do more than signal the excess produced by God's presence. It can also buttress and substantiate the legitimacy of deeply unequal political and economic regimes.

The exhibit was made up of two components: "fashion" items created by designers in the twentieth and twenty-first centuries with implicit or explicit reference to Catholic themes or modes of dress, and donations of regalia and jewels from the Vatican. The exhibit's fashion items were liberated from their place in the cellar to enjoy a powerful display mingled among numerous Christian media in the museum's medieval and byzantine galleries. The donations from the Vatican, which, theoretically at least, could claim more kinship with the objects and images in these galleries, were relegated to the basement level Costume Institute, where they were displayed alone and without much in the way of commentary. Implicitly and explicitly the exhibit encouraged viewers to make connections between medieval or ancient Christian objects and contemporary fashion items. In a somewhat jarring contrast, however, the donations offered by the Vatican dated from a very different era. The majority of the objects displayed in the Costume Institute from the Vatican were created in the nineteenth century.

In his analysis of *Heavenly Bodies*, historian Stephen Schloesser argued that the Vatican donations are "profoundly political" objects that "symboliz[ed] church-state conflicts" during an era marked by the widespread rise of liberal nation-states and the ultimate demise of the Papal States. In other words, these remarkable objects replete with gold metal thread, silver, diamonds, emeralds, sapphires, and other precious materials were produced at the height of a crisis of legitimation of the authority of the Roman Catholic Church and the nobility and monarchies with which it had long been intertwined in Western Europe. The display of abundant wealth served as a means of defending a political-religious entanglement that was coming to appear increasingly illegitimate. In David Morgan's summation of the period found in the exhibit catalogue: "the symbolic value of ritual, art, and costume bloom in times of rhetorical efflorescence and political shrinkage" (2018: 101).

What are we to make of the fact that—a decade following the financial crisis of 2008—the abundance of the Catholic imagination made for such a powerful pairing with an industry emblematic of neoliberalism? The political theologian Adam Kotsko (2015, 2018) has argued that events of the early twenty-first century, including the financial crisis and the Trump presidency, have highlighted the illegitimacy of the neoliberal age. For Kotsko, this illegitimacy exists in tension with governments' ongoing and powerful commitment to the market as a mechanism for the distribution of goods and the good. While Schloesser critiqued the explanatory panels that accompanied the Vatican's donations for their focus on the materiality of the objects, rather than the political claims they had upheld, I want to highlight how their abundance is part and parcel of their politics, in both the past and the present. By relying on Catholic majestic abundance, *Heavenly Bodies* made a clamorous appeal to the legitimacy of the inequalities that structure the neoliberal age.

According to Schloesser, "had this exhibition taken place a century ago, it would have generated enormous controversy… given the objects' profoundly political nature symbolizing church-state conflicts. However, as the historical context is set aside the political is transformed into the purely aesthetic" (Schloesser 2018). I would argue that both religious and aesthetic modes of mediation are inevitably political. And, what is more, the political claims buttressed or dismantled by aesthetic and religious modes of mediation are deeply intertwined with economic systems of domination.[7] A number of scholars have offered insightful commentary on the kind of Catholicism mediated in the exhibition (in addition to Schloesser see, for example, Elliott 2018; Heartney 2018; and Orsi 2018). I will argue that the popularity of *Heavenly Bodies* exemplifies how Roman Catholic abundance can offer a powerful means by which to legitimate increasingly illegitimate political and economic forms.

In what follows, I will first address the place of museums in the Catholic and capitalist imaginaries. I will then explore the exhibit in some detail, highlighting the ways in which the fashion items gained a level of legitimacy by being "Catholicized" through the exhibition display. Finally, I will place my argument on Catholic abundance in conversation with literature on a variety of prosperity religious practices in the twenty-first century.

Museums and Catholicism

In this section, I will address both the Catholicism and capitalism underlying modern public art museums. Museums—especially those formed in Europe and the United States during the nineteenth century—have often been seen as institutions that detracted from the authority and wealth of the Roman Catholic Church, as numerous national governments expropriated the paintings, altarpieces, and sculptures that had once adorned churches and began to display them in museums as national, rather than religious, treasures. This sense of loss was a refrain among Catholic parishioners I met in Paris in 2017. When I toured a church in western Paris, for example, the parishioner tour guides took pride in pointing to how, unlike many of Paris's Roman Catholic churches, this church had been able to hold onto a number of its most valuable objects. I asked the guide how this had been possible, given that the 1905 law separating Church and state in France made most of the churches built prior to that date, along with their contents, the property of the state. While most of the expropriation of Catholic media by the French state occurred a century prior, during the French Revolution, at the turn of the twentieth century, all parish churches were required to produce detailed summaries of their contents, which the state then used in order to transfer some of the more valuable objects to national and municipal holdings. In response to my question, the parishioner's eyes sparkled mischievously, and he smiled and put a finger to his lips. "We hid everything when they came looking," he said conspiratorially. Whether or not his account was accurate, his depiction of turn-of-the-century parishioners hiding the church's art objects when the state demanded them exemplifies how, for many Catholics, the state expropriation of Catholic media and their placement in national museums has long been deemed a threat to the power of the Church that must be combatted.[8]

The historian Louis Ruprecht (2014) has demonstrated, however, that the Roman Catholic Church played a powerful role in the rise of public art museums. It was, in fact, the Roman Catholic Church that created the first public art museum, also known as the "Profane Museum," in the Vatican Palace in 1767. In the decades that followed its initial opening, the Profane Museum quickly expanded, with a new wing of the Apostolic Palace added to "house many of the Vatican's most important Greek and Roman statuary" (2014: 134). Thus, while Catholic objects were not on display in this first museum, it was the Catholic Church that first encouraged the public viewing of objects in a comparative, de-contextualized fashion in the space of the museum.

Beyond this very material role played by the institutional Church in the formation of public art museums, I also want to highlight how certain Catholic practices bear significant resemblance to the effects and affects of museum display. From the time of the French Revolution, commentators both Catholic and otherwise have decried museums as sites in which the power of sacred objects is compromised and drained. One of the most famous critics from this period, Antoine-Chrysostome Quatremère de Quincy (1989), lamented the formation of museums as a process through which objects would lose the context that gave them meaning. While he understood the educative ends of many of these new museums, and their potential significance for the rising category of "citizens," he saw museums as defeating their own goals. By exhibiting objects outside of the contexts that give them a "moral purpose," museums "depriv[e] the public of the 'accessory impressions' that make clear art's purpose, and of the multitude of moral ideas, of intellectual harmonies' that act upon our sensibility" (Sherman 1994: 128, citing de Quatremère de Quincy).

In contrast to Quatremère's concerns about the moral significance of art objects as most readily apparent when displayed in particular contexts, the work of art historian Cynthia Hahn points us to how certain Catholic practices may inform museum rituals. Hahn has described in some detail what she calls the "reliquary effect." For Hahn, the reliquary—the bejeweled, intricate objects that contain relics—"finds its purpose in stimulating attention and capturing desire" (2017: 14). For Hahn, the "reliquary effect" provides the "value, presentation, and context" that establishes the object held within as sacred, valuable, and deserving of wonder (2017: 6), "endow[ing] these objects with significance out of proportion to any intrinsic worth" (2017: 283). I want to point to some interesting overlaps between the effects of reliquaries and museums. Many of the nineteenth century public art museums were, like the Met, built to mimic classical temples that served to signal the sacrality of the objects found within. Unlike temples, however, these "containers" were intended to recede into the background as the objects held within became the primary site of the ritual of viewing. Just as a reliquary, "even when itself constructed of precious materials aimed at attracting attention," the museum is able to "simultaneously erase[] its own existence, standing only as a setting or context for the staging of" (2017: 10) the ritual encounter with the object.

According to the museum theorist Carol Duncan, the ritual that occurs in the space of the museum is that of creating an "ideal bourgeois citizen" (Duncan 1995: 49). Over the course of the nineteenth century, a "consensus" that the best means of constructing such a citizen was to "unfold" for them "the origins and development of the schools, highlighting whenever possible their outstanding geniuses.... The supposition was that by walking through this history of art, visitors would live the spiritual development of civilization" (1995: 49). Thus, the powerful setting of the museum signals to the viewer that the objects found within are those deserving of wonder. Establishing this context of wonder then creates the conditions of possibility for a ritual act through which citizens can position themselves in relation to "the spiritual development of civilization."

I am arguing that as a site of mediation, the museum functions in a similar way to the reliquary. It sets the stage for awe and wonder, and then recedes and effaces itself as the ritual experience unfolds. Humans and objects do not simply encounter one another as agentive subject and mute object. Rather, human-material encounters are dialectical processes that form and shape both actors in a variety of ways, according to the particular contexts and communities in which these encounters occur. The national public art museums that came to seem so necessary to public life over the course of the nineteenth century throughout Europe and North America, I argue, relied upon Catholic modes of mediation and human-material encounters in order to give the objects found within a value, aura, and power far exceeding their material components.

Equally significant to the history of museums like the Met is a certain form of capitalism. Like the catholicity underlying the nineteenth-century public art museum, this influence is both material and conceptual. Duncan has described how the interests of the capitalist class drove the creation of these reliquaries.

> The Republican bankers, merchants, and lawyers who founded the first great American public art museums had certainly arrived economically—they owned or controlled vast shares of American capital. Now they were in the process of securing both their political base and their social prestige. The power of high culture to identify them as members of an elite social network with international connections was not simply a luxury; it was necessary to their political and economic objectives. (Duncan 1995: 54)

These spaces would beautify cities, lending legitimacy to the private capital motoring the wealth underwriting these efforts. Moreover, by engaging visitors in edifying rituals of national belonging, such populations could be distracted from the material concerns (and revolutionary ideas) that otherwise threatened capitalist hierarchies.

In some respects, the creation of museums stood as an ultimate symbol of the decline of noble and monarchical power by making the objects that were once their purview alone available to a broader category of (white, middle-class) citizens (Bennett 1995). In her account of the significance of museums in France, Chantal Georgel argues that "if the eighteenth century in France had declared the right of the people to come to full possession of what rightfully belonged to all mankind, the nineteenth century museum saw the museum as the accomplishment of this idea" (1994: 113). And yet, the manner of possession that could occur through the museum ritual was deeply constrained. In the whiteness of faces displayed, and the relegation of art objects produced outside of Europe to ethnographic museums separated from the public "civilizing" art museums also served to constrain ideals of citizenship and equality in terms of race, class, and gender. In addition, "the museum allowed its visitors symbolically to possess objects that were inaccessible—objects that could neither be bought, since they were inalienable, nor fully understood, except by an elite of *amateurs* or art appreciators—and as such invested with high cultural prestige" (1994: 119).

This constrained possession, I would argue, also helped to fuel the unending desire for commodities so essential to capitalism's reproduction. According to Duncan, the founders of these museums legitimated their own exorbitant wealth by insisting upon the public nature of these reliquaries, allowing the museums' (limited) openness to symbolically belie the hierarchies and inequalities capitalism produced. In sum, as a reliquary, the nineteenth-century museum relied upon Catholic modes of mediation to assert both the value and the limited possession visitors might experience of the objects fueling and aestheticizing capitalist inequality found within.

Heavenly Bodies

In the *Heavenly Bodies* exhibit, a variety of mechanisms worked to elevate the value of the fashion items, arguing for their legitimacy alongside more classical representations of high culture. The primary means through which this argument was made, however, was through proximity to Catholic media. It was, I argue, by being Catholicized that the fashion items were able to gain greater prestige. In using the term "Catholicized," I do not intend to argue that, through the exhibit, the works of Dolce and Gabbana became capable of serving as reliable conduits of God's presence. Catholic media perform a variety of functions, including the buttressing of political and economic regimes and serving as a symbol of "civilization." Here, the proximity of fashion items to Catholic media increased their power and aura, allowing them to enter into the category of "fine art" or "high culture." As Catholicized objects, they could offer legitimation to the distinctions in wealth and power increasingly significant in a late capitalist age.

The fashion items exhibited in *Heavenly Bodies* are, in many respects, strange objects in the museum. Articles of clothing are more difficult for the museum as reliquary to contain in ways that effectively induce the same wonder as paintings and sculptures. They bear, perhaps, the most resemblance to the objects found in the "decorative arts" section of the Met, which includes furnishings and table settings of wealthy families. I am not making an argument that these are similar objects, but instead pointing to how both put the viewer in a similar position before them. As Duncan argues, museums display paintings and sculpture in such a way as to emphasize them as universal "spiritual goods" in which all can partake. In contrast, in the rooms devoted to the decorative arts, "the museum now casts you as a visitor come to admire the possessions" (Duncan 1995: 61) of others who are able to enjoy such riches. Clothing cannot help but call to mind the position of the wearer, a position most are unlikely to occupy.

When she wrote *Civilizing Rituals* nearly thirty years ago, Duncan recognized that, in contrast to the repeated emphasis on the *public* interest of these spaces in the nineteenth and early twentieth centuries, by the 1990s, the museum's Board of Trustees seemed far less concerned with ensuring these spaces continued to appear so. "If the Met's trustees have less commitment to public service than their grandfathers, it is also true that the elitist interests that brought American public art museums into existence now go virtually unchallenged—in the realm of public culture as in the realm of political discourse" (1995: 70). If, in the nineteenth and twentieth centuries, revolutionary ideals could offer working-class citizens alternative utopian visions to those offered in public art museums—as well as a clear ideology through which to critique the wealth of their founders—today, such alternatives and critiques are noticeably diminished. Global events have clearly reduced the legitimacy of neoliberalism. And yet, the fantasy of unbridled consumption and wealth powerfully constrain the increasing need to effectively imagine alternatives to the present. Exhibitions like *Heavenly Bodies* use Catholic abundance to refuse the necessity of such alternatives and reassure the viewer of the legitimacy of a deeply unequal and destructive system.

The process of Catholicization occurred in numerous ways in *Heavenly Bodies*. First, the exhibit was notable for the evocative way in which it took up the space of the Met's permanent exhibits. Rather than being isolated in a basement or a special exhibitions space, the fashion items were distributed throughout the Byzantine and medieval galleries in ways that, at times, equated the objects with those of the permanent collections, and, at others, amplified the fashion items against the permanent objects that became a mere background. Second, the fashion objects were admired for their materiality, while the objects with which they were supposedly in conversation were reduced to the narratives they conveyed. Third, text panels, the exhibition catalogue, and accompanying events helped to create a powerful discursive framework for the overlap between Catholic media and twentieth- and twenty-first century fashion. I will now offer examples of each of these modes of Catholicization.

The fashion items were distributed in a variety of often surprising ways throughout the Byzantine and medieval galleries in the Fifth Avenue Met, and throughout the Cloisters in Upper Manhattan. Upon entering the museum and moving to the left of the grand staircase, visitors were immediately and powerfully confronted by a series of gowns displayed far above both eye-level. The white mannequins with blank faces and varying white hairstyles had been elevated via simple black metal platforms, one in front of another, recalling both the movement of models in a fashion show and, according to the language often used by the curators, the "procession" of a church mass.[9] While most of the garments were made to stand out among the surrounding art, much of the jewelry was simply added into the glass cases that displayed Byzantine and medieval objects. A quick glance, in fact, might not have allowed viewers to realize that they were looking at pieces from the twenty-first century alongside of those from the sixth or the eighth. The only indicator that such objects were distinct from those surrounding them was the labels that used the same muted color palette—dark gray background and white letters—as the larger explanatory panels found throughout the exhibition.

Moving into the larger medieval sculpture gallery—which is laid out as a church with a nave and two side aisles, and includes a large choir screen—visitors found the immense space filled with gowns relating to "the earthly and celestial hierarchies." The choir screen served to separate the earthly from the heavenly. Items that played on the garments worn by the highest figures of the earthly hierarchy—bishops, cardinals, and popes—populated the center of the nave, while those that resembled habits worn by nuns and priests and monks filled the right and left side aisles, respectively. The intermingling of the fashion items and long-admired Byzantine and medieval objects of the Met's collection made a rather powerful argument for their equality and the necessity of viewing them together.

The interconnections between these objects were further amplified through their pairing with Catholic images found in paintings, sculptures, and mosaics. Take, for example, a Dolce & Gabbana dress displayed in the Byzantine galleries at the Fifth Avenue Met. The bejeweled dress with an image of the Madonna was displayed elevated above the fragments of sixth- and twelfth-century mosaics found on the museum walls. In the catalogue it appears on the page opposite two images of such mosaics: "Fragment of a Floor Mosaic with a Personification of Ktsis," Byzantine, 500–50, and "Madonna in Orans from the Duomo Di Cefalù," Byzantine, 1145–160. Similarly, a black silk jersey robe laid over a white cotton poplin by Riccardo Tisci was displayed directly next to a tapestry of Mary Magdalene similarly attired in black and white. According to the accompanying text, the "propriety" of "this 'habit'... is both tenuous and temporary, as a flip of the wrist and a toss of the head bring the veil tumbling down in a gesture suggestive of a striptease. It is shown alongside a tapestry depicting Mary Magdalene dressed in an ensemble that later became associated with the habit of Dominican nuns." In this case, the exhibit also added one of their gray and white labels to the tapestry, adding more detail to the piece that they were attempting to bring into conversation with the fashion item. According to the panel,

> In the Gospel of John (20:11-17), Mary Magdalene arrives at Jesus's empty tomb and asks a nearby gardener where she can find the body. Calling her by name, the gardener reveals himself as Christ and asks that she report his resurrection to the disciples. In this tapestry, Mary wears a sumptuous cloak, shimmering with golden thread. She kneels with her hands extended, eyes fixed on Christ's body. Christ raises his right hand, commanding Mary to keep her distance, and presents his wound. Christ is captured in the exact moment of his revelation, still holding a humble spade even as he appears in his resurrected majesty. Gilded threads blaze forth from his head to create a cruciform halo.

Here, the tapestry (entitled "The Resurrected Christ Appearing to Mary Magdalene in the Garden," made of wool, silk, and gilt-metal-wrapped thread, South Netherlandish, Woven *c.* 1500–30) is explored for the story found within it, rather than the particular form it takes in this representation, or the time and context in which it was produced. In other words, the tapestry is reduced to what Jacques Rancière (2004) would describe as a "poetic regime," as visitors are encouraged to admire it for its mimetic relationship to a Christian narrative. The fashion, in contrast, is admired through an "aesthetic regime," according, that is, to criteria internal to it. The connection between the two items is made through the "revealing" central to both: the striptease of the garment and the "revelation" of Jesus's resurrection.

At the Cloisters, many of these pairings were less direct, such as the simple cotton dresses displayed alongside of the baptismal fonts in the Longon and Fuetidueña Chapels. In the catalogue, a white cotton dress from An Vandevorst and Flip Arickx's "Religion" collection is displayed next to images of a dark calciferous limestone "Baptismal Font," South Netherlandish, *c.* 1155–75. The dress is described in the following terms.

> Made from white cotton poplin, in includes an internal corset, a fetishistic detail typical of the fashions of their house. Here it is juxtaposed with a baptismal font from the church of Saint John the Baptist at Wellen. According to … legend … a holy woman named Christina, troubled by an evil spirit as she passed the Wellen church, leapt into this very font, emerging from the water salved.
>
> (258)

Once again, the pairing allows the curators to emphasize the poetic regime through which the Catholic object is viewed, but by pairing it with the Catholic object, the fashion item is able to rise to the status of the "aesthetic regime."

Finally, a number of discourses surrounding the exhibit broadened these interconnections by arguing that the work of producing fashion—as well as its effects—is similar to the efforts that go into the production of Catholic objects and the manner in which they have been viewed historically and in the present. I went to visit the Cloisters portion of the exhibit on a sunny and hot summer day. I was one of the few to seek out the stones of various medieval French monasteries reconstructed atop the Hudson River on such a glorious afternoon, and so I was able to spend ample time in the space and view the various elements unimpeded by the crowds that tend to make any visit to the Fifth Avenue Met a challenge. While the Fifth Avenue exhibit aimed to emphasize the "processional and ceremonial" components of the Catholic imagination, in the Cloisters, the exhibit focused on the "reflective and monastic" aspects of Catholic sensibilities. According to a summary of the exhibition found at the entrance to the Cloisters, the exhibit

> unfolds as a series of short stories through conversations between religious artworks in the Met collection and fashions of the twentieth and twenty-first centuries.... While the fashions might seem far removed from the sanctity of the Catholic Church, these contexts illuminate the myriad ways in which they embody the imaginative traditions of Catholicism. Taken together, the fashions and artworks in *Heavenly Bodies* sing in unison with distinctly enchanted and enchanting voices.

By presenting the exhibit in such terms, the curators argued that the link between fashion and the Catholic imagination was not limited to mere metaphor or inspiration, but that fashion—although seemingly remote—could, in fact, "embody" Catholic sensibilities.

At a public talk during the exhibition, I listened as the curator for the Cloisters (Barbara Boehm), the curator for the Costume Institute (Andrew Bolton), and the envoy from the Vatican who had helped to secure the loans of papal garments for the exhibit (Bishop Paul Tighe, the Secretary of the Pontifical Council for Culture) discussed the array of linkages they saw between fashion and Catholicism. Boehm suggested that the fashion helped to complete the permanent exhibit at the Cloisters and to increase its sacredness. The Chapter House of a monastery, she explained, is not sacred until everyone gathers there. And the presence of these clothed figures helped to populate spaces in the Cloisters that otherwise felt empty. For Bolton, the exhibit was not merely "a history of fashion's engagement with Catholicism," but rather "a series of conversations between fashion and Catholic works of art." In other words, the inspiration could not be unidirectional, but he instead wanted to emphasize the conversation between these two art forms.

For his part, Bishop Tighe carefully took the time to express his admiration for museums. He even went so far as to describe them as "sacred spaces," that house beautiful objects "to open us up, stimulate us." He explained that part of his role is to get church-goers looking at art and art viewers to see something transcendent. He seemed comfortable with the idea that "many people go to churches as if they were museums." He even wanted to see parishioners bringing a few more museum practices to their encounters with pilgrimage sites. He pointed to the example of the Chartres Cathedral in France. Here, he wants parishioners to see the beauty of the art that is present and other visitors who are there primarily for the beauty to become pilgrims. The beauty found in both museums, he explained, is the work of human hands, but even more importantly, it is the work of the human spirit.

In attempting to explain how fashion could be an expression of the human spirit, he recounted his earlier parish work in which he had chastised his mostly impoverished parishioners for spending more money than they had available on lavish clothing and celebrations for events such as confirmations. One day during mass, he implored those gathered to save their money and approach these events with the knowledge that God cares not for the clothes one wears. The older priest in his parish brought him in after this incident and reminded him that he had not been assigned to this parish "in order to impose middle class values." He explained that his error had taught him that there is "something gratuitous in celebration and in art," just as there is in the way God loves us. "It is given to us without our merit."

This brief mention of those whose desire to inhabit luxury might also require them to forego rent or groceries disrupted a conversation otherwise devoted to the celebration of the creation of luxury available only to a few as a potentially "spiritual practice." In her critique of the exhibit, Religious Studies scholar Emma Anderson highlights how the emphasis on majestic Catholic abundance overlooked an opposing Catholic sartorial tradition: the use of clothing such as hairshirts and identical robes to reduce wearers' earthly desires. The current Pope (who played no direct role in the donation of the objects for the exhibit) has made a reputation for his stripped-down choices, and his refusal to make use of objects like the ones displayed (a practice in which his predecessor, Benedict XVI, had often indulged). The choice to emphasize only one component of Catholic media, she argues, "prompt[ed] gazes less awestruck than acquisitive, less ascetic than aspirational" (Anderson 2018). I am arguing here that this was precisely the exhibition's aim. That some forms of Catholic media lend themselves so easily to such a project is an uncomfortable fact that scholars of Catholic mediation need to do more to address.

Occult Economies and Religious Practices of Prosperity

Before concluding, I want to briefly explore how Catholic abundance fits into a variety of religious practices aimed at inducing prosperity, which have become increasingly common in our neoliberal era. In the decade leading up to the new millennium, a number of economies that had been closed to foreign capital investment were forced open through a series of structural adjustment programs. As foreign investment moved in to spaces where it had previously been forbidden, it tended to bring images of widespread abundance along with it. Shopping malls and a variety of advertising images made this abundance appear easily available. The gap between images of abundance and the lived reality of many of the people in these regions created powerful desires to inhabit these lifestyles of consumption. At the same time, many of the social institutions that had historically determined the distribution of wealth in these areas were increasingly disrupted, giving the appearance that those who were able to engage in these modes of consumption had done so in ways that might potentially be available to anyone. Jean and John Comaroff (2000) have described how many have turned to magical means in order to increase their access to that wealth, describing the neoliberal era as one shaped by "occult economies."

These types of practices have found expression in a variety of religious traditions, from the expansion of the prosperity gospel among Pentecostals in sub-Saharan Africa (Haynes 2017), to Buddhists possessed by the spirits of the guardians of the treasure trove in Burma (Foxeus 2017). These practices have tended to be marked by desires of immediacy: being directly inhabited by the Holy Spirit or possessed by spirits in ways that appear to bypass the traditional institutional, material, and semiotic frameworks that might otherwise shape one's encounters with God. Experiences of possession aimed at securing more possessions speak to an impossible desire to secure wealth in a neoliberal age.[10]

The Catholic modes of mediation found in *Heavenly Bodies* and in public art museums share with practices of possession aimed at securing possessions the effect of upholding and legitimating the consumption necessary for neoliberalism's reproduction. They differ significantly, however, in their approach to mediation. The majestic and deeply material modes of mediation

I have referenced with the term "abundance" contrast significantly with these desires for immaterial encounters with transcendent spirits. We can best understand these distinctions not by presuming a purity to immateriality and a corruption that accompanies all material forms, but by looking at those who are most likely to engage in them. Practices of possession, both among Pentecostals in sub-Saharan Africa, and Buddhists in Burma, tend to be the purview of lower middle classes. According to Foxeus, those involved in trade, the sale of goods, and other uncertain and uneven modes of wealth acquisition are most likely to turn to the spirits of the guardians of the treasure trove at Buddhist temples in Burma. Similarly, Haynes has described how expansive notions of "prosperity" have allowed the working poor to see themselves as blessed, despite an ongoing lack of economic security.

An image in the *New York Times* just ahead of the opening of *Heavenly Bodies* spoke volumes about those who can most fully engage in the rituals surrounding *Heavenly Bodies*. Gazing at a liturgical vestment of Pope Benedict XV are Christine Hearz Schwarzman, Donatella Versace, and Stephen A. Schwarzman. Mr. Shwarzman is the CEO of Blackstone, a private equity investment firm who, along with the designer Donatella Versace, was one of the major donors who supported the exhibit. While *Heavenly Bodies* was the most attended exhibit at the Met, the primary audience of the Costume Institute's exhibits has largely been an elite audience. As evidenced by the annual Met Gala which opens the Institute's annual exhibit, these events are a means of using the aura of celebrity in order to celebrate (and fundraise among) the super-rich. As Duncan suggested, the fact that these events are highly exclusive is not something with which the trustees appear to concern themselves. While the working poor seek the economic security images of abundance promise, as Weber has argued, the wealthy look for assurance that their good fortune is deserved. Such a claim requires an infrastructure of "high" culture that legitimates the fortunate and the abundance they have secured.

Conclusion

That fashion could be Catholicized in order to legitimate an increasingly illegitimate political-economic formation is particularly interesting given the historical imbrications of fashion and anxieties surrounding the sacrality and transcendent nature of Catholic media. Matthew Engelke (2009) has explored the transcendent experiences of time Christians understand to be made available through the reading of the Christian Bible. In summarizing St. Augustine's account of the unique temporality of the Bible, Engelke points to how "Scripture is in time, but not wholly of time because the Word of God is eternal. Reading Scripture, then, is an act that can take one out of time" (159). Historically, images, statues, and spaces that functioned as "icons" operated in a similar manner. Within the Byzantine and Roman Catholic traditions from at least the eighth century, "iconic" images were understood through a kind of substitutionary logic. Their producers aimed to replicate images that were purported to date back to the life of Jesus, Mary, and the saints on earth. The artists and particular works were substitutable, as it was the resemblance between the images and their "prototypes" that served as the primary concern. Humans standing before icons could venerate them in ways that would allow the devotion they offered before them at particular moments in time to be passed on to those beings situated outside of time. The authority of icons, therefore, rested in their ability to appear time*less*. However, by the thirteenth century, in art historian Alexander Nagel's account of critics at the time, many such images had failed to maintain their logics of substitution and, instead, betrayed the moments in time in which they were produced, as painters paid increasing attention to details of dress, interiors, and hairstyles.[11]

By the time of the Renaissance, according to Nagel, anxieties surrounding the apparent shallowness of painting had grown. These images looked increasingly distant from their prototypes, bearing as they did the ever-changing dress, hairstyles, and décor of the periods in which they were made. Nagel sees the introduction of perspective in painting—generally conceived of as visual evidence of modernity's march of progress—as one of a series of "reactionary" responses to the "modernizing" tendencies in painting that made them appear outdated, rather than timeless. The visual innovations that occurred during the Renaissance—innovations, moreover, that often stand in as visual evidence of a rising modernity—may have been aimed at upholding the possibility of a painting's proximity to its transcendent origin or destination. This apparent contradiction need not surprise us. Catholic abundance, as I have demonstrated here, moves in multiple directions, allowing it to express God's majesty as well as upholding what Kotsko has described as His "provisional servants'" (2018: 293) illegitimate political regimes.

In his review of the exhibit, Orsi argues that "one of the major themes of the *Heavenly Bodies* exhibition is that aesthetics provides access to the sacred in Catholicism. But the connection between beauty and the sacred in Catholic culture is not a direct one. It is always mediated by and implicated in power"

(Orsi 2018). When reflecting upon Catholic media, I argue, it is important to attend to the other "itineraries" (Napolitano 2016) this material abundance encounters along its way to and from the transcendent. We need to reflect carefully on the various powers, hierarchies, and political projects in which it is implicated.

Notes

1   "1,659,647 Visitors to Costume Institute's *Heavenly Bodies* Show at Met Fifth Avenue and Met Cloisters Make It the Most Visited Exhibition in The Met's History." The Metropolitan Museum of Art. Press Release. October 11, 2018. https://www.metmuseum.org/press/news/2018/heavenly-bodies-most-visited-exhibition.

2   "The Met Store Launches Exclusive Cosmetics and Apparel with PAT McGRATH LABS in Celebration of The Costume Institute's Spring 201 Exhibition, *Heavenly Bodies: Fashion and the Catholic Imagination*." The Metropolitan Museum. Press Release. May 7, 2018. https://www.metmuseum.org/press/news/2018/pat-mcgrath-labs.

3   Returning to this topic nine months into a global pandemic in which the fashion industry has been decimated and gatherings of any size have become potentially deadly affairs, the confident and unabashed celebration of abundance that characterized this exhibit seems almost quaint. And yet, the stock market's ability to further enrich the richest at a time when poverty and unemployment soared speaks to the necessity of critiquing such imaginaries. When gatherings can once again commence, we need new ideals to celebrate.

4   Matthew Engelke (2007) has persuasively argued that the semiotic ideology that prefers direct and unmediated access to God expressed by a variety of Protestant groups overlooks the impossibility of immediacy. He has highlighted how a variety of practices—including those centered on language—are also mediating and material forms. David Morgan (2007, 2012) has demonstrated the ongoing power of visual culture in the production and reproduction of Protestant imaginaries.

5   This summary of the field is informed by the work of Annalisa Buttici (2016). Andrew Greeley's work on the Catholic "imagination" is explicitly referenced in the exhibit's title and his work is cited throughout the exhibit on text panels. Both his work and that of David Tracy are cited by the exhibit curator, Andrew Bolton, in the opening essay of the exhibit catalogue (Bolton 2018). Tracy (2018) also wrote an essay for the catalogue. By the term "semiotic ideologies," I refer to commonly accepted standards of what counts as a sign and how it operates in the world (see Engelke 2007 and Keane 2007 for more on how various semiotic ideologies structure religious life).

Mediating Catholicism

6   The first objects to fill middle-class homes were, in fact, religious objects, which
    opened the way, some have argued (Coleman 2021), to the power of consumption
    in domestic spaces.

7   The economist Thomas Picketty (2014) has demonstrated how the nineteenth and
    early twenty-first centuries share similar levels of inequality.

8   The church in which we stood was built in the nineteenth century during the
    Second Empire, a moment when conservative voices reigned and the city of
    Paris was being extensively rebuilt to make way for private capital and increased
    consumption (Harvey 2006). This was also a time in which many new Roman
    Catholic churches were built in a historicizing fashion, mimicking many of the
    medieval and byzantine styles that appeared so attractive to Heavenly Body
    curators a century and a half later.

9   Many critics have pointed to how "cold" these mannequins appeared. According
    to the Curator of the Costume Institute Andrew Bolton, the sculptor of the female
    mannequins was given an image of Michelangelo's *Pietà* for inspiration (although,
    Bolton acknowledged, the sculptor was no Michelangelo). The sculptor of the
    male mannequins was given an image of Jared Leto, who, Bolton suggested, is the
    contemporary celebrity who looks the most like Jesus.

10 I am grateful to Angela Zito for noting the overlap between these terms.

11 This attention to such details, Nagel recounts, has been largely explained by the
    growing significance of private devotional practices, "prompt[ing] the development
    of techniques to coordinate" references to the life of Christ "with the circumstances
    of devotion" (2004, 37).

9

Miraculous Sovereignties: Mediation and the Señor de los Milagros in Lima, Peru

Kristin Norget

On the hot afternoon of October 19, 2013, a representative of the Confederation of Peruvian Workers (Confederación de Trabajadores del Perú, or CTP), one of the country's largest public-sector unions, delivered a solemn discourse at one of the scheduled stops (*paradas*) in the annual two-day procession of the Señor de los Milagros (Lord of Miracles) in the central district of Lima, Peru. The man's speech began, in typical manner, as a passionate litany of appeals to the beloved saint, known as the patron saint of Lima and the focus of the largest Catholic processions in Latin America:

> The Confederation of Peruvian Workers pays tribute to the Lord of Miracles, asking for blessings for our leaders, for all of Peru, so that together we can fight for a country that is more just, with social justice, with enough bread and freedom [*pan y libertad*]. Lord of Miracles, Lord Christ of the poor, Lord Christ of Pachacamilla: here are your people, your community, here are the people of Lima who present themselves to beg for your forgiveness [*clemencia*]. My Lord, Christ of all peoples, Christ of the ill, Christ of miracles, Señor, your mercy for our faith.[1]

This chapter stems from a broader research project (carried out over 2011–17) on media technologies and mediation in current forms of Catholic evangelism in Peru and Mexico, funded by the Social Sciences and Humanities Research Council of Canada. I acknowledge the invaluable research collaboration of Dr. Margarita Zires Roldán. Assistance by a wonderful group of undergraduate students at the Pontificia Católica Universidad de Perú (PCUP) was also critical to the success of fieldwork in Lima: Diana Safra, Alexandra Díaz; Sergio Sarabia, Sergio Tirado, Sebastian Delgado, Eliana Caballero. Also crucial was support from Dr. Véronique Delecaros, José Carlos Paredes, and Dr. Marcel Valcarcel, Fernando Lino, Dr. Mañuel Orillo (the Mayordomo of the Hermandad de las Nazarenas), Sra. Glaver Fátima, and other Hermanos who generously shared their experiences. I am grateful to the insightful reflections on this chapter by my colleagues at the Mediating Catholicism symposium in Québec City, and to subsequent feedback and comments especially by Valentina Napolitano, Rafael Sánchez, and Marc Loustau. Amazing research assistance from Damian Arteca sharpened key arguments of this essay. Sections of this chapter appeared in an article published in *Journal of Global Catholicism* 3 (2): 50–83 (2019).

Figure 9.1 The Señor de los Milagros procession in Lima, Peru, 2017 (photo by author).

The man's forceful words, initiating with a typical petitional script for blessings from the Señor de los Milagros, were met with polite attentiveness from the crowd. But suddenly his speech veered away from more routine religious themes and, having invoked the leftist revolutionary slogan "Pan y libertad" (Bread and Freedom), launched into sharp criticism of the government's pro-Fujimori (a reference to the imprisoned former President and dictator) political line:

> Here are Christ and the workers that were victims of a *fujimontesinista* dictatorship, that got rid of 35,0000 workers. Just like the new law just passed, which is also against workers.[2] My Lord, blessings, give us your protection, your blessing. Lord, you are so great, my Lord, what a blessing it is for all of us to have you so close.

At this point, shrill whistles, hisses, and screams erupted from the crowd: "Booooh! Booooh!", "Ssssssssssss!". Noticing this opposition, a woman on the stage beside the representative promptly removed the microphone from his hands and began to pray. The crowd joined her in reciting a series of Hail Marys and quickly calmed down. A large man standing in the throng, a member of the Brotherhood of the Señor de los Milagros de las Nazarenas, the lay Catholic organization charged with executing the procession each year, extended his disapproval: "That guy came to speak about his own problems" he muttered loudly, to no one in particular, "and there was nothing there for the Señor."[3]

"Nothing there for the Señor." The Brother's words suggested that the man's allusion to the consequences of a horrifically violent period and one of the most controversial, yet still popular, presidents in contemporary Peruvian history, his appeal for just treatment of Peruvian workers, was somehow unacceptable. The man's spontaneous mixing of devotion to the Señor and an overtly anti-*Fujimorista* line of politics ruffled what had been up to that moment a smooth procession. Apparently, at least for most people there, a tacitly enjoined reciprocity of some kind—in this very public, sacred space, at this specific moment—had not been fulfilled. A kind of mixing of religion and politics had been repudiated. And yet it seemed to me that at the same time "the political" reverberated throughout the procession.

This chapter unpacks the signification sparked by this seemingly inconsequential incident, one that distinguished this stop from others in the Señor's procession that day. For the small confrontation was unleashed by a defiant enunciation of agency and historical memory met with a sudden insistence on its erasure. The man's words were an invocation of the miraculousness of the Señor de los Milagros, a call for divine justice that spoke to a particular consciousness of the authoritarian violence of the Peruvian state. Yet I had to ask myself, why had this speech's open blending of religion and politics been treated as "matter out of place" (Douglas 1966) when other such blendings were tacitly accepted, even normative? My claim is that the Señor de los Milagros procession illustrates the need to attend to the role of public religious performances as mediations of political power which speak to the Church's complicity with "secular" authority and modes of enchantment that might be overlooked if they are seen to be "merely religious."

Every year, the image of the Señor de los Milagros is taken out of the Church of the Nazarenas on the shoulders of Brotherhood members, and over two long days (October 18 and 19) snakes through the heart of Lima's colonial center past the public institutions emblematic of the country's national political identity—the Cathedral, the Archdiocese of Lima, the Government Palace (*Palacio del Gobierno*), the Republican Congress, and the Judicial Palace (*Palacio de Justicia*), among others (see Figure 9.1).[4] In this highly charged context, as a complexly interpellated, vital entity, the Señor has a central role in an ornate ritual worlding in which Catholics nurture their devotion to this much-beloved saint while the Peruvian nation and its constitutive powers are underlined, performatively, materially, and affectively.[5] This orchestrated ideal world may exist for just a couple of days, but its effects—and affects—are enduring.

Scholarly writings on the procession have drawn attention to complex history of the Señor, including his syncretic (pre-Hispanic and African) origins (e.g., Banchero 1976; Vargas Uguarte 1966; Rostworowski 1992; Sanchez Rodriguez 2002; Costilla 2015, 2016; Gómez 2015); and the saint's role in the shaping of identity in Peruvian diasporic communities (e.g., Ruiz 1999; Paerregaard 2008; Napolitano 2016, 2017). I analyze here this procession not as a reiteration of timeless Catholic Peruvian or local Lima-based ("*Limeño*") tradition, but as a mediation of Catholicism constituted at interlinked local, national, and global scales, and across a range of terrains, bodies, and objects. I understand mediation as both an intrinsic aspect of religious practice (Morgan 2008; Meyer 2014) and a fertile conceptual ground for examining the dynamics of Catholicism as both local and global religion and as a fundamentally political form.

This chapter thus attends to themes of aesthetics and materiality in approaching the celebration of the Señor de los Milagros in Lima as having an active regulating political role in Peruvian society. The theme of mediation and saints emerges from a basic yet critical concept of Catholic theology, as divine beings like the Señor de los Milagros are seen as crucial intercessors of God's will and grace. Yet throughout the contemporary Catholic world massive public celebrations of certain historically resonant saints, as multidimensional triggers of affective forces of identification and attachment, also figure in the *emplacement* of both Catholic Church presence and authority and a sacred anchoring of apparently secular national political orders (Norget 2011, 2017, 2021). I argue we should not underestimate the role of such public religious ritual performances in the constitution of governance, where processes of commodification, transnational relationships, and values and desires of secular, global modernity are entangled in such public events that triumph Catholic tradition and push for the continued centrality of religion in national social life.

In what follows, I will examine dimensions of the Señor de los Milagros celebration as an arena that throws into sharp relief what normally remains largely hidden: the deeply religious nature of the foundation of social authority and sovereignty in Peru. I explore this specific celebration of the Señor de los Milagros in contemporary Lima not only as a symbolically rich arena for devotees' mutual engagement with the saint, but also the production of a specifically *Catholic* Peruvian national identity and the legitimation of power by representatives of both Church and state. I regard legitimation not as a certainty or *fait accompli* secured or underlined by the procession, but as an uncertain ritual end that is performatively emergent and socially contingent. The legitimation-seeking performances in the procession I focus on here are interactions with the Señor by prominent leaders of the Catholic Church (most notably, the Archbishop), the State (the President), and a range of government and public organizations. In this context, I examine "the miraculous" (*lo milagroso*), a particular mode of discourse and behavior that is both the referent for a petition to the saint for his blessing and protection and an appeal for public vindication of the petitioner's actions and status. As we will see, the Señor's procession appears in some ways to defy and *counter* the public space of the state and its monopoly over "rightful" rule, while other performances of the miraculous during the procession articulate and uphold these.

Theopolitics of the Miraculous

The Señor's procession in Lima is a dynamic, exceptional space in which multiple political and social forces, as well as experiential worlds, converge. In his reiterative tracing of a sacred path through the heart of Lima's colonial urban terrain, the Señor recreates the city as a palimpsest, in De Certeau's terms, a cumulative layering of heterogeneous places which bears traces of multiple significations and practices (De Certeau 1984; see also Gandolfo 2009). Along these lines the procession itself is a "spatial practice" (Lefebvre 1974), condensing over centuries myriad "moving layers" (De Certeau 1984: 108) of the violences of race and class conflict that have produced Lima as a distinct place.

Much in the same way the procession emerges as a confluence of various vying political and social interests, the Señor's history is a series of transformations and iterations that enclose multifarious communities, identities, and sovereignties. The cult emerged in the seventeenth century within the African and indigenous neighborhood of Pachacamilla (Vargas 1966; Costilla 2015).[6] Promoted since by Jesuit catechists, the cult drew devotion among the *criollo* (American-born European) population before ultimately becoming the public spectacle we see today.

Most city residents I spoke to during the procession and members of the Hermandad of the Nazareñas acknowledged the African-inflected origins of the cult. This association lingers today in the conspicuous predominance of Black and *mulato* Peruvians in the Brotherhood, despite the fact even they and other Limeños still affirmed their perception of the "mestizo" (i.e., national) character of the procession's significance in its contemporary form. Yet the celebration is steeped in signs of indigeneity and afro-identity which flout the dominant homogenizing claims of Peruvian nationalism. The Señor's heterogeneous identity is seen, for example, in the names by which he is known—the Lord of Pacachamilla (*Señor de Pachacamilla*), the Brown Christ (*Cristo Moreno*), the Lord of Earthquakes (*Señor de los Temblores*), and the Lord of Marvels (*Señor de las Maravillas*).[7] The saint is hence interpellated in complex ways as he bears traces of an Andean or African telluric deity while being a powerful symbol of Catholic faith and the Peruvian nation.

The Señor also travels through diverse religious terrain. For although the procession (and the majority of the national population) is Catholic, over 14 percent of Peruvians are now evangelical Protestants, whose numbers continue to grow.[8] Moreover, despite the advent of Catholic liberation theology in the 1980s, Peru is dominated by a particular breed of conservative Catholicism, originating in early twentieth century, and shaping the country's mode of neoliberal governance arising since the 1980s (Klaiber 2016; Casey 2017). Espoused by several Peruvian Church leaders since the republican period, including Cardinal Juan Luis Cipriani (Archbishop of Lima 1999–2019), this fundamentalist, "integral" Catholic ideology sees Catholic faith as the rightful foundation for all social and political action, and rejects *a priori* the separation of church and state.[9] While a new 1979 Peruvian Constitution finally legally formalized the principle of "religious freedom" and thus the separation of church and state, the Constitution also declares that "the State recognizes the Catholic Church as an important element of Peruvian historic, cultural and moral formation and cooperates with it."[10] Also marking the beginning of Peru's ambiguous status as a modern, "confessional" yet nominally secular nation was the government's signing, in 1980, of an official agreement or "concordat" with the Holy See.[11]

Neo-liberalist reforms and successive campaigns of urban renewal in Lima in the 1990s have enabled the privatization of public properties and natural resources, and an alteration of the meaning of public, urban civic space, as exemplified by attempts (through, for e.g., vast projects of architectural restoration, or the expulsion of street vendors) to recuperate the "lost splendor" (Gandolfo 2009) of its colonial center. In this context, the Señor de los Milagros procession today is a defiant, lavish enactment of vibrant, syncretic (heterogeneous) divine presence within and across contested (and ambivalently secular) public city space.

In the procession of the Señor de los Milagros, public verbal entreaties to the Señor's miraculousness (what I refer to as *miracle-talk*) are not "just" devotional petitions. In Lima, they are part of the miraculous (*"lo milagroso"*), a wider register of auratic, embodied affective experience with both popular *and* elite theopolitical force (Norget 2021). That is, as a publicly legible experiential idiom, the miraculous is constituted as much by theological teachings or Church directives as it is by the diverse lifeworlds of the devout. *Limeños* can readily recount moving stories of the saint's miraculousness, as demonstrated by particular occurrences of good fortune or healing in their lives, especially in moments of acute distress, suffering, or precariousness (e.g., "When my baby was about to die, the Señor arrived to me [*me llegó*] and saved him"; "At the worst moment, when our family had nothing to eat, and after I prayed and prayed, the Señor appeared to me in a dream, saying everything would be OK. The next day, my father found a job."). As an all-powerful and compassionate healer, savior, consoler, and companion, the Señor de los Milagros offers an intimate sense of connection for millions of devotees, of all social backgrounds. For the masses of poor Limeños and Peruvians especially, intimate interactions with the Lord of Miracles are a source of personal or collective agency and autonomy within a deeply unequal social order.

Nevertheless, I concentrate here in how Church and government representatives make performative appeals to the Señor's miraculousness to cloak their public statements and actions in the garb of ultimate truth and morality. These utterances and acts take on particular significance within Peru's current neo-liberal democratic regime, where pressures from civil society groups are ongoing for religious pluralization, secular education, and gender, sexual, and reproductive rights, and more transparency in governance, challenging the Catholic Church's previously privileged social and cultural status and eroding the ideal and fantasied image of the state as *polis*, an integrated, ordered political community.

During the Señor's procession, the Catholic Church and the state carry out a theopolitical staging of the miraculous force and presence as they assert their social authority. My use of the concept *theopolitical* here, highlighting the need to engage with the theological dimensions of politics, deserves more explanation. It is precisely in relation to performances of legitimation that I suggest that forms of miracle-talk "from above" dovetail with the potentiality that Agamben underlined was key to the power of systems of sovereignty in relation to the state of exception, a sovereignty exercised partially by the potential "legal" suspension of law. Indeed, in his *Political Theology* (1922) political theorist (and ex-Catholic) Carl Schmitt, following Rousseau, uses the divine miracle as the theological paradigm of "the state of exception," as both manifest sovereign or divine power inhering in the interruption or suspension of the order of normal or natural law (Honig 2007: 79; Bussolini 2010). The key analogy here is one between God and the human sovereign, so that "[j]ust as a voluntarist deity sustains the universe's natural laws through miracles, so too a human sovereign sustains the state's juridical laws through inscrutable acts of will" (Lesch 2018: 3). From this classic political theological perspective, both political and religious spheres afford a power of authority naturalized (grounded in "truth") by their "exemptive" ability—that is, each sphere's ability to (paradoxically) root the authority of its conventional doctrine by appeal to its capacity *to step outside* this conventional order. In these terms, in a secular nation-state, sovereignty is located in "a transcendental and atemporal political legitimacy" that rightly "belongs" exclusively to the juridico-political order of the state (McAllister and Napolitano 2021: 5).

Yet Schmittian concepts of political theology, rooted as they are in western European experience and histories, fail to illuminate the particular workings of power vis-à-vis church-state relations in postcolonial nominally secular Catholic settings like Peru. Along this vein, Carlotta McAllister and Valentina Napolitano (2021) have developed a revised concept of theopolitics *from the Americas*, acknowledging the Church's participation in the conjoining of capitalism and colonialism wherein violent processes of accumulation shaped particular "regimes of the senses" and agendas of inclusion and exclusion within a cultural formation composed of specific "incarnated" forms of power, labor, and gender and race (2021: 2). Recognition of the theological elements in current political dynamics in the Americas (and implicitly elsewhere) then demands an awareness of the potentiality of a "God otherwise" or of God's sovereignty in the everyday, an attunement to the pervasive immanence of the divine, one not exclusively subsumed by the state's power of exception. Drawing on Walter Benjamin's concept of the "theologico-political," McAllister and Napolitano argue that such an idea of politics approaches sovereignty (which can be both "from above" and "from below") "as a practice in and of movement, governed less by concepts and ideologies than by rhythms and aesthetics, and always in provisional form" (2021: 6).

Theopolitics in these material terms allow us to grasp the particular complex sensational baroque texture of the Señor's procession—its extravagant, spectacular form enfolding indigenous, African and European ontologies and continuous oscillations between instability and rigidity, silence and intense sound, timelessness and immediacy, tender sentimentalism and abrupt aggression, humility and authority, and intimacy and formality (Norget 2021). The procession's illusion of majestic unity depends on the stable containment of such abundance of signification, even if such efforts can never succeed in any complete sense.

Thus, the procession of the Señor de los Milagros makes ethnographically tangible the link between the miraculous and performances of a right-of-rule. Here I stress the performative force of *lo milagroso* as it references a transcendent, indisputable truth, one that is outside itself and denies any contestation. In this way then, representatives of both Church and state undergird their social and moral authority and status by means of their simple presence during the procession, or through public addresses and devotional acts they offer to the Señor. In such public declarations, this miracle-talk "from above" should not be seen as a petition of the devout or simple ritual utterance but rather a practical bid to directly influence the social world, even if such attempts are only provisional. Murmurs of "subaltern politics"—hidden transcripts (Scott 1990) of intimate lay devotion to the Señor, exemplified by the CTP representative's words that began this chapter—are also alive in the procession. My focus however is on how the Church's formal structuring of the procession operates to stifle these. The Señor's Lima celebration thus displays the dynamics of a particular form of theopolitics in which different and vying sovereignties can be seen to "collide but also provisionally resonate with one another" (McAllister and Napolitano 2021: 11).

The Procession

The procession of the Señor de los Milagros affects individual pilgrims as part of a trajectory of personal devotion as they seek out the Señor for favors, for healing, or to fulfill a *promesa* or vow. The event is also a (controlled) rupture in daily life in civil, religious, and political spheres as they blend, transforming the city's profile visually, symbolically, and materially. *Limeños* hang purple balloons, images, and banners from the balconies of homes or on businesses. Traffic is re-routed, wreaking havoc and eliciting complaints from many members of the general public. The procession is replicated at various local and regional scales throughout the country, and in Lima, in schools, businesses, hospitals, and prisons. The Señor de los Milagros becomes the leading topic of local newscasts, newspapers, and magazines.

In the procession's unfolding ritual drama, the Señor—alive and interactive— is a central actor and interlocutor. He is "charged" (in all senses) as the consummate mediator, joining the bodies of *Limeños* (and national body of

Peruvians) of all classes and races. He is addressed during the event not as "just" an image, a mimetic copy or representation of "something else," but as a vibrant, sentient entity.[12] Along his path, the Señor engages devotees in dialogue, and they welcome him with affectionate reverence: *"Fuerte el aplauso para el Señor de los Milagros!!"* (Let's give strong applause for the Lord of Miracles!); or *"Le damos gracias por el amor de la familia, por la salud…"* (Let's give him thanks for the love of our family, for our good health…).

The Señor is shown love, devotion, passion, and respect and, according to *Limeños* we spoke to, he returns it in abundance, bestowing the gift of his spectacular presence and sacred blessing. He sometimes interacts with other saints (e.g., the Virgen de Santa Rosa de Lima, the Virgen de Corchacas, and San Martín de Porres), with whom he engages in a dynamic, gestural salutation. He is also said to "sleep" on the night of October 18 (the first main procession day), in the Church of Carmen in the poor Lima neighborhood Los Barrios Altos. Adding to this conflation of divine aura and everyday familiarity, Señor is the Spanish version both of "Mister" or "Sir," and of "Lord," denoting his sacred status. The saint is spoken of as "visiting" each place where he stops, and he is welcomed with endearment—my Padre, *Mi Viejo* (my Old Man) or *"Papa Lindo"* (Beautiful Father), *"Nuestro Cristo Moreno"* (Our Brown Christ)—as a beloved, sacred guest. At each of the Señor's programmed stops, he receives an official homage (*homenaje*), and act of tribute, consisting of an offering (*ofrenda*) of a spoken greeting by representatives, and an instrumental or choral performance, from *"criollo"* or *"chicha"* (popular genres blending African, European, and Andean music) to classical genres, and extravagant flower bouquets.

The Señor de los Milagros, this Lord of Miracles, is a transcendent yet immanent presence who is nurtured and re-nurtured during his traversal through the city. The visceral effect of the procession's overwhelming beauty, a multi-sensory aura-affect of communitas, is seductive. Nonetheless we should not forget the rigid structure that also pervades the event, exemplified by members of the Hermandad (Brotherhood, composed of around 6,000 members—men and women) who are responsible for carrying out the core activities of the procession. If the Señor de los Milagros is the star of this ritual show, the Brotherhood distinguishes itself from the crowd as the event's formal *collective* actor. It performs, at least for duration of the Señor's *recorrido* or perambulation, a microcosm of hierarchical order. The event is tightly orchestrated, with members of the national police corps (PNP), security, municipal police, and even soldiers strictly maintaining the separation between members of the crowd and those of the Hermandad by means of a thick rope or *soga*. Thus, the *soga* marks an arbitrary dividing line between the potentially unruly ("excessive") crowd outside of it, and the sacred space inside, focused on the Señor's litter or *anda*, and the group or *cuadrilla* of Hermanos who bear it.

The strictly sealed and hierarchical nature of the Hermandad reproduces a certain kind of Catholicism essential to the moral ideals of traditional Peruvian society. We have here a replication of forms, an idealized national political body and that of the Hermandad—a convergence highlighted in the strict separation of the Señor and his brotherhood-protectors from the crowd. The Hermandad, a hybrid entity of lay Catholics who also work in close cooperation with the Church, therefore manifests the appropriate transitional body, its ambivalent status corresponding to the liminal zone which the *hermanos* and *hermanas* occupy during the procession between saint and everyday devotees.

These principles of structural and moral order extend to the gendered division of labor in the procession. Brothers of the Hermandad conduct themselves according to masculine ideals of physical might, stoicism, and honor. Carrying the Señor is a matter of (masculine) physical strength but also encompasses an experience of suffering and penitence (sacrifice) that is profoundly corporeal and sensual. In the words of one Hermano, who had carried the *anda* for hours, "Afterwards there is no pain, you don't feel tired; it's magic." ("*Luego no hay dolor, uno no siente cansado. Es magia.*")[13]

As *sahumadoras* (incense blowers) and *cantoras* (hymn-singers), the veiled women perform a different kind of enduring, sacrificial devotional body (see Figure 9.2). They walk, sometimes barefoot, slowly backwards in rows before the image, *limpiando* (cleaning or purifying) the path of the Señor, singing his praises as they gaze at the image of the Virgen de la Nube painted on the other side of the Cristo image of the Señor. In the words of Gisela, the leader of the Cantoras, "The Señor is rarely without song; the whole route we sing to him, the whole route," adding, "For all of us the Nazarene [*el Nazareno*] is a marvel, the emotion is indescribable My Señor! He is omnipotent, he softens the heart of even the toughest [*mas rudo*] men and women, the toughest human being."[14]

At many of the pre-designated *anda* stops there is a change in the *cuadrilla*, following a script of elaborate gestures and acts (the placement of the litter on the ground, the removal and replacement of the candles and flowers, the arranging of the new *cuadrilla* of Hermanos, and the raising of the litter), down to the last detail.

By means of a continual series of repeated ritual action, a scripted and patterned constant flow of people, objects (candles, flowers), the Señor thus

Figure 9.2 Sahumadoras (photo by author).

performs a poetic mapping through central Lima of sensorily vibrant sacred space. Yet as mentioned, members of the Hermandad (and thus ultimately, the Archbishop and Church hierarchy) carefully manage the spaces through which the Señor moves in terms of public accessibility to the *anda*. The controlled division and occupation of space in Lima's civic core create an impression that the Señor de los Milagros is a seamless extension of ecclesiastical property and identity, even while the diverse devotional and spatial practices of other participants along the route (e.g., the impromptu cheers, and shout-outs to the Señor as he passes, the intimate personal prayers and petitions whispered in his presence, devotees who sneak into the sacred cordoned off area around the *anda* to get closer to the Señor), are eruptions of an alternative social vision or even a divine politics "otherwise" (McAllister and Napolitano 2021) which seem to contest and escape this total control.

Miraculous Acts of Legitimation

The procession thus affords a constant and compressed interaction between Peruvians, the Church, state institutions, and the Señor himself. The event is organized over several months by the Hermandad del Señor de los Milagros, yet this coordination is supervised by the Archbishop of Lima (in the years of fieldwork, Cardinal Juan Luis Cipriani). The Señor's planned trajectory changes slightly from year to year: petitions for stops of the *anda* are vetted first at the Archdiocese by the Archbishop, who then chooses what he deems as the appropriate stops (twenty-four in total) before they can be made official.

Many public and political institutions appear during the procession offering *homenajes*, each with their own agenda. The Señor is the mediator or arbiter of these intentions. This public and conspicuous space exudes a moral resonance—a certain theopolitical affect—with the Señor de los Milagros as its sacred referent. The event thus becomes a very visible site or arena of interlocution: rich, patterned rhetorical statements are made at each stop of the Señor, when people take advantage of the moment to thank the saint for his blessings, and to solicit more for the year to come; the saint is asked to "illuminate those governing," "protect the workers," and so on. Such examples of miracle-talk emitted at some of the official stops in the procession emphasize collective fates as placed in the hands of the Señor: the good performance (*desempeño*) of the institutions, the well-being of the economy (the lifeblood of Peru's national political body), and so on.

In this context, the space of the miraculous sanctifies and legitimates political action, at least as a potentiality. On the Señor's sacred stage, those watching are scrutinizing and judging the behavior of all: there are deeply entrenched expectations of how one should demonstrate respect to the saint, and so the site becomes a space for evaluating people's moral worth. The pragmatics of this ritual context demand that each interlocutor be recognized as a credible addressee of the Señor, to insert themselves in a particular language of identification vis-à-vis the saint, and to appeal to the Señor de los Milagros, as interlocutor, to accept their petition.[15] With their ritual performances, such speakers can be seen to claim public space through a delicate balance of improvisation and routine, a script of sanctioned and expected techniques and gestures. If such public acts of discourse deviate from acceptable themes of address (as shown in the case of the CTP union representative mentioned at the start of this essay), their speakers run the risk of being ostracized. For in these spaces such moments represent communication ruptures, a breakdown of the tacit, delicate pact of sacrifice and exchange, one of words and of the unimpeachable purity and intimacy of acts of penitence and devotion. These ruptures expose the heavy weight of the Señor in the creation and disciplining of political credibility and integrity and of moral Peruvian (Catholic) subjects.

At certain stops (*paradas*) on the official route, expectations of propriety of comportment are particularly elevated, for these are sites most closely associated with social status and state/Church authority. Nowhere is more exemplary of this point than the Señor's stops in the Plaza de Armas (Plaza Mayor) of Lima, where Peru's religious and political powers are concentrated. When the Señor arrives at the Plaza on October 18 (the first of the main procession days), he makes stops, in turn, at the Governmental Palace (where he is received by the President), the Municipality of Lima (where the saint is "greeted" by the city's mayor), the Archdiocese of Lima, and the Cathedral (where the Archbishop delivers an important speech), and then the national Congress building, where he is paid homage by the *congresistas* (congressmen and women). At this stage in the *anda*'s route, the physical juxtaposition of buildings and of

Figure 9.3 The Señor de los Milagros procession in the Plaza de Armas, Lima, Peru, 2017 (photo by author).

representatives of Church and state throws into relief a symbiosis of religious and "secular" powers.

When the Señor arrives at the governmental palace, the president (accompanied by his cabinet members) is expected to come out to welcome him and pay their respects, customarily stepping in to help carry the litter for a few minutes. While such displays of deference would likely offend in more liberalist, secular Latin American (though still majority Catholic) countries such as Mexico, in Peru such gestures of pious humility by politicians occur regularly and are quite normal. The salient point, however, is not so much the openness of this apparent collusion, but rather its strongly moral aura. Formal, official greetings made to the Señor are utterances and actions that both index and produce this particular space of Lima as part of the core of national authority.

In this potent encounter of the respective heads of "earthly" and "heavenly" realms, the actions and behavior of the president are subject to public judgment. The president makes no public verbal greeting but remains entirely silent throughout his interaction with the Señor. His "proper" or competent execution of expected rites is therefore especially salient. This point in the procession is covered carefully by local and national media outlets, who tend to focus on matters demonstrating moral character: for example, did the president carry the image? Did he don the purple tunic? Was he respectful before the Señor? Behavior deemed appropriate becomes the stuff of photo-ops, while missteps are condemned (see Figure 9.3). In 2012, in President Ollanta Humala's second year in power, he and First Lady Nadine Heredia exited the Palacio de Gobierno to greet the Señor over ten minutes "late," and were subject to boos, jeers, and whistles from the crowd, and harsh criticism nationwide. One man in the crowd commented loudly: "He [Humala] thinks that even God is going to wait for him!"; "He lacks manners!", yelled another.

The gaffe was also seized upon by television and newspapers, which sported headlines such as, "Ollanta Humala and Nadine Heredia booed ['*pifiados*'] in the procession of the Brown Christ [*el Cristo Moreno*]." Such highly mediatized moments echo Ludovic Lado's point (this volume) regarding how Catholic radio in Chad offers a channel through which the members of the public can voice complaints about institutions of authority not possible through other means. In Lima however, it appears the stain of such complaints is erasable: the next year, in 2013, Ollanta Humala appeared quickly from the governmental palace and even carried the Señor, thereby redeeming himself in the eyes of the public.[16] And over the remaining years of his tenure (which ended in July 2016), it seems he made sure to fulfil his *compromiso* (obligation) to the saint, down to the last detail. There is a vicarious excitement here, in this reversal of roles, the sight of the head of government deferring to the Lord of Miracles, the savior of the poor and powerless. Yet while the rules of gift and sacrifice enjoined by the performance are in principle relevant to all participants, they must be followed in an exact manner.

If such moments can be seen to display a certain vulnerability of moral authority, they do not unsettle the overarching frame in which political authority is located in the figure of the president, whose access to the Señor is open and direct. This frame also affords the Catholic Church the use of the space of the miraculous to couch its political statements as transcendent, absolute Truth. A polemical homily delivered by then Archbishop Juan Luis Cipriani in 2015 during the main procession day (October 18) illustrates such a purposing of miracle-talk:

> We ask the Señor de los Milagros, protect the family, so that they may be close to their children and grandparents and so the family may be the central place [*el lugar central*] of the entire country: the family, made up of father, mother, children, grandchildren, grandparents. *The Señor de los Milagros wants that miracle.* That the family rises again, united, and so we say to him: "have compassion."
>
> The Señor de los Milagros *takes care of human life*. We don't want to treat anyone badly, but we cannot say that abortion is a right. Abortion is not a right, it's a crime. So we ask the Señor de los Milagros, *please make for me that great miracle*: "abortion no, *life yes*." These are *normal* things: life, the sick, the marriage of a man and a woman. The Church, with much love [*cariño*] is holding out its hand to everyone to help us, but it is not saying that we should keep quiet about what Jesus has taught us.[17] [my emphases]

Cipriani's words here address the Señor as the recipient of his solicitation. By means of statements such as "The Señor de los Milagros wants that miracle...," Cipriani can also be seen to ventriloquize the Señor, conveying the saint's (supposed) message in his stead. In this type of discourse the Archbishop uses the publicity of the procession to elaborate on the Roman Catholic Church's current theological discourse of "life," centered on the heterosexual family, as the grounding of a locally and nationally rooted *Peruvian* way of life.[18] In this and other homilies, the Archbishop speaks to Peruvian Catholics through the image of the Señor, and affective metaphors such as love (*amor, cariño*, compassion) and the (nuclear, heteronormative) family, the privileged unit for the reproduction of ("integrist") Catholic faith and moral society (Norget 2021).

The above examples illustrate how aspects of the Señor's procession appear to both defy and counter the public space of the state, as seen in the criticisms of Humala. Yet prominent performances of the miraculous during the procession also serve to articulate and uphold the state. Countless local and national news stories are full of comments on other politicians, from judges to ministers and members of congress, who have made a point of being seen to take part in the ritual, including all of Peru's presidents during two decades of military dictatorship and since then (see Figure 9.4).[19] Alan García (president 1985 to 1990, and from 2006 to 2011), often carried the image as an Hermano (for almost fifty years) in the 9th Cuadrilla. Politician Alberto Andrade carried the Señor during his first year as mayor of Lima in 1996. Even outside the official days of his annual celebration, during a heated presidential campaign in May of 1990, then Archbishop Augusto Vargas authorized the "taking out" of the saint in a procession in protest of support given to Fujimori's presidential candidacy by evangelical Christian groups. The event was condemned by progressivist Catholic bishops who accused the Archbishop of promoting a "crusade-like" Catholicism (*catolicismo de cruzada*),[20] thereby exposing again the fissures in local and national Peruvian Catholicism, and the Church's influence.

These acts support my argument that the procession of the Señor de los Milagros is a public performance of the miraculous and a vital resource in the public affirmation of the rightness and moral legitimacy of rule, or simply the assertion of a political position. Yet the gap between such performances and what occurs behind the scenes can be jarring. For example, both presidents whose tenure spanned this body of research (2011–17)—Ollanta Humala and Pedro Kuczynski—are currently, respectively, awaiting trial (Humala) and imprisoned (Kuczynski) for human rights crimes or corruption.[21] Humala's predecessor, Alejandro Toledo (2001 to 2006), is also entangled in a corruption scandal, and is fighting extradition to Peru from the United States. Alan García (1985–90/2006–11) was accused of "financial irregularities" during his two presidential terms and committed suicide in 2019. And García's second presidency followed that of Alberto Fujimori, Peru's autocratic ruler from 1990 to 2000, who in 2009 was sentenced to twenty-five years in jail for human rights breaches in the war against the Shining Path (*Sendero Luminoso*) guerrillas and was later convicted of embezzlement and corruption.

These cases point to something striking in the apparent normalization and "invisibilizing" in Peru of the ethical ruptures of crisis, hypocrisy, and betrayal at the same time as these politicians' regimented but "authentic" displays of humility and piety before the Señor. In this sense then the

Figure 9.4 President Pedro Kuczynski and Vice-President Mercedes Aráoz greeting Apostolic Nuncio Nicola Girasoli and Mayordomo of the Hermandad de las Nazarenas, Manuel Orillo outside the Palacio de Gobierno (Lima, October 18, 2017) (photo from Secretaría de Prensa, Presidencia del Perú).

miracle and the miraculous appear to express both the limits of power and its legitimation. Yet public performative solicitations—in word or deed—for the blessing or help of the Señor made by such political figures are only entreaties; they are not perlocutional. In classical political theological terms, the miracle or the miraculous makes sovereign or divine power evident by means of the arrest or interruption it represents in the normal or natural law governing the mundane order. It refers to an exceptional, unassailable truth whose potency lies in invisibility, in faith. Miracle-talk and related acts in this sense can be read as "sacraments of power" in Agamben's terms; like the oath, public invocations of the miraculous are "situated at the junction between religion and politics," speech acts "that only possesses a signifying content, without stating anything in itself. Their function is the *relation* they establish between the word uttered and the *potential* invoked" (Benaviste, in Agamben 2010: 11; emphasis added), the potential here residing in the "efficacity" of the connection with the realm of the divine (Bussolini 2010). Peruvian politicians' miracle-talk and in other devotional acts thus appear as earnest demonstrations of faith, a sincerity that is not manifest in behavior or actions in the mundane world, but rather in the ritual space of the Señor, which allows a moral status to stick, even if only temporarily, to those who invoke it.

Yet, I stress the ambivalent, provisional nature of such acts of legitimation. Such invocations of the miraculous afford "religious culture," and its proponents, an independent appeal to a stable truth relative to, and outside of, "state/secular culture." At the same time, this is a delicate balancing act. During the procession, as evidenced by ex-president Humala's gaffe, the titular head of the state cannot ignore the Señor. Likewise, the CTP representative brought politics into an honoring of Señor de los Milagros in a manner that signified a denial of the "miracle as exception" as accessible only to and locatable only *within* the state—which might partly explain why the man was punished for his assertion of a popular theopolitical legitimacy or sovereignty.

Thus, the history of the Señor de los Milagros, like the procession, is one in which the divine purchase of the Miracle is in constant negotiation as communities and institutions vie for its "grounding." My point however is that this grounding or naturalizing of a theopolitical doctrine (paradoxically) in the exception *from* the order (i.e., which the doctrine represents) operates to both mystify the site of authority and exclude the validity of attempts to contest or counter it. Affirmed is the ideal that the proper place of politics and legitimate authority is the state and those who uphold it; multiple past and present violences of the Peruvian state are merged with "the law" as implicitly divinely sanctioned. This mystification, while strengthening the authority, also means that contact with it is never direct but rather *mediated*, either imagistically, aesthetically, performatively, or otherwise.

Conclusion

Through processes of repetition, the differentiation of space and actors, and the enforcement of certain ritual acts and discourses, the annual procession of the Señor in Lima projects a worlding of ideal Catholicism and Peruvian life. The resulting potent ritual defies certain neo-liberal and other democratizing forces in Lima that push toward the recognition of religious diversity and a stronger civil society, along with a greater separation of religion (i.e., Catholicism) from education, public affairs, and state governance or *laicización* (Blancarte 2016). Thus, the Señor's procession as event mirrors the structure of the "miracle" that it depicts: in the same way that the miracle grounds doctrine by means of its power to interrupt it, the procession effectively operates as a rupture of everyday life that grounds the structure of the everyday and performatively legitimates the sovereignty (i.e., having access to the "sovereignty of miracle" or "miracle of sovereignty") of parties involved.[22]

I have focused on the miraculous/*lo milagroso* as implicated in legitimation processes for a range of social actors from the state or church. Yet miracles hover at the tenuous fold between the visible and the invisible, the potential and the impossible, of (invisible) inner, subjective personal experience and (visible) "exterior" socially accepted extra-ordinary reality. As a mediation of personal, intimate faith, the framework or field of *lo milagroso* is an ambiguous and ambivalent experiential ground as it draws from both popular class sensibilities and theological categories and logics (Zires 2006; Norget 2021). And it is precisely the procession's oscillation between poles of intimate immediacy and distant transcendence that is key to its compelling power. As the chapters by Julius Bautista and Eric Hoenes (this volume) also show, this necessary imbrication of intimacy and public, spectacular performance is characteristic of many contemporary large Catholic processions and events, an imbrication that has only been amplified by the increasing mediatization of such performances through multiple media technologies and platforms (see Norget 2017, 2021).

Contemporary Catholic saint celebrations like that of the Señor de los Milagros in Lima allow us to rethink the constitution of the "political" in interaction with the "religious" both as spheres of experience and as institutions (i.e., as Church or State). The procession of the Señor also signals the provisional, unstable nature of the post-colonial Peruvian state and its theopolitical performances of sovereignty, made as they are from centuries of political violence, terror, crisis, and enduring agendas of social exclusion. The Señor himself condenses these and other local national and histories, and reveals the power of saints within a wider infrastructure of institutional bureaucracy public events, organizational forms, objects, and networks that allows the movement of images and discourse which constitute Catholicism as a dynamic, globalized religion (Larkin 2013).

Notes

1   Stop (*estrado*) at the Confederación de Trabajadores de Peru (CTP), October 18, 2013.

2   The colloquial term merges the names of former autocratic president of Peru Alberto Fujimori (1990–2000) and of Victor Montesinos, head of Peru's intelligence service, who were complicit in a series of crimes and human rights abuses, including bribery, corruption, embezzlement, drug-trafficking, illegal arrests, torture, and genocide (in 2009 Fujimori was sentenced to twenty-five years in prison). The Law the CTP director referred to was then President Ollanta Humala's extension of a neo-liberalist labor reform project begun by Fujimori: "La Ley del Servicio Civil," passed in July 2013, which worsened the conditions of employment of public service employees and led to the termination of some 320,000 workers. Unions such as the CTP were strongly opposed to the reforms. https://puntoedu.pucp.edu.pe/noticias/informe-puntoedu-todo-sobre-la-ley-de-servicio-civil/.

3   "*Este pata viene a hablar de sus cosas, y nada para el Señor.*"

4   Processions also take place on October 6 and October 28 that are part of the wider annual celebration of the Señor; we focus here on the main procession days of October 18th and 19th.

5   I understand affect here as introduced by Brian Massumi, in his translation of Deleuze and Guattari, as a dynamic "prepersonal" relational force, irreducible to human experience, but inherent in interactions and encounters. In this context of the Señor's procession, desire or passion for God is part of the event's politics of affect (see also Jane Bennett 2016).

6   African slaves and free Blacks, members of a *cofradía* or religious brotherhood gathered regularly in a small building where one of them had painted an image of a crucified Christ (Vargas 1966; Costilla 2015). After an earthquake in 1655, the building collapsed, except for the wall containing the Christ image. Spurred by this miracle, and promoted by Jesuit catechists, the saint's cult gradually gained visibility and popularity among local *criollo* (American-born European) elites and regal authorities who made attempts to contain and manage it (Costilla 2015: 154). Eventually, in 1671, the Viceroy ordered the shed holding the painting to be converted into a chapel, and the subsequent appropriation of the saint's image and his cult by crown and Church authorities.

7   See Gómez Torres (2015) for more on the significance of the names by which the saint is known.

8   Instituto Nacional de Estadística e Informática [INEI] 2017, (http://www.censos2017.pe/inei-difunde-base-de-datos-de-los-censos-nacionales-2017-y-el-perfil-sociodemografico-del-peru/) (accessed January 13, 2021). The National Evangelical Council (CONEP) however estimates that evangelicals represent at

least 15 percent of the population. Evangelical Christianity arrived in Peru in the early 1900s. See also Lecaros (2013).

9   Cipriani is also a member of Opus Dei, a semi-secretive rightist Catholic organization active in Peru since the late 1950s. Another prominent conservative movement in Peru is Sodalitium Christianae Vitae (Romero 2008).

10 See Article 50, http://www.congreso.gob.pe/eng/constitution/.

11 The Concordat guarantees clergy salaries similar to state employees and exemption from certain taxes, and that Catholicism remains the only religion taught in public schools (Romero 2008; Valderrama Adriansen 2010).

12 In Lima there are two images of the Señor de los Milagros: the original painted image in the Church of the Nazarenas, which is visited throughout the year by pilgrims from all over the world, and a replica or surrogate of this original painted image which moves in the procession. This replica and the Holy *anda* or litter on which it sits are permanently housed in a special room within the Church. Here, politicians and members of elite families may seek private audiences with the Señor to pray and request his blessings. At one moment in the year the two images are side by side, an occasion that attracts more visitors since anyone is allowed to touch, even if briefly, the image and the *anda* (Gómez Torres 2015: 32–3).

13 One can see here a mimetic echo of modes of devotional labor of African slave bodies in the Viceroyalty of Peru and in Lima, where people of African origin composed around 60 percent of the urban population.

14 Interview with Glaver Fátima, leader of the Cantoras, Hermandad de las Nazarenas, May 2017.

15 I owe this insight to my research collaborator Dr Margarita Zires Roldán.

16 See, for example, https://peru.com/actualidad/mi-ciudad/ollanta-humala-cargo-anda-senor-milagros-multitudinaria-procesion-fotos-noticia-203189 (accessed September 20, 2021).

17 Homily of Cardinal Juan Luis Cipriani, "Santa Misa por la Nación y la familia peruana," Sunday, October 18, 2015. Plaza Mayor de Lima (available at: http://www.arzobispadodelima.org/blog/2015/10/18/homilia-en-el-santa-misa-por-la-nacion-y-la-familia-peruana/) (accessed July 18, 2019).

18 See Napolitano (2016) for an explanation of the "culture of life" in the Church's theology of the "New Evangelization." See also Bennett (2016: 86–9).

19 Juan Velasco Alvarado (1968–75); Francisco Morales Bermúdez (1975–80).

20 Evangelical Christian members of Congress are also expected to pay formal respects to the Señor. (Personal communication, Dr. Véronique Lecaros, Lima, Peru.)

21 In 2017, Ollanta Humala and his wife were arrested on charges of corruption and served eighteen months of pretrial detention while being investigated on money-

laundering and conspiracy charges. Humala's successor Pedro Kuczynski resigned in 2018, just ahead of the public exposure of another corruption scandal. See "Does Peru Need a Special Prison for Former Presidents?", by Sonia Goldenberg, *New York Times*, August 7, 2017.
22 Thanks to Damian Arteca for this valuable insight.

10

The Mediatization of Catholicism: Some Challenges and Remarks

Luís Mauro Sá Martino

In this concluding chapter, I would like to draw attention to certain insights and questions that arose for me as I read through these essays. Rather than offering a synthesis of the authors' many stimulating ideas or providing a detailed account of the discussions, this closing text intends only to outline some common problems that underline the research in mediatization of Catholicism from the perspective of a scholar who conducts research in Brazil.

The titles of this book and its individual chapters offer a glimpse of more general phenomena than the case studies and theoretical insights address—namely, the changes that have been taking place in the relationship between media and religion over the past several decades. We might now directly address the two main words of the title: What do we mean by religion and, particularly, by "Catholicism"? What do we mean by "media"?

There is no single, or simple, definition of each of these words; the very meaning of "media" and "religion" refers to a broader, much more inclusive and plural group of social practices and discourses; even if, at first sight, it is possible to understand what these words mean, a closer look points to various understandings of each one. It would be a truism to say that both media and religion have been changing; the book provides a documented and detailed account of some of the key characteristics of those changes.

Media and Religion research is not a new subject. It has a history, recorded in at least two main journals, the *Journal of Communication and Religion* and the *Journal of Media and Religion*, both of which have been active for over two decades. These are, of course, in addition to a considerable number of scientific papers on the subject published in media and communications periodicals that do not include "religion" in their titles. There is also a Media and Religion working group at the International Association for Media and Communication Research (IAMCR), which secures a place for academic exchange on the subject. Along with these journals and conferences, it is easy to find books titled *Media and Religion, Mediated Religion, Mediating Religion, Mediatization of Religion*, and so on. The relationship between media and religion has thus become an institutionalized part of the research agenda in media and communication studies (Block 2000; Stout and Buddenbaum 2002, 2008; Meyers and Moors 2006; Martino 2016).

Media and religion has become a well-defined interdisciplinary research area that draws on and combines insights from communication studies, the social sciences, and humanities. As an interdisciplinary field there is not a single theoretical or conceptual approach, but a variety of ways to deal with a changing and challenging subject. While this goes beyond the scope of this text, it is interesting to note that in the process of institutionalizing this field, universities have usually placed media and religion studies in media and communication departments or schools, but this book's contributors show that it would equally fit well in social sciences or cultural studies departments. As an interdisciplinary field of inquiry, researchers have approached this area of studies in different ways throughout the last decades, which led to the current shape and characteristics of the field. For those researching media and religion, it is rewarding to note that the subject is now receiving increased and long-deserved academic attention. At the same time, however, that increased recognition creates new challenges for scholars to consolidate their ideas and "ferment in the field." As the field of inquiry grows, its avenues for research develop in new and unexpected directions, resulting in not only the integration of preexisting and emerging subjects and topic areas but also the development of new perspectives on established ones. This book provides a combination of these approaches, including studies of the uses of established broadcast media (Lado, Loustau) and emerging social media channels (Dugan, Hoenes del Pinal) in contemporary religious life, critical analyses of the representational logics of mediatization (Norget, Oliphant, Csordas), and examinations of the consequences of media and mediatization for religious imaginaries and ethics (Bautista, Kaell).

Taken at face value, the mediation of Catholicism is not exactly news. Media has been an important part of the Roman Catholic Church for nearly a century now, from the Vatican's first radio broadcasts in February 1931 to Pope Benedict XVI's first Twitter post in December 2012. The radical changes in the media in the last thirty years in particular, and the sped-up pace of its everyday transformations, nonetheless pose a constant challenge for those who research media and Catholicism. If one could talk about "mass media and religion" not so long ago, what would be the challenges for those who research social media and religion or, in a broader sense, the mediatization of religion? There was a not-so-distant time when "the media" meant radio and television broadcasts and newsprint; today it would be difficult to place "the media" as a unique or integrated entity, as every single smartphone around the planet now accesses a wide range of mediated forms of communication.

It would be impossible to talk about this subject, too, without taking into account the many changes that the Roman Catholic Church itself has been through during the last thirty years. Three Popes have been on St. Peter's throne in the first two decades of the twenty-first century alone, each of them with his own view and approach to the contemporary world, including distinct thoughts and engagements with the media. The Catholic Church may have been the first global organization in the past, but now more than ever it exists as one religion among others and many feel it struggles to matter in increasingly secular states and religiously plural societies. Scholars must also address the complex ways that media and mediatization play in promoting or countering religious fundamentalism and intolerance, as well as ecumenism, toleration, and cooperation.

In what follows, I will outline some general aspects of the questions raised throughout this book, while keeping in mind that this is "a" reading, not "the" reading of its content.

Catholicism: One or Many?

When a person declares himself or herself to be a "Catholic," what does it mean? At first sight the answer is clear: they believe in the doctrine of the Roman Catholic Church, follow the teachings of the Church, and act in conformity with its ethical indications. However, reality is never so simple. The meaning of "being a Catholic" may be very different according to the context. Being a Catholic in a mostly Protestant country like Sweden, England, or the United States, for example, differs greatly from being a Catholic in a traditionally Catholic Latin American country.

The question is not only geographical or geopolitical. Inside the Catholic Church there are many views on what it means to be a believer, on how to interpret the teaching of the Church, and of the place of the Catholic religion in the contemporary world. There is no single approach for understanding the teachings of the Church, and interpretations may change in time and place. The Church may officially be a unity, but it is hardly monolithic, and different interpretations of what it means to be a Catholic may arise.

In Brazil, for example, traditionalist Catholics believe the Church should be more engaged with spiritual and doctrinaire matters, while progressives argue it should side with the poor in their struggle for social justice and actively help society to diminish economic inequalities. While traditionalists have their Masses said and sung in Latin, Pentecostal Catholics perform their celebrations with guitars, drums, and dance showing the aesthetic differences that exist alongside but not necessarily in lockstep with doctrinal ones (Rolim 1980; Prandi 1997; Souza 1997; Martino 2016). In the middle of this path lies the bigger slice of Roman Catholics, living their faith in a plethora of ways. Which of them is truly "Catholic"? Is it the same to be a Roman Catholic in Brazil as it is in Canada, the United States, Guatemala, Peru, Chad, or the Philippines?

In Brazil, and, generally, in Latin America, the Spanish and Portuguese colonizers brought Catholicism with them, which makes it very difficult to think of a non-Catholic ruling class in this context. Yet, following colonizers' forced conversion and evangelization efforts, as the Catholic Church's doctrine further spread among local indigenous and other inhabitants, it also developed in more "popular" forms that sought to address the needs of the poor, the marginalized, and the excluded. One could thus speak of "elite" and "popular" forms of Catholicism, yet despite those class divisions, all of them would proclaim themselves to be "Catholic." It is therefore possible to ask if the meaning and experience of being a Catholic are the same for all of them. The debatable nature of El Señor de los Milagros' "visit" to the president of Peru discussed in Kristin Norget's essay in this volume shows how these classed interpretations of what Catholicism means can clash in the public sphere.

As this book's contributors have done, a closer look at everyday practices reveals that there are many "Catholicisms." I am not referring, of course, to the core set of doctrinal beliefs that define the Catholic Church, but the living everyday experience of religion (Fausto Neto 2004; Carranza 2011; Miklos 2012). From a sociological point of view, religion is not important just as a set of beliefs and doctrines, but it also provides the ground for people's behavior and actions toward one another. The social importance of religion depends mostly on how people perceive the world through a religious lens and act in accordance to it. For example, the theme of "Christian love" is central to the Catholic institutions that both Kaell and Loustau discuss in their chapters, but that very idea seems to mean slightly different things and engage different groups even within the organizations in question. Although there is only one Catholic doctrine, individuals have their own way of being a Catholic in everyday life.

In addition, modern Brazilian society is also a multi-faith society. Family bonds are no longer defined only by religious affiliation, and one could question how many people actually take faith into account when choosing their partners. Of course, this depends on how strong an individual feels toward their religious beliefs, but the main point is that religious affiliation has become ever more fluid (Martin 2005; Martinez 2011). In a context characterized by a similar shift away from Catholic hegemony as Pentecostalism has grown, worries about that fluidity motivate the Guatemalan Catholics Hoenes del Pinal studies to find new ways to use media to consolidate the community.

At the same time, religious affiliation—or the lack of it—is still a powerful element in defining individual identity. Contemporary modern life might affect some aspects of religion, but it has not placed religion outside the realm of everyday experience. Religion is an important answer to the challenges of Modernity, its problems, conflicts, and anxieties, by providing a coherent ground for persons and groups to interpret the social reality. As Katherine Dugan shows in her essay on Catholic family planning and social media, religion also might provide a strong sense of belonging in a fast-changing world, where personal and social ties are constantly challenged and weakened by the constraints of everyday life and its endless demands. Religious ties may be more or less tight, according to each person: there is no single way to be committed to religion as it becomes increasingly a matter of choice—an "invisible religion," as Thomas Luckmann (1970) has put it.

The Catholic Church in the Religious Field

In contemporary Brazilian society, the diversity of religious offerings has also dramatically increased. French sociologist Pierre Bourdieu (1971, 1980) defines a "field" as a structured social space where people and institutions dispute a common symbolic aim (which might be prestige, success, status, and its derived prerogatives) using the available (and legitimate) strategies. A field is a place of dispute and competition between those who share the same interests and aim for the same goals—frequently, the hegemony of the said field, which is to say, the right to define its rules. Bourdieu (1971) developed the notion of "religious field" to explain the competition between churches, which seek not only to amass the greatest number of members but also struggle to impose their own concepts of what is right or wrong. According to Bourdieu, such a field is like a "market of symbolic goods," where there is competition among the churches to engage the largest number of people and so become socially relevant as the dominant group. The advantages of "dominance" in a given field refer not only to prestige but also to the power to set the rules of the game or competition (the field) and to influence other fields, as well. Thus, dominance in the religious field can also lead to influence in politics and culture more generally (Hoover 1997; Birman and Lehmann 1999; Marsden 2008; Martino 2014).

All fields must have their players: people, and institutions sharing a common ground and disputing the same goals. In the religious field, Bourdieu argues, churches and their denominations are the players fighting amongst each other and sometimes within themselves not only for the largest number of worshippers but also for the definition of what is correct in matters of religion. Therefore, to study the development of the Roman Catholic Church in Brazil, it is important to place it in the broader picture of the Brazilian religious field.

The use of media communication has been one of the most important strategies to gather more worshippers. Chronologically, the Roman Catholic Church was the first to employ mass media (especially, radio and television) to convey its message in Brazil, beginning in the early 1950s. However, it was only after Protestant Evangelicals increased their reach through a robust engagement with broadcast media in the late 1970s that the Catholic Church fully adopted the media as part of its strategies in the religious field as well.

Brazilian sociologist Antonio Flávio Pierucci has stated that "the sociology of religion in Brazil has been the study of the decline of the Roman Catholic Church" (2004: 14). As bold as this statement might be, the fact still stands that although Brazil has one of the largest Roman Catholic populations in the world, it is also now a nation split between Catholics and Protestants, with a lesser presence of other religions. A survey from early 2020 by the Datafolha Institute, one of the most reliable research centers in Brazil, showed that 50 percent of Brazilians declare themselves to be Roman Catholics, 31 percent Protestants (mostly Pentecostals), with 5 percent also belonging to other religions and 10 percent declaring themselves Atheists. Nearly fifty years before, in 1971, 90 percent of the population was nominally Roman Catholic.

There are a considerable number of reasons for this change, which would include historical, social, and political factors. The study of media and religion in Brazil cannot afford to ignore the close relationship that denominations have with the media, from the main broadcast media companies to social media, and how this shapes the country's overall cultural milieu.

While in Latin America Catholicism has been the dominant religion for centuries, the presence and growth of Protestant denominations since the early twentieth century have challenged its hegemony (Ramirez 2009; Gaytán 2018; Sepúlveda 2018). The increase in the number of members also augments the importance of a church, including its ability and perceived right to have a say on political and social matters that involve citizens of all religions. Today in Brazil, there are both Catholic and Protestant representatives in Parliament, but this would have been very difficult as recently as the 1970s when Protestants were only 10 percent of the population (Souza 1969; Camargo 1973). The rapid growth of Evangelical Protestant churches between 1970 to 2000 has meant that in the twenty-first century their members play a larger part in electing politicians who represent their perspectives on issues such as same-sex marriage, the adoption of religious teaching in public schools, and so forth (Pierucci and Prandi 1996; Figueiredo Filho 2005; Aguiar 2019).

Brazilian society is increasingly religiously plural, and this variety is also reflected in the ways people understand their own affiliations. For example, a person who declares himself or herself to be a Catholic, but has only a loose tie with the Church, may be only nominally a Catholic, and perhaps they would be willing to marry a Protestant and raise children with no religious affiliation. A more committed and traditional Catholic might not, nor might they approve of some of the newer social teachings of the Church and even be reproachful of some of Pope Francis's statements concerning equality and justice. There are also equally committed Catholics who would feel at home with those same statements and approve of these new social engagements. Finally, a Pentecostal or Charismatic Catholic might be more concerned with their personal connection to the spiritual side of the religion than with its involvement in social issues. This is to say, finally, that there is an endless range of combinations among these Catholic positions. This book's chapters have shown some of this plurality around the world, and the challenges faced by researchers trying to understand what it means to be a Catholic in the contemporary, media-saturated world.

What "Media"? From Media to Mediatization

If "Catholicism" does not fit into a single concept, settling on a definition of "media" is no easier task either. "The media" usually refers to a wide range of elements more or less related to a networked or broadcasted message (news, advertising, movies, comics), the devices (smartphones, tablets, television sets), and the companies or platforms that produce such messages. This was not always the case. Decades ago, "the media" referred to big companies broadcasting news or entertainment and the messages produced by them alone. Its major product was broadly mentioned as "popular culture" and there was a clear split between the media as producers and its public as consumers.

The internet and digital media have changed this scene by today connecting people to an unprecedented degree. Large media companies still exist, and they seem to be as powerful as ever, standing alongside other groups, such as NGOs and civil society groups, and pressure groups that have benefited from expansion of network technologies ever further into everyday life. With the transition to digital media, massive corporate media conglomerates such as Organizações Globo and Grupo Abril—which own multinational television networks, radio stations, newspapers, and magazines—remain hugely influential, but are steadily losing audiences to non-Brazilian international digital news and social media platforms (e.g., Facebook, WhatsApp, Buzzfeed, and Netflix). Today, Brazilians spend an estimated 65 percent of their daily media consumption online—a percentage that in coming years will only continue to climb (WNPI 2019).

In the last three decades, several concepts and labels were developed in order to define this new media scenario, including "cyberculture," "digital culture," "connection culture," "digital media," and "virtual world," among other ephemeral names. None of them are broad enough to encompass the profound social changes that have been taking place since the advent of the internet and new media devices, such as the personal computer, tablets, and increasingly sophisticated smartphones. So, the notion of "media," it seems, still fills the conceptual gap to explain what is going on in society.

The place of the media in society has changed, too. As Sonia Livingstone (2009) points out, not so long ago it was possible to distinguish "the media" quite cleanly from "the society." Now that we're all connected and that every person is able, given possession of a simple smartphone or a similar device, to produce and share information with a larger number of people, there is no longer a gap between the people and the media. Instead of "media and society," we now talk about a "mediated society" since everyone now seems to be connected all the time, and every single action, like having dinner or watching a TV series, is meticulously posted and shared through social media. This is one of the key features of contemporary culture—the "mediation of everything," as Livingstone (2009) puts it. The notion of "mediation" seems to have quickly spread among researchers to define the way ordinary actions have become related to the media.

Etymologically, the word "mediation" refers to the "action of the media," or the part played by the media in everyday life. This leads to another concept employed by several researchers in the last three decades to refer to a more specific phenomenon involving media and society: the idea of "mediatization." Just as "mediation" refers to the use of media in everyday actions, "mediatization" points to a broader process of articulation between the media environment and social practices (Veron 1986; Hjarvard 2008; Livingstone 2009; Gomes 2010; Couldry and Hepp 2013; Martino 2016, 2019; Valdettaro 2016). In order to understand this notion of mediatization, we must define three elements: "media environment," "social practices," and "articulation."

Researcher Joshua Meyrowitz (1999, 2000) was one of the first to talk about the "media environment." In the early 2000s, he wrote a paper defining "media" as a group of elements—the devices and the broadcasting companies, but also their messages, such as news or entertainment. In other words, there is not a single "place" or location for the media; it surrounds us, both as devices, such as TV sets or smartphones, and as one of our primary cultural frames. It is around us; the media becomes the environment we live in, true to its name since the word "environment" comes from the Latin *ambiens*, meaning "what is around."

As social practices become mediatized, learning to speak the language of media becomes one of the major challenges faced by social institutions and practices, such as politics, sports, and religion. For example, the broadcasting of a Roman Catholic Mass or a Protestant service, without any change in the way it unfolds, does not characterize the "mediatization" of Catholicism; it is simply a broadcasting of an event, with no alterations to the core practice. However, when there is an alteration in the celebration, for example when the priest or minister speaks to the camera as if talking to the people at home watching on television, the Mass or the service is no longer simply being broadcasted; at least some feature of it has been changed to fit the media environment. In this case we can speak of it becoming mediatized, since the event now unfolds according to the language of the media.

In modern society, social practices have increasingly become articulated with the media environment. "Articulation," a concept coined by British sociologist Stuart Hall (1996), refers to the dynamic, unbreakable connection between two elements that mutually influence each other. The media environment and social practices seem to be connected this way; there is no center or focal point, but a continuous interaction between them. The media environment and social practices are articulated in such a way that we cannot fully understand one without the other—although each one of them retains its independence in principle.

As a social practice, religion does not need any sort of connection with the media environment. One does not need a smartphone to attend Mass, nor a radio to pray. However, in order to be connected with people in a modern society, religious denominations need to learn how to fit in the media environment by adapting their message to it. When Pope Benedict posted his first Tweet on December 12, 2012, he had to write it with the same 140 characters everybody else is afforded, his status as leader of the world's largest church gave him no special license to write more. When a reporter interviews Pope Francis, the conversation follows the broadcaster's coverage rules. When you see a Catholic Mass on YouTube, you see that there are cuts and close-ups, camera moves and wide views, just as there are in any television show or in a movie; how the Mass is represented follows the language of cinema now, not just that of ritual. The Pope and the ritual of the Mass remain the same; it would be a media-centric exaggeration to argue they have changed fundamentally. But although they are the same, they have also now been adapted to fit with the language of the media environment; they are now articulated with the media.

The mediatization of religion refers to a broad social process by which religious practices articulate with the media environment resulting in a lived experience of religion that is mediatized (Martino 2016). In 2020, during the first months of the Covid-19 pandemic, broadcasted services from nearly empty churches were the only way to experience the celebration while in lockdown. There might be several theological debates on the validity of attending Mass through the screen of a smartphone, but, from the point of view of communications research, it seemed to be the crowning of mediatized religion. Eric Hoenes del Pinal's chapter in this volume shows some of the issues that this rapid mediatization created for one community.

The broadcasting of a religious ceremony is not the only way religion has been mediatized; it may not even be the most prominent example of this. We may better grasp this process if we focus on some other ways religious media have been used to spread religions' messages—for example, many churches feature gospel music that resembles popular songs, and certain priests have been "celebrified" (to use Julius Bautista's term from this volume) into internet stars with millions of followers on social media. We might see as another example of this trend in *The Catholic Link* cartoon video depicting the life of Pope Francis from his early years as the priest Jorge Bergoglio in Argentina to his election to the Holy See in 2013.[1] Produced in fifteen languages, the video demonstrates the use of a widely accessible media form (animation) to enhance the global popularity of the new Pope.

Mediating Catholicism: From "Show masses" to Movies

One of the best examples of the high mediation of Catholicism in Brazil came in the middle of the 1990s, when the Charismatic priest Father Marcelo Rossi began to attract media attention with his so-called "showmasses" (a mix of "show" and "Mass"), religious celebrations filled with pop-style songs and choreographed dances alternating with devout prayers. He soon became famous for his "pop" style of celebrating Mass which seemed more akin to a popular music concert or to a TV program than to a religious service. By the early 2000s, he had become a media celebrity; he had a regular broadcast of his celebrations, appeared in several popular television shows, and, finally, was given his own television program. He also produced and appeared in two dramatic theatrical films—*Brothers of Faith* (2004), about the life of Apostle Paul, and *Mary, the Mother of the Son of God* (2003), about Saint Mary. Although his message was traditional, his way of preaching and celebrating Mass was framed in a style close to pop culture, especially pop music and television, illustrating again how aesthetic innovation and doctrinal content articulate in contemporary Catholic contexts.[2]

Father Rossi was followed in the 2010s by another priest, Fábio de Melo, who has also drawn heavily on pop culture to convey his religious message through pop songs, television appearances, and profiles in several social media—he is a constant social media user, regularly interacting online with his followers. Father Reginaldo Manzotti has become increasingly popular in the last ten years, mostly through social media and particularly on YouTube. Like the Filipino lay participant in Catholic Holy Week festivals and human rights activist Bishop who Bautista discusses in his chapter, these priests are not just people who are well-known Catholics, they are celebrities whose images circulate widely and impact larger audiences sometimes in unexpected ways.

The three main television broadcast channels owned by the Catholic Church in Brazil are TV Aparecida, Rede Vida, and TV Canção Nova, which broadcast not only religious programming, but also celebrations of the Mass, talk shows, news, and variety shows that focus on contemporary issues. These television channels as well as their radio counterparts reach large audiences in hopes of influencing the broader culture of the nation. These references are in service of escaping from a certain "media-centrism," that is, the tendency of giving the media the primacy in social transformations. Social processes, such as politics or religion, have their own characteristics. However, as they articulate with the media environment, some of these characteristics are partially reorganized in order to fit the particularities of the media environment, such as has been shown in several studies examining the interfaces of religious and entertainment media (Dias 2001; Fausto Neto 2004; Patriota 2008, 2013; Carranza 2011; Cunha 2011, 2013; and Martino 2016). In spite of their different approaches, they all show that religious celebrations have drawn heavily on the "media languages" that originated in secular television shows and, more recently, the internet and social media.

In empirical terms, there is also a progressive presence of digital media and internet environments as research subjects, supported by specific bibliography added to studies on mass communication such as the works by Martino (2016) or Klein (2005). Sbardelotto (2012) studies how religion has changed to fit digital media, and Miklos (2012) investigates the forms of elaboration and activation of religious bonds, also thought of in the sense of the Latin roots of the word "religion," "*religare*," from different backgrounds, in cyberspace, tensioned with the physical space, or "non-virtual."

Final Remarks

When I was younger, I usually spent my summer vacations at my grandfather's house, in a beautiful seaside town. He was a devout Roman Catholic, who attended Mass regularly. One day, on returning from church, he looked a bit upset.

"What's wrong, grandpa?" I asked. "Was there something wrong in the church?"

"You know," he answered, "they've changed everything"

There was no need to ask what he meant by "everything" as he continued:

Now they have a band. Guitars. Even drums. They play rock and roll during the Mass. The people sing along with the band, move to the rhythm, and clap their hands.

He had just had a first-hand experience of mediation of Catholicism, with the adoption of media-related songs and a television-inspired celebration. Instead of a traditional choir and pipe organ, there were rock instruments, pop music, and an intense participation by the congregants. My grandfather's surprise was due to the novelty of what he saw and heard; his old church was now part of a broader mediatization of Catholicism.

In this last chapter, I have tried to address some conceptual questions concerning the notions of "media" and "religion" from a Brazilian perspective. As I read the previous chapters, the first thought that crossed my mind was that it is impossible to talk about "Catholicism" (or "religion" in general) without mentioning the plurality of concepts, ideas, and practices associated with it.

The comparison of this book's case studies with some aspects of Brazilian Catholicism was inevitable, and several times I was surprised by both the similarities and the differences with the situations described in the chapters concerning the link between media, religion, and society. In most chapters there seemed to be a tension between "old" and "new" ways of being Catholic, which I have also found to be a recurrent concern in my research in Brazil. On the other hand, because of the historical circumstances surrounding how the Catholic Church and the media system developed in each country are unique, it can be challenging to draw exact comparisons between cases. There are many ways of being a Catholic, even inside the same country; and although all Catholics may expect to share the same set of core principles, their living experience of being a Catholic in a modern and unequal world is sometimes widely divergent.

Of course, many other questions could be addressed here. For example, what about the public? Inside the religious field, mediatized religion has a particularly important goal: to maintain the audience, be it by attracting new members or retaining the old ones. The mediatization of society has brought new challenges to Catholicism, as it must reach people more and more familiar with the form and contents of the media. What do new Catholic publics look like?

The spreading of a religious message also follows the pace of technological change and adapts itself to it. It is possible to download religious texts or to hear a service from anywhere in the world, to follow priests on social media and be part of online celebrations. What effect does this have on living experiences of Catholicism? How much does this interfere in the everyday life of the faithful? How can a church or a denomination deal with the appeals of worldly messages? What should a priest do on YouTube so as not to be skipped in favor of the next cute dog-playing-with-cat video?

There is, of course, no single answer, as the contributors to this book show. The Catholic Church has been facing the challenges of a mediatized society, sometimes relying on more traditional approaches, and sometimes fully adopting the potentialities of the media. Is there a correct answer? Maybe not—but, as the chapters have shown, embracing diversity and plurality may be a good start.

Notes

1   Catholic Link. 2013. *The Life of Pope Francis in Cartoon*, https://www.youtube.com/watch?v=_rHL4P1_GFM (accessed July 25, 2021).
2   See De Abreu (2021) for an in-depth look at the dynamic practices of Rossi and other Charismatic priests in fomenting the distinct aesthetic properties by means of which Catholicism is mediated in contemporary Brazil.

Bibliography

Adama, H. (2015), "Islamic Communication and Mass Media in Cameroon," in
F. Nyamnjoh and R. Hackett and B. Soares (eds), *New Media and Religious
Transformations in Africa*, 137–56, Bloomington: Indiana University Press.

Adesokan, A. (2017), "'Jesus Christ, Executive Producer': Pentecostal Parapolitics in
Nollywood Films," in T. Olaniyan (ed.), *State and Culture in Postcolonial Africa:
Enchantings*, 191–206, Bloomington: Indiana University Press.

Adumitroaie, E. and I. Dafinoiu (2013), "Perception of Parental Rejection in Children
Left behind by Migrant Parents," *Revista de Cercetare si Interventie Sociala*, 42:
191–203.

Agamben, G. (2010), *The Sacrament of Language: An Archaeology of the Oath*, trans. A.
Kotsko Stanford: Stanford University Press.

Aguiar, C. E. S. (2019), *Secularização em questão: O ativismo religioso digital e as eleições
presidenciais de 2018*. Paper presented at the Pensacom Brasil Conference, Bela
Vista, São Paulo, Brazil, December 9–10.

Ahmad, A. (2017), *Everyday Conversions: Islam, Domestic Work, and South Asian
Migrant Women in Kuwait*, Durham: Duke University Press.

Airoldi, M. (2018), "Ethnography and the Digital Fields of Social Media," *International
Journal of Social Research Methodology*, 21 (6): 661–73.

Altheide, D. L. (2016), "Media Logic," in *The International Encyclopedia of Political
Communication*, 1–7, Chinchester: John Wiley and Sons.

Alvarez, E. H. (2016), *The Valiant Woman: The Virgin Mary in Nineteenth-century
American Culture*, Chapel Hill: University of North Carolina Press.

Anderson, B. (1983), *Imagined Communities: Reflections on the Origin and Spread of
Nationalism*, London and New York: Verso.

Anderson, E. (2018), "The Cardinal's New Clothes," *The Immanent Frame. Couture
and the Death of the Real: A Response to Heavenly Bodies*. October 5. https://tif.ssrc.
org/2018/10/05/the-cardinals-new-clothes/

Anzelmo, A. (2017), "Eglise catholique et technologies informatisées: interaction
médiatiques avec un public de masse," *Journées thématiques 2017, école doctorale
Cognition, Comportements, Langage(s)*, Juin 2017, Poitiers, France. https://hal-
univpoitiers.archives-ouvertes.fr/hal-01726665/document.

Asad, T. (2003), *Formations of the Secular: Christianity, Islam, Modernity*, Stanford:
Stanford University Press.

Asamoah-Gyadu, J. (2015), "'We Are on the Internet': Contemporary Pentecostalism
in Africa and the New Culture of Online Religion," in F. Nyamnjoh R. Hackett

and B. Soares (eds), *New Media and Religious Transformations in Africa*, 157–70, Bloomington: Indiana University Press.

Associated Free Press (2020), "Guatemala ordena cierre de playas, ríos y lagos en Semana Santa por coronavirus," *Prensa Libre*, April 2. https://www.prensalibre. com/guatemala/comunitario/guatemala-ordena-cierre-de-playas-rios-y-lagos-en-semana-santa-por-coronavirus/ (accessed April 3, 2020).

Balázs, K. (2016), "Mária Rádió, A Szűzanya ajándéka," *Krónika online*, April 10, 2016. https://kronikaonline.ro/eklezsia/maria-radio-a-szuzanya-ajandeka/print.

Banchero Castellano (1976), *La Verdadera historia del Señor de los Milagros*, Lima: Intisol.

Barker, N. (1998), *The Revival of Ritual Self-Flagellation and the Birth of Crucifixion in Lowland Christian Philippines*, Nagoya: Graduate School of International Development Nagoya University.

Baugh, L. (2011), "The African Face of Jesus in Film: Part Two: Mark Dornford-May's 'Son of Man,'" *Gregorianum*, 92 (2): 317–45.

Bautista, J. (2017), "Hesukristo Superstar: Entrusted Agency and Passion Rituals in the Roman Catholic Philippines," *TAJA The Australian Journal of Anthropology*, 28 (2): 152–64.

Bautista, J. (2018), "On the Anthropology and Theology of Roman Catholic Rituals in the Philippines," *International Journal of Asian Christianity*, 1 (1): 143–56.

Bautista, J. (2019), *The Way of the Cross: Suffering Selfhoods in the Roman Catholic Philippines*, Honolulu: University of Hawai'i Press.

Bautista, J., and Peter J. Bräunlein (2014), "Ethnography as an Act of Witnessing: Doing Fieldwork on Passion Rituals in the Philippines," *Philippine Studies: Historical and Ethnographic Viewpoints*, 62 (3) (October 10, 2014): 501–28.

Belo, C. F. X. (1996), "Carlos Filipe XImenes Belo: Nobel Peace Prize Lecture 1996." https://www.nobelprize.org/prizes/peace/1996/belo/facts/ (accessed June 18, 2020).

Belo, C. F. X. (2016), "Speech by the Most Reverend Bishop Carlos Filipe Ximenes Belo, at the Ceremony to Award the Collar of the 'Order of Timor-Leste,'" Office of the President of Timor-Leste. https://presidenciarepublica.tl/2016/08/speech-reverend-bishop-carlos-filipe-ximenes-belo-ceremony-award-collar-order-timor-leste/?lang=en (accessed June 30, 2020).

Belting, H. (1994), *Likeness and Presence: A History of the Image before the Era of Art*, Chicago: University of Chicago Press.

Bennett, J. (2016), *Vibrant Matter*, Durham: Duke University Press.

Bennett, T. (1995), *The Birth of the Museum: History, Theory, Politics*, New York and London: Routledge.

Berecski, S. (2016), "Az erdélyi Mária Rádió tizedik születésnapjára készülve". April 16, 2016. https://vasarnap.verbumkiado.ro/14-szam-2016-aprilis-3/2334-panorama/4326-az-erdelyi-maria-radio-tizedik-szueletesnapjara-keszuelve-1

Birman, P., and D. Lehmann (1999), "Religion and the Media in a Battle for Ideological Hegemony: The Universal Church of the Kingdom of God and TV Globo in Brazil," *Bulletin of Latin American Research*, 18: 145–64.

Blancarte, R. J. (2016), "Secularism and Secularization," (trans. J. A. Barragán), in *The Cambridge History of Religions in Latin America*, 331–45, Cambridge: Cambridge University Press.

Blanton, A. (2015), *Hittin' The Prayer Bones: Materiality of Spirit in the Pentecostal South*, Chapel Hill: University of North Carolina Press.

Block, E. (2000), "The Media and Religion: A Decade of Publications," *Communication Booknotes Quarterly* 31: 5–16.

Boltanski, L., and E. Chiapello (1999), *The New Spirit of Capitalism*, New York: Verso.

Bolton, A. (2018), *In Heavenly Bodies: Fashion and the Catholic Imagination*. Part II: Fashioning Worship. Exhibition Catalogue, New York: Metropolitan Museum of Art.

Bolton, R. (1979), "Machismo in Motion: The Ethos of Peruvian Truckers," *Ethos*, 7 (4): 312–42.

Bornstein, E. (2005), *The Spirit of Development: Protestant NGOs, Morality, and Economics in Zimbabwe*, Palo Alto: Stanford University Press.

Bottoni, S. (2008), *Sztálin a székelyeknél. A Magyar Autonóm Tartomány Története (1952–1960),* Miercurea Ciuc: Pro-Print Könyvkiadó.

Bourdieu, P. (1971), "Genèse et Structure du Champ religieux," *Revue Française de Sociologie*, 12 (3): 295–334.

Bourdieu, P. (1977), *Outline of a Theory of Practice*, Cambridge: Cambridge University Press.

Bourdieu, P. (1980), *Questions de Sociologie,* Paris: Minuit.

Bourdieu, P. (1998), *Raisons Pratiques*, Paris: Seuil.

Bräunlein, P. J. (2009), "Negotiating Charisma: The Social Dimension of Philippine Crucifixion Rituals," *Asian Journal of Social Science*, 37: 892–917.

Bräunlein, P. J. (with Bautista, Julius) (2014), "Ethnography as an Act of Witnessing: Doing Fieldwork on Passion Rituals in the Philippines," *Philippine Studies: Historical and Ethnographic Viewpoints*, 62 (3): 501–28.

Brown, P. (1971), "The Rise and Function of the Holy Man in Late Antiquity," *The Journal of Roman Studies*, 61: 80–101.

Brubaker, R., M. Feischmidt, J. Fox and L. Grancea (2007), *Nationalist Politics and Everyday Ethnicity in a Transylvanian Town*, Princeton: Princeton University Press.

Bussolini, J. (2010), "Critical Encounter between Giorgio Agamben and Michel Foucault: Review of Recent Works by Agamben," *Foucault Studies*, 10: 108–43.

Butticci, A. (2016), *African Pentecostals in Catholic Europe: The Politics of Presence in the Twenty-First Century*, Cambridge: Harvard University Press.

Camargo, C. P. F. (1973), *Católicos, Protestantes, Espíritas*, Petrópolis: Vozes.

Bibliography

Campanella, B. (2019), "Celebrity Activism and the Making of Solidarity Capital," in N. Farrell (ed.), *The Political Economy of Celebrity Activism*, 35–50, London: Routledge.

Campbell, B. (2015), 'Three Things I Learned at My First Compassion Christmas Party', *Compassion*, October 23. https://blog.compassion.com/3-things-i-learned-at-my-first-compassion-christmas-party/.

Campbell, H., ed. (2012), *Digital Religion: Understanding Religious Practice in New Media Worlds*, New York: Routledge.

Campbell, H. and S. Garner (2016), *Networked Theology (Engaged Culture): Negotiating Faith in Digital Culture*, Grand Rapids: Baker Academic.

Carey, P. (1999), "The Catholic Church, Religious Revival, and the Nationalist Movement in East Timor, 1975–98," *Indonesia and the Malay World*, 27 (78): 77–95.

Carranza, B. (2011), *Catolicismo Midiático*, Aparecida: Ideias e Letras.

Casanova, J. (1994), *Public Religions in the Modern World*, Chicago: University of Chicago Press.

Casey, M. (2017), "Del fascismo a la pastilla del día siguiente: La derecha católica y sus propósitos en el Perú contemporáneo," Paper presented at the annual meeting of the Latin American Studies Association, April 30, Lima, Peru.

Catholic Link (2013), *The Life of Pope Francis in Cartoon*. https://www.youtube.com/watch?v=_rHL4P1_GFM (accessed July 25, 2021).

Chen, C. and J. Zhang (2016), "Exploring Background Risk Factors for Fatigue Crashes Involving Truck Drivers on Regional Roadway Networks: A Case Control Study in Jiangxi and Shaanxi, China," *Springerplus*, 5: 582–90.

Chojnacki, R. J. (2010), *Indigenous Apostles: Maya Catholic Catechists Working the Word in Highland Chiapas*, Amsterdam and New York: Rodopi.

Chouliaraki, L. (2006), *The Spectatorship of Suffering*, London: Sage.

Chua, L. (2012), "Conversion, Continuity, and Moral Dilemmas among Christian Bidayuhs in Malaysian Borneo," *American Ethnologist*, 39 (3): 511–26.

Clark, L. S. (2003), *From Angels to Aliens: Teenagers, the Media, and the Supernatural*, Oxford: Oxford University Press.

Cojtí Cuxil, D. (aka Waqi' Q'anil) (2004), *Configuración del Pensamiento Político del Pueblo Maya (Primera Parte)*, 2nd edn, Guatemala: Cholsamaj.

Coleman, C. (2021), The Spirit of French Capitalism: Economic Theology in the Age of Enlightenment. Stanford: Stanford University Press.

Coleman, S. (2000), *The Globalisation of Charismatic Christianity*. Cambridge, UK: Cambridge University Press.

Coleman, S. (2009), "Transgressing the Self: Making Charismatic Saints," *Critical Inquiry*, 35 (3): 417–39.

Coleman, S. (2017), "We're All Catholics Now," in K. Norget, V. Napolitano and M. Mayblin, (eds), *The Anthropology of Catholicism: A Reader*, 273–81, Berkeley, CA: University of California Press.

Comaroff, J. and J. Comaroff (2000), "Millennial Capitalism: First Thoughts on a Second Coming," *Public Culture*, 12 (2): 291–343.

Conseil Pontifical pour les Communications Sociales (2002), "L'église et Internet," Vatican, le 22 février. http://www.vatican.va/roman_curia/pontifical_councils/pccs/documents/ rc_pc_pcs_doc_20020228_church-internet_en.html

Corrigan, J. (2002), *Business of the Heart: Religion and Emotion in the Nineteenth Century*, Berkeley: University of California Press.

Costilla, J. (2015), "'Guarda y custodia' en la Ciudad de los Reyes: la construcción colectiva del culto al Señor de los Milagros (Lima, siglos XVII y XVIII)," *Fronteras de la Historia*, 20 (2): 152–79.

Costilla, J. (2016), "Una práctica negra que ha ganado a los blancos: símbolo, historia y devotos en el culto al Señor de los Milagros de Lima (siglos XIX–XXI)," *Anthropologica* 34 (36): 149–76.

Couldry, N. (2008), "Mediatization or Mediation? Alternative Understandings of the Emergent Space of Digital Storytelling," *New Media & Society*, 10 (3): 373–91.

Couldry, N. and H. Andreas (2013), "Conceptualizing Mediatization: Contexts, Tradition, Arguments," *Communication Theory*, 23: 191–202.

Csordas, T. J. (2014), "Malediction, Exorcism, and Evil," *The Immanent Frame. Aggressive Prayers, Curses, and Maledictions.* November 17. http://blogs.ssrc.org/ tif/2014/11/17/malediction-exorcism-and-evil/

Csordas, T. J. (2017), "Possession and Psychopathology, Faith and Reason," in K. Norget, V. Napolitano, and M. Mayblin (eds), *The Anthropology of Catholicism*, 293–304, Berkeley: University of California Press.

Csordas, T. J. (2019a), "From Theodicy to Homodicy: Evil as an Anthropological Problem," in W. C. Olsen and T. J. Csordas (eds), *Engaging Evil: A Moral Anthropology*, 35–50, London: Berghahn Books.

Csordas, T. J. (2019b), "Spectre, Phantom, Demon," *Ethos*, 47 (4): 519–29.

Cunha, M. N. (2011), *Explosão gospel*, Rio de Janeiro: Mauad X: Instituto Mysterium., 201.

Cunha, M. N. (2013), O lugar das mídias no processo de construção imaginária do "inimigo" no caso Marco Feliciano. *Comunicação, Mídia e Consumo*, São Paulo, 10, 51–74.

Dalsgaard, S. (2016), "The Ethnographic Use of Facebook in Everyday Life," *Anthropological Forum: A Journal of Social Anthropology and Comparative Sociology*, 26 (1): 96–114.

Damome, E. (2018), "Religions et médias au Ghana et au Togo," *Revue française des sciences de l'information et de la communication*, 13 | 1 juin 2018. http://journals. openedition.org/rfsic/3710.

de Abreu, M. J. (2021), *The Charismatic Gymnasium: Breath, Media, and Religious Revivalism in Contemporary Brazil*, Durham: Duke University Press.

de Certeau, M. (1984), *The Practice of Everyday Life*, trans. S. Rendall, Berkeley: University of California Press.

de La Cruz, D. (2009), "Coincidence and Consequence: Marianism and the Mass Media in the Global Philippines," *Cultural Anthropology*, 24 (3): 455–88.

Demeter, C. (2011), *Rurbanizáció: Területfejlesztési és modernizációs politika Székelyföld elmaradott régióiban—1968–1989*, Miercurea Ciuc: Státus Kiadó.

de Vries, H. and S. Weber (2001), *Religion and Media*, Stanford: Stanford University Press.

de Witte, M. (2003), "Altar Media's 'Living Word': Televised Charismatic Christianity in Ghana," *Journal of Religion in Africa*, 33 (2): 172–202.

Dias, A. P. (2001), *Domingão do Cristão,* São Paulo: Salesianas.

Doss, E. (2005), "Elvis Presley as Saint and Savior," in J. F. Hopgood, et al. (eds), *The Making of Saints: Contesting Sacred Ground,* 152–68, Tuscaloosa: The University of Alabama Press.

Douglas, M. (1966), *Purity and Danger*, London: Routledge and Keegan Paul.

Douyère, D. (2015), "De la mobilisation de la communication numérique par les religions," *tic&société*, 9 (1–2) | 20 avril 2019. http://journals.openedition.org/ticetsociete/1822 (accessed August 17, 2019).

Douyère, D. (2015), "Présentation," *tic & société*, 9 (1–2) | 8 janvier 2016. http://journals.openedition.org/ticetsociete/ (accessed August 17, 2019).

Douyère, D. and F. Antoine (2017), "Penser l'entrelacs des religions et des médias," *Revue française des sciences de l'information et de la communication,* 13 | 2018, 1 juin 2017. http://journals.openedition.org/rfsic/3756 (accessed August 17, 2019).

Douyere, D., S. Dufour, and O. Riondet (2014), "Introduction—Étudier la dimension communicationnelle des religions," in D. Douyere, S. Dufour, and O. Riondet (dir.), *Religion & Communication thematic issue of Médiation & Information*, 38: 7–20.

Dulles, A. (1974), *Models of the Church*, New York: Doubleday.

Duncan, C. (1995), *Civilizing Rituals: Inside Public Art Museums*, New York: Routledge.

Dunn, J. (1983), *Timor: A People Betrayed*, Milton: John Wiley & Sons Inc.

Early, J. D. (2006), *The Maya and Catholicism: An Encounter of Worldviews*, Gainesville: University Press of Florida.

Eisenlohr, P. (2010), "Materialities of Entextualization: The Domestication of Sound Reproduction in Mauritian Muslim Devotional Practices," *Journal of Linguistic Anthropology*, 20 (2): 314–33.

Eisenlohr, P. (2011), "Media Authenticity and Authority in Mauritius: On the Mediality of Language in Religion," *Language and Communication* 31: 266–73.

Elliott, D. (2018), "Time, Gender-bending, and the Medieval Church," *The Immanent Frame. Couture and the Death of the Real: A Response to Heavenly Bodies.* October 26. https://tif.ssrc.org/2018/10/26/time-gender-bending-and-the-medieval-church/

Engelhart, K. (2013), "The PR Guru behind the Pope Who Is Charming the World," *Vice* (blog), November 21, 2013. https://www.vice.com/en_us/article/exmd5k/greg-burke-pope-pr (accessed June 25, 2020).

English, J. F. (2005), *The Economy of Prestige: Prizes, Awards, and the Circulation of Cultural Value*, Cambridge: Harvard University Press.

Engelke, M. (2007), *A Problem of Presence: Beyond Scripture in an African Church*, Berkeley: University of California Press.

Engelke, M. (2009), "Reading and Time: Two Approaches to the Materiality of Scripture," *Ethnos*, 74 (2): 151–74.

Engelke, M. (2012), "Angels in Swindon: Public Religion and Ambient Faith in England," *American Ethnologist*, 39 (1): 155–70.

Engelke, M. (2013), *God's Agents: Biblical Publicity in Contemporary England*, Berkeley: University of California Press.

Escobar, I. (2020), "Coronavirus: Giammattei suspende actividades de sector público y privado," *Prensa Libre*, March 16. https://www.prensalibre.com/guatemala/politica/coronavirus-giammattei-suspende-actividades-de-sector-publico-y-privado/ (accessed April 2, 2020).

Escobar, I., W. Cumes, and Y. A. Domínguez (2020), "Alejandro Giammattei confirma el primer case de coronavirus en Guatemala," *Prensa Libre*, March 13. https://www.prensalibre.com/guatemala/comunitario/coronavirus-alejandro-giammattei-confirma-el-primer-caso-de-covid-19-en-Guatemala/ (accessed April 2, 2020).

Evangelium Vitae (1995). http://w2.vatican.va/content/john-paul-ii/en/encyclicals/documents/hf_jp-ii_enc_25031995_evangelium-vitae.html

Farrow, M. (2019), "Why Some Catholic Women Say an NFP-shaming Article Was 'off the Charts'," *Catholic News Agency*, July 25. https://www.catholicnewsagency.com/news/why-some-catholic-women-say-an-nfp-shaming-Article-was-off-the-charts-79734.

Fassin, D. (2011), *Humanitarian Reason: A Moral History of the Present*, Berkeley and Los Angeles: University of California Press.

Fausto Neto, A. (2004), "A Igreja Doméstica," *Cadernos IHU* 2 (7), São Leopoldo: Unisinos.

Fehérváry, K. (2013), *Politics in Color and Concrete: Socialist Materialities and the Middle Class in Hungary*, Bloomington: University of Indiana Press.

Ferge, Z. (1997), "Women and Social Transformation in Central-Eastern Europe: The 'Old Left' and the 'New Right'," *Czech Sociological Review*, 5 (2): 159–78.

Fewkes, J., ed. (2019), *Anthropological Perspectives on Religious Uses of Mobile Apps*, New York: Palgrave MacMillan.

Figueiredo Filho, V. (2005), *Entre o púlpito e o palanque*, São Paulo: Annablume.

Fincher, M. (2013), "Christian Foundation for Children and Aging co-founder Bob Hentzen dies," *National Catholic Reporter*, October 11. https://www.ncronline.org/news/people/christian-foundation-children-and-aging-co-founder-bob-hentzen-dies

Foxeus, N. (2017), "Possessed for Success: Prosperity Buddhism and the Cult of the Guardians of the Treasure Trove in Upper Burma," *Contemporary Buddhism*, 18 (1): 108–39.

Freidenfelds, L. (2020), *The Myth of the Perfect Pregnancy: A History of Miscarriage in America*, New York: Oxford University Press.

Funk, N. and M. Mueller, eds. (1993), *Gender Politics and Post-Communism: Reflections from Eastern Europe and the Former Soviet Union*, London: Routledge.

Gal, S. and G. Kligman (2000), *The Politics of Gender after Socialism: A Comparative-Historical Essay*, Princeton: Princeton University Press.

Gandolfo, D. (2009), *The City at Its Limit*, Chicago: University of Chicago Press.

Garbarino, S., P. Durando, O. Guglielmi, G. Dini, F. Bersi, S. Fornarino, A. Toletone, C. Chiorri, and N. Magnavita (2016), "Sleep Apnea, Sleep Debt and Daytime Sleepiness Are Independently Associated with Road Accidents. A Cross-Sectional Study on Truck Drivers," *PLoS ONE*, 11 (11): 1–12.

Gard, J. (2015), "Pope Francis Says Catholics Don't Need to Breed 'Like Rabbits'," *National Public Radio*, January 20. https://www.npr.org/sections/thetwo-way/2015/01/20/378559550/pope-francis-says-catholics-dont-need-to-breed-like-rabbits

Gaytán, F. (2018), "La invención del espacio político en America Latina: Laicidad y secularización en perspectiva," *Religião e Sociedade*, 2: 119–47.

Geddes, J. and E. Scarry (2000), "On Evil, Pain, and Beauty: A Conversation with Elaine Scarry," *The Hedgehog Review*, 2 (2). https://hedgehogreview.com/issues/evil/articles/on-evil-pain-and-beauty-a-conversation-with-elaine-scarry (accessed June 28, 2020).

Georgel, C. (1994), "The Museum as Metaphor in Nineteenth-Century France," in D. J. Sherman and I. Rogoff (eds), *Museum Culture: Histories, Discourses, Spectacles*, 113–22, Minneapolis: University of Minnesota Press.

Gershon, I. and P. Manning (2014), "Language and Media," in N. J. Enfield, P. Kockelman, J. Sidnell (eds.), *The Cambridge Handbook of Linguistic Anthropology*, 559–76, Cambridge: Cambridge University Press.

Goffman, E. (1981), *Forms of Talk*, Philadelphia: University of Pennsylvania Press.

Gomes, P. G. (2010), *Da igreja eletrônica à sociedade em midiatização*, São Paulo: Paulinas.

Gómez Torres, C. (2015), "The Procession of the Señor de los Milagros: A Baroque Mourning Play in Contemporary Lima," (MA thesis, Dept. of Anthropology, McGill University).

Gonzalez, G. (2015), *Shape-shifting Capital: Spiritual Management, Critical Theory, and the Ethnographic Project*, New York: Lexington Press.

Gordon, P. (1992), "Cold Blood: The Massacre of East Timor," *Yorkshire Television*. https://www.bfi.org.uk/films-tv-people/4ce2b7b8da954 (accessed July 1, 2020).

Greeley, A. (2001), *The Catholic Imagination*, Berkeley: University of California Press.

Guttmacher Institute (2012), "Guttmacher Statistics on Catholic Women's Contraceptive Use," *Guttmacher.org*. February 15. https://www.guttmacher.org/article/2012/02/guttmacher-statistic-catholic-womens-contraceptive-use (accessed January 31, 2020).

Gunderson, C. (2010), "The Making of Organic Indigenous-Campesino Intellectuals: Catechist Training in the Diocese of San Cristóbal and the Roots of The Zapatista Uprising," *Research in Social Movements, Conflicts and Change*, 31: 259–95.

Hackett (1998), "Charismatic/Pentecostal Appropriation of Media Technologies in Nigeria and Ghana," *Journal of Religion in Africa*, 28 (3): 1–19.

Hackett, Rosalind I. J. and Benjamin F. Soares eds (2015), *New Media and Religious Transformations in Africa*, Bloomington: Indiana University Press.

Hahn, C. (2017), *The Reliquary Effect: Enshrining the Sacred Object*, London: Reaktion Books.

Hall, S. (1996), "On Postmodernism and Articulation: An Interview with Stuart Hall," in D. Morley and C. Kuan-Hsing (eds), *Stuart Hall: Critical Dialogues in Cultural Studies*, 131–50, London: Routledge.

Han, S. and K. M. Nasir, eds (2015), *Digital Culture and Religion in Asia*, London: Routledge.

Harding, S. (2000), *The Book of Jerry Falwell: Fundamentalist Language and Politics*, Princeton: Princeton University Press.

Harvey, D. (1989), *The Condition of Postmodernity*, Oxford: Blackwell.

Harvey, D. (2006), *Paris, Capital of Modernity*, New York and London: Routledge.

Hattrup, K.N. (2019), "Unbound Serves the Poor across the Globe," *Catholic Digest*, July 23. http://www.catholicdigest.com/from-the-magazine/love-your-neighbor/unbound-serves-the-poor-across-the-globe/

Haynes, N. (2013), "Standing in the Gap: Mediation in Ethnographic, Theoretical, and Methodological Perspective," *Swedish Missiological Themes*, 101 (3–4): 251–66.

Haynes, N. (2017), *Moving by the Spirit: Pentecostal Social Life on the Zambian Copperbelt*, Oakland: University of California Press.

Heartney, E. (2018), "The Met's 'Heavenly Bodies' Show Minds Catholicism for Eye Candy, and the Result Is Both Gorgeous and Unsettling," *Artnet News*, May 10. https://news.artnet.com/exhibitions/heavenly-bodies-fashion-and-the-catholic-imagination-1282631.

Hege, A., M. Lemke, and S. Sönmez (2018), "Occupational Health Disparities among U.S. Long-haul Truck Drivers: The Influence of Work Organization and Sleep on Cardiovascular and Metabolic Disease Risk," *PLoS One*, 13 (11): 1–18.

Heinich, N. (2014), "Limits of Religious Analogy: The Example of Celebrity," *Social Sciences*, 3 (1): 71–83.

Hepp, A. (2013), *Cultures of Mediatization*, Cambridge, UK: Polity Press.

Hernández Sandoval, B. L. (2018), *Guatemala's Catholic Revolution: A History of Religious and Social Reform, 1920–1968*, Notre Dame: University of Notre Dame Press.

Hirschkind, C. (2006), *The Ethical Soundscape Cassette Sermons and Islamic Counterpublics*, New York: Columbia University Press. http://site.ebrary.com/id/10183540 (accessed May 31, 2013).

Hjarvard, S. (2008a), "The Mediatization of Society," *Nordicom Review*, 29 (2): 102–31.

Hjarvard, S. (2008b), "The Mediatization of Religion: A Theory of the Media as Agents of Religious Change," *Northern Lights: Film & Media Studies Yearbook*, 6 (1): 9–26.

Hjarvard, S. (2011), "The Mediatisation of Religion: Theorizing Religion, Media, and Social Change," *Culture and Religion*, 12 (2): 119–35.

Hjarvard, S. (2013), *The Mediatization of Culture and Society*, London: Routledge.

Hjarvard, S. (2014), "From Mediation to Mediatization: The Institutionalization of New Media," in A. Hepp and F. Krotz (eds), *Mediatized Worlds*, 123–39, London: Palgrave Macmillan.

Hodge, J. (2013), "The Catholic Church in Timor-Leste and the Indonesian Occupation: A Spirituality of Suffering and Resistance," *South East Asia Research*, 21 (1): 151–70.

Hodge, J. (2017), *Resisting Violence and Victimisation: Christian Faith and Solidarity in East Timor*, London: Routledge.

Hoenes Del Pinal, E. (2016), "From Vatican II to Speaking in Tongues: Theology and Language Policy in a Q'eqchi'-Maya Catholic Parish," *Language Policy*, 15 (2): 179–97.

Hoenes Del Pinal, E. (2017), "The Paradox of Charismatic Catholicism," in K. Norget, V. Napolitano, and M. Mayblin (eds), *The Anthropology of Catholicism: A Reader*, 170–83, Berkeley: University of California Press.

Hoenes Del Pinal, E. (2019), "The Promises and Perils of Radio as a Medium of Faith in a Q'eqchi'-Maya Catholic Community," *Journal of Global Catholicism*, 3 (2): 42–62.

Honig, B. (2007) "The Miracle of Metaphor: Rethinking the State of Exception with Rosenzweig and Schmitt," *Diacritics*, 37: 78–102.

Hoopes, O. (2015), "Emptying Yourself for Christ," *Unbound Newsletter*, May 11.

Hoover, S. (1997), "Media and the Construction of the Religious Public Sphere," in S. Hoover and K. Lundby (eds), *Rethinking Media, Religion, and Culture*, 283–97, London: Sage.

Hoover, S. M. (2006), *Religion in the Media Age*, New York: Routledge.

Hoover, S. (2016), *The Media and Religious Authority*, University Park: Pennsylvania State University Press.

Hornbeck, T. (2015), "Imitating the Self-Emptying Love of Christ," *Unbound Newsletter*, 23 March.

Hovland, I. (2018), "Beyond Mediation: An Anthropological Understanding of the Relationship between Humans, Materiality, and Transcendence in Protestant Christianity," *Journal of the American Academy of Religion*, 86 (2): 425–53.

Howe, J. (2000), "Revisiting the Holy Man: Review Article," *The Catholic Historical Review*, 86 (4): 640–4.

Humanae Vitae (1968). http://w2.vatican.va/content/paul-vi/en/encyclicals/documents/hf_p-vi_enc_25071968_humanae-vitae.html

Ilboudo, J. P. (2014), "Les étapes d'implantation de la radio en Afrique noire," *Conférence prononcée à l' occasion de la Journée Mondiale de la Radio à Dakar*,

Février 13, 2014. http://www.unesco.org/new/fileadmin/MULTIMEDIA/FIELD/ Dakar/pdf/ConferencesuraradioenAfriqueNoire130214.pdf

Jackson, M. (1995), *At Home in the World*, Durham: Duke University Press.

Jackson, M. D. (2013), *Lifeworlds: Essays in Existential Anthropology*, Chicago: University of Chicago Press.

Jacobs, L. (2018), "Heavenly Bodies: Fashion and the Catholic Imagination Review: A Gift from the Sartorial Gods," *Wall Street Journal*, May 10, 2018. https://www.wsj. com/articles/heavenly-bodies-fashion-and-the-catholic-imagination-review-a-gift-from-the-sartorial-gods-1525907633

Kaell, H. (2012), "Of Gifts and Grandchildren: American Holy Land Souvenirs," *Journal of Material Culture*, 17 (2): 133–51.

Kaell, H. (2014), *Walking Where Jesus Walked: American Christians and Holy Land Pilgrimage*, New York: New York University Press.

Kaell, H. (2016), "Seeing the Invisible: Ambient Catholicism on the Side of the Road," *Journal of the American Academy of Religion*, 85 (1): 136–67.

Kaell, H. (2019), "Catholic Globalism in the United States: Notes on Conversion and Culture," *Exchange*, 48: 280–90.

Kaell, H. (2020), *Christian Globalism at Home: Child Sponsorship in the United States*, Princeton: Princeton University Press.

Kalanit, E. and A. Shoham (2013), "The Theory of Planned Behavior, Materialism, and Aggressive Driving," *Accident Analysis & Prevention*, 59: 459–67.

Keane, W. (2003), "Semiotics and the Social Analysis of Material Things," *Language and Communication*, 23 (3–4): 409–25.

Keane, W. (2007), *Christian Moderns: Freedom and Fetish in the Mission Encounter*, Berkeley: University of California Press.

Kim, B. and Y. Chen (2020), "Effects of Religious Celebrity on Destination Experience: The Case of Pope Francis's Visit to Solmoe Shrine," *International Journal of Tourism Research*, 22 (1): 1–14.

King, D. (2019), *God's Internationals: World Vision and the Age of Evangelical Humanitarianism*, Philadelphia: University of Pennsylvania Press.

Klaiber, J. L. (2016), *Historia Contemporánea de la Iglesia Católica en el Perú*, Pontificia Universidad Católica del Peru.

Klein, A. (2005), *Imagens de culto, imagens da mídia*, Porto Alegre, Sulina.

Kligman, G. (1998), *The Politics of Duplicity: Controlling Reproduction in Ceaușescu's Romania*, Berkeley: University of California Press.

Kligman, G. and K. Verdery (2011), *Peasants under Siege: The Collectivization of Romanian Agriculture, 1949–1962*, Princeton: Princeton University Press.

Kohen, A. S. (1997), *From the Place of the Dead: A Biography of Bishop Carlos Ximenes Belo, Winner of the Nobel Prize for Peace, 1996*, New York: St. Martin's Press.

Kotsko, A. (2015), "The Problem of Evil and the Problem of Legitimacy: On the Roots and Future of Political Theology," *Crisis and Critique*, 2 (1): 285–99.

Kotsko, A. (2018), *Neoliberalism's Demons: On the Political Theology of Late Capital*, Stanford: Stanford University Press.

Krüger, O. (2018), "The 'Logic' of Mediatization Theory in Religion: A Critical Consideration of a New Paradigm," *Marburg Journal of Religion*, 20 (1): 1–31.

Lado, L. (2009), *Catholic Pentecostalism and the Paradoxes of Africanization*, Boston: Brill.

Lado, L. (2019), "The Catholic Charismatic Renewal as Ecumenical and Intercultural Experience," in S. C. Ilo (ed.), *Pentecostalism, Catholicism and the Spirit in the World*, 192–210, Eugene: Cascade Books.

Laki, L. and Z. Bíró (2001), *A globlizáció peremén: Kunhegyes térsége és a Csíki-medence az ezredfordulón*, Budapest: MTA Politikai Tudományok Intézete.

Lakoff, G. and M. Johnson (1980), *Metaphors We Live By*, Chicago: University of Chicago Press.

Laneri, R. (2018), "Millennials Ditch the Pill for High-tech Pull & Pray," *New York Post*, March 19. https://nypost.com/2018/03/19/why-millennial-women-are-ditching-the-pill/

Lanuza, G. (2017), "Making and Selling the 'Rock Star Pope': The Celebritization of Pope Francis during His Five-Day Visit to the Philippines," *Humanities Diliman*, 14 (1): 1–45.

Larkin, B. (2008), *Signal and Noise: Media, Infrastructure, and Urban Culture in Nigeria*, Durham: Duke University Press.

Larkin, B. (2013), "The Poetics and Politics of Infrastructure," *Annual Review of Anthropology*, 42: 327–43.

Laurin, N. (2012), "Le discours sur la chasteté dans les communautés religieuses de femmes au Québec de 1900 à 1970," in J-P Warren (ed.), *Une Histoire des sexualités au Québec*, 54–67, Montreal: VLB Editions.

Lebner, A. (2012), "A Christian Politics of Friendship on a Brazilian Frontier," *Ethnos*, 77 (4): 496–517.

Lecaros, V. (2013), *Eglise catholique face aux évangéliques: Le cas du Pérou*, Paris: L'Harmattan.

Lefebvre, H. ([1974] 1991), *The Production of Space*, trans. D. Nicholson-Smith, Oxford: Basil Blackwell.

Lesch, C. H. T. (2018), "Theopolitics Contra Political Theology: Martin Buber's Biblical Critique of Carl Schmitt," *American Political Science Review*, 113 (1): 1–14.

Lichtenstein, B., E. Hook, D. Grimley, and J. St. Lawrence (2008), "HIV Risk among Long-haul Truckers in the USA," *Culture Health & Sexuality*, 10 (1): 43–56

Liebelt, C. (2011), "On Global Happenings in the Name of Jesus, Rubbing Shoulders with 'VIPs' and Domestic Work in the 'Holy Land': Notes on Celebrity and Blessing in the Filipino Diaspora," *South East Asia Research*, 19 (2): 225–48.

Lim, F. K. G., ed. (2009), *Mediating Piety: Technology and Religion in Contemporary Asia. Mediating Piety*, London: Brill.

Livingstone, S. (2009), "On the Mediation of Everything," *Journal of Communication*, 59: 1–18.

Lofton, K. (2011), "Religion and the American Celebrity," *Social Compass*, 58 (3): 346–52.

Loustau, M. R. (2019), "Belief beyond the Bugbear: A Propositional Theology and Intellectual Authority in a Transylvanian Catholic Ethnographic Memoir," *Ethnos*. https://doi.org/10.1080/00141844.2019.1640262 (accessed July 31, 2020).

Loustau, M. R. (2021), "Politics of the Blessed Lady: Catholic Art in the Contemporary Hungarian Culture Industry," *Religions*, 12 (8): 577–96.

Lövheim, M. (2014), "Mediatization and Religion," in K. Lundby (ed.), *Mediatization of Communication*, 547–70, Berlin and Boston: De Gruyter.

Luckmann, T. (1970), *The Invisible Religion*, London: Macmillan.

Lundby, K. and B. Meyer, eds (2013), "Material Mediations and Religious Practices of World-Making," in *Religion across Media from Early Antiquity to Late Modernity*, 1–19, New York: Peter Lang.

Lundry, C. (2002), "From Passivity to Political Resource: The Catholic Church and Nationalism in East Timor," *Asian Studies*, 38 (1): 1–33.

Lyon, A. (2013), "The Activist Catholic Church in Post Portuguese East Timor: 'The Church Is Not a Political Institution'," in C. M. Paul, C. Wilcox, and A. Lyon (eds), *Religion and Politics in a Global Society: Comparative Perspectives from the Portuguese—Speaking World*, 75–92, Lyneham: Lexington Books.

Maigret, S. (2015), *Sociologie de la Communication et des medias*, Paris: Armand Colin.

Malara, D.M. and T. Boylston (2016), "Vertical Love: Forms of Submission and Top-Down Power in Orthodox Ethiopia," *Social Analysis*, 60 (4): 40–57.

Malkki, L. (2015), *The Need to Help: The Domestic Arts of International Humanitarianism*, Durham: Duke University Press.

Manovich, L. (2008), *The Language of the New Media*, Cambridge: MIT Press.

Marsden, L. (2008), *For God's Sake: The Christian Right and US Foreign Policy*, London: Zed Press.

Martin, D. (2005), *On Secularization*, London: Ashgate.

Martinez, A. T. (2011), "Secularización y laicidad: Entre las palabras, los contextos y las políticas," *Sociedad y Religión*, 21: 66–88.

Martino, L. M. S. (2013), *The Mediatization of Religion: When Faith Rocks*, Burlington: Ashgate.

Martino, L. M. S. (2014), "Midiatização da religião e esfera pública nas eleições paulistanas de 2012," *Revista Brasileira de Ciência Política*, 14: 7–26.

Martino, L. M. S. (2016), *The Mediatization of Religion*, London: Routledge.

Martino, L. M. S. (2019), "Rumo a uma teoria da midiatização," *InTexto*, 45 (1): 16–34.

Mayblin, M. (2012), "The Madness of Mothers: Agape Love and the Maternal Myth in Northeast Brazil," *American Anthropologist*, 114 (2): 240–52.

Mayblin, M. (2014), "People Like Us: Intimacy, Distance, and the Gender of Saints," *Current Anthropology*, 55, Sup. 10: S271–80.

Mayblin, M., K. Norget, and V. Napolitano (2017), "Introduction: The Anthropology of Catholicism," in K. Norget, V. Napolitano, and M. Mayblin (eds), *The Anthropology of Catholicism: A Reader*, 1–29, Berkeley: University of California Press.

Mayer, S. (2013), "En-Nobeling Literary Celebrity: Authorial Self-Fashioning in the Nobel Lectures of Elfriede Jelinek and Harold Pinter," in A. Colvin (ed), *The*

Performance of Celebrity: Creating, Maintaining and Controlling Fame, 67–80. Oxfordshire: Inter-Disciplinary Press.

McClory, R. (1995), *Turning Point: The Inside Story of the Papal Birth Control Commission, and How Humanae Vitae Changed the Life of Patty Crowley and the Future of the Church*, New York: Crossroad.

McDannell, C. (1986), *The Christian Home in Victorian America, 1840–1900*, Bloomington: Indiana University Press.

McDannell, C. (2007), *Material Christianity: Religion and Popular Culture in America*, New Haven: Yale University Press.

McLuhan, M. (1962), *The Gutenberg Galaxy: The Making of Typographic Man*, Toronto: University of Toronto Press.

McLuhan, M. (1964), *Understanding Media: The Extensions of Man*, New York: McGraw-Hill.

Meisenzahl, M. (2019), "The Facebook Groups Where Catholic Women Shame Each Other about Sex," *The Outline*, July 18. https://theoutline.com/post/7696/catholic-natural-family-planning-facebook-groups?zd=6&zi=ycdzmhs3.

Merra, L. (2013), *Pour une sociologie des médias sociaux. Internet et la révolution médiatique: nouveaux médias et interactions*, Sociologie: Paris Sorbonne Cité—Paris Descartes.

Meyer, B. (2004), "'Praise the Lord': Popular Cinema and Pentecostal Style in Ghana's New Public Sphere," *American Ethnologist*, 31: 92–110.

Meyer, B. (2006), *Religious Sensations: Why Media, Aesthetics, and Power Matter in the Study of Contemporary Religion*, Amsterdam: Vrije Universiteit.

Meyer, B. (2009), "Pentecostalism and the Modern Audiovisual Media," in K. Njogu and J. Middleton (eds), *Media and Identity in Africa*, 114–23. Edinburgh: Edinburgh University Press.

Meyer, B. (2011), "Medium," *Material Religion*, 7 (1): 58–64.

Meyer, B. (2014), "Mediation and Immediacy: Sensational Forms, Semiotic Ideologies, and the Question of the Medium," in J. Boddy and M. Lambek (eds), *A Companion to the Anthropology of Religion*, Malden and Oxford, UK.

Meyer, B. (2015), "Film as Revelation," in *Sensational Movies: Video, Vision, and Christianity in Ghana*, 153–91. Oakland: University of California Press.

Meyer, B. (2017), "Catholicism and the Study of Religion," in K. Norget, V. Napolitano, and M. Mayblin (eds), *The Anthropology of Catholicism: A Reader*, 305–15, Berkeley: University of California Press.

Meyer, B. (2020), "Religion as Mediation," *Entangled Religions*, 11 (3).

Meyer, B. and A. Moors (2006), "Introduction," in A. Moors and B. Meyer (eds), *Religion, Media, and the Public Sphere*, 1–25, Bloomington: Indiana University Press.

Meyrowitz, J. (1999), "Understandings of Media," *Et Cetera*, 56: 44–52.

Meyrowitz, J. (2000), "Medium Theory," in D. Crowley and D. Mitchell (eds), *Communication Theory Today*, 50–77, Palo Alto, CA: Stanford University Press.

Miklos, J. (2012), *Ciber-Religião*, Aparecida-SP: Ideias e Letras.

Miller, P. (2014), *Good Catholics: The Battle over Abortion in the Catholic Church*, Berkeley: University of California Press.

Mitchell, J. (2017), "A Catholic Body? Miracles, Secularity and the Porous Self in Malta," in K. Norget, V. Napolitano, and M. Mayblin (eds), *The Anthropology of Catholicism: A Reader*, 211–26, Oakland: University of California Press.

Mitler, M., J. Miller, J. Lipsitz, J. K. Walsh, and C. D. Wylie (1997), "The Sleep of Long-Haul Truck Drivers," *New England Journal of Medicine*, 337 (11): 755–61.

Moeller, S. D. (1999), *Compassion Fatigue: How the Media Sell Disease, Famine, War and Death*, New York and London: Routledge.

Moore, B. (2015), "Friendship and the Cultivation of Religious Sensibilities," *Journal of the American Academy of Religion*, 83 (2): 437–63.

Morgan, D. (2007), *The Lure of Images: A History of Religion and Visual Media in America*, New York and London: Routledge.

Morgan, D. (2011), "Mediation or Mediatisation: The History of Media in the Study of Religion," *Culture and Religion,* 12 (2). Routledge: 137–52.

Morgan, D. (2012), *The Embodied Eye: Religious Visual Culture and the Social Life of Feeling*, Berkeley: University of California Press.

Morgan, D. (2013), "Religion and Media: A Critical Review of Recent Developments," *Critical Research on Religion*, 1 (3): 347–56.

Morgan, D. (2018), "Vestments and Hierarchy in Catholic Visual Piety," in A Bolton (ed), *Heavenly Bodies: Fashion and the Catholic Imagination. Volume II: Fashioning Worship*, 97–105. New York: Metropolitan Museum of Art.

Morgan, D., ed. (2008). *Keywords in Religion, Media and Culture*, New York: Routledge.

Mouthe, G. (2015), "Catholicisme et usages religieux de l'internet au Cameroun," *TIC & Société* (online), 9 (1–2).

Muehlebach, A. (2013a), "The Catholicization of Neoliberalism: On Love and Welfare in Lombardy, Italy," *American Anthropologist*, 115 (3) 452–65.

Muehlebach, A. (2013b), "The Catholicization of Neoliberalism," in J. Boddy and M. Lambek (eds), *A Companion to the Anthropology of Religion*, 507–27, New York: Wiley Blackwell.

Müller, L. (2014), "On the Demonization and Discrimination of Akan and Yoruba Women in Ghanaian and Nigerian Video Movies," *Research in African Literatures*, 45 (4): 104–20.

Murchison, J. (2015), "Ethnography of Religious Instants: Multi-Sited Ethnography and the Idea of 'Third Spaces'," *Religions*, 6 (3): 988–1005.

Nagel, A. (2004), "Fashion and the Now-Time of Renaissance Art," *RES: Anthropology and Aesthetics*, 46: 32–52.

Napolitano, V. (2016), *Migrant Hearts and the Atlantic Return: Transnationalism and the Roman Catholic Church*, New York: Fordham University Press.

Napolitano, V. (2017), "On a Political Economy of Political Theology: El Señor de los Milagros," in K. Norget, V. Napolitano and M. Mayblin (eds), *The Anthropology of Catholicism: A Reader*, 243–55, Oakland: University of California Press.

Napolitano, V. and C. McAllister (2021), "Incarnate Politics beyond the Cross and the Sword," *Social Analysis*, 64 (4): 1–20.

Natale, S. (2013), "Spiritual Stars: Religion and Celebrity in the Careers of Spiritualist Mediums," *Celebrity Studies*, 4 (1): 94–6.

The Nation (1996), "A Shepherd in the Midst of Suffering in East Timor." December 12. Bangkok.

Nayar, P. K. (2009), *Seeing Stars: Spectacle, Society, and Celebrity Culture*, New Delhi: SAGE Publications.

Ngardiguina, A. (2013), *Tchad: Radioscopie des médias*, Yaoundé: Editions Ifrikiya.

Nikunen, K. (2019), *Media Solidarities: Emotions, Power and Justice in the Digital Age*, Los Angeles: Sage.

Noome, I., S. Aupers, and D. Houtman (2012), "In Their Own Image? Catholic, Protestant, and Holistic Spirituality Appropriations of the Internet," in D. Houtman and B. Meyer (eds), *Things: Religion and the Question of Materiality*, 379–92, New York: Fordham University Press.

Norget, K. (2011), "Pope. Saints, *Beato* Bones and Other Images at War: Religious Mediation and the Translocal Roman Catholic Church," *Postscripts*, 5 (3): 337–64.

Norget, K. (2017), "The Virgin of Guadalupe and Spectacles of Catholic Evangelism in Mexico," in K. Norget, V. Napolitano and M. Mayblin (eds), *The Anthropology of Catholicism: A Reader*, 184–200, Berkeley: University of California Press.

Norget, K. (2021), "Mediat(iz)ing Catholicism: Saint, Spectacle, and Theopolitics in Lima, Peru," *Journal of the Royal Anthropological Institute (JRAI)*, 27 (4): 757–99.

Nyamnjoh, F. (2015), "Introduction: New Media and Religious Transformations in Africa," in R. Hackett and B. Soares (eds), *New Media and Religious Transformations in Africa*, 1–16, Bloomington: Indiana University Press.

Octobre, S. (2014), "Mutations des pratiques culturelles à l'heure du numérique," *Bulletin d'études et Synthèses de l'Observatoire de la jeunesse, Numéro* Septembre 21: 1–4.

Oha, O. (2002), "Yoruba Christian Video Narrative and Indigenous Imaginations: Dialogue and Duelogue," *Cahiers D'Études Africaines*, 42 (165): 121–42.

Ong, J. C. (2014), "'Witnessing' or Mediating' Distant Suffering? Ethical Questions across Moments of Text, Production, and Reception," *Television & New Media*, 15(3): 179–96.

Ong, J. C. (2015a), *The Poverty of Television: The Mediation of Suffering in Class-Divided Philippines*, London: Anthem Press. http://public.eblib.com/choice/publicfullrecord. aspx?p=2051144 (accessed June 15, 2020).

Ong, J. C. (2015b), "Witnessing Distant and Proximal Suffering within a Zone of Danger: Lay Moralities of Media Audiences in the Philippines," in *International Communication Gazette*, 1–16, London: SAGE Publications.

Oosterbaan, M. (2011), "Virtually Global: Online Evangelical Cartography," *Social Anthropology*, 19 (1): 56–73.

Orejas, T. (2005), "Getting Nailed for Good Friday." http://baptistwatch.websitetoolbox. com/post/Getting-Nailed-For-Good-Friday-371087 (accessed November 9, 2012).

Orsi, R. A. (1994), "'Mildred, Is It Fun to Be a Cripple?' The Culture of Suffering in American Catholicism in the Middle Years of the 20th Century," *South Atlantic Quarterly*, 93: 547–90.

Orsi, R. A. (1996), *Thank You, St. Jude: Women's Devotion to the Patron Saint of Hopeless Causes*, New Haven: Yale University Press.

Orsi, R. A. (2005), *Between Heaven and Earth: The Religious Worlds People Make the Scholars Who Study Them*, Princeton: Princeton University Press.

Orsi, R. A. (2010), *The Madonna of 115th Street: Faith and Community in Italian Harlem, 1880–1950*, 3rd edn, New Haven: Yale University Press.

Orsi, R. A. (2016), *History and Presence*, Cambridge: The Belknap Press of Harvard University Press.

Orsi, R. A. (2018), "Something Old, Something New, Something Borrowed, Something Blue, Something Dead," *The Immanent Frame. Couture and the Death of the Real: A Response to Heavenly Bodies*. September 21. https://tif.ssrc.org/2018/09/21/something-old-something-new-something-borrowed-something-blue-something-dead/

Orta, A. (2004), *Catechizing Culture: Missionaries, Aymara, and the "New Evangelization"*, New York: Columbia University Press.

Orubuloye, I. O., J. Caldwell, and P. Caldwell (1991), "Sexual Networking in the Ekiti District of Nigeria," *Studies in Family Planning*, 22 (2): 61–73.

Ozsváth, J. (2011), "Ez a Rádió Csak Szeretetből Működik," *Keresztény Szó*. May 5, 2011.

Paerregaard, K. (2008), "In the Footsteps of the Lord of Miracles: The Expatriation of Religious Icons in the Peruvian Diaspora," *Journal of Ethnic and Migration Studies*, 34 (7): 1073–89.

Pascale, M. (2016), "Macabre Fascination and Moral Propriety: The Attraction of Horror," *Contemporary Aesthetics,* 14. https://contempaesthetics.org/newvolume/pages/article.php?articleID=764 (accessed June 21, 2020).

Patriota, K. (2008), "O Fragmentado sujeito pós-moderno e a religião midiática," *Revista Brasileira de História das Religiões*, 1: 14–28.

Patriota, K. (2013), "Ensinando sobre o amor inteligente," *História Agora*, 13: 282–99.

Peña, E. A. (2011), *Performing Piety: Making Space Sacred with the Virgin of Guadalupe*, Berkeley: University of California Press.

Pertierra, R. (2006), *Transforming Technologies, Altered Selves: Mobile Phone and Internet Use in the Philippines*, Manila: De La Salle University Press.

Péter, A. (2011), "Öt éves az erdélyi Mária Rádió: Péter Arthur OFM beszéde," *Gloria TV*. March 11, 2011. https://gloria.tv/reply/rZ73NaC12VQj2KNCBetipD3nm.

Peters, J. D. (1999), *Speaking into the Air: A History of the Idea of Communication*, Chicago: University of Chicago Press.

Pew Forum on Religion & Public Life (2011), *Global Christianity: A Report on the Size and Distribution of the World's Christian Population*.

Philpott, S. (2006), "East Timor's Double Life: Smells like Westphalian Spirit," *Third World Quarterly*, 27 (1): 135–59.

Picketty, T. (2014), *Capital in the Twenty-First Century*, trans. Arthur Goldhammer. Cambridge: The Belknap Press of Harvard University Press.

Pierucci, A. F. (2004), "Secularização e declínio do catolicismo," in B. M. Souza and L. M. S. Martino (eds), *Sociologia da religião e mudança social*, 13–21, São Paulo: Paulus.

Pierucci, A. F. and R. Prandi (1996), *A Realidade Social das Religiões no Brasil*, São Paulo: Hucitec.

Poovey, M. (1998), *A History of Modern Fact: Problems of Knowledge in the Sciences of Wealth and Society*, Chicago: University of Chicago Press.

Pope, S.J. (1991), "The Order of Love and Recent Catholic Ethics: A Constructive Proposal," *Theological Studies*, 52: 255–88.

Prandi, R. (1997), *Um sopro do Espírito*, Sao Paulo: FAPESP.

Premawardhana, D. (2018), *Faith in Flux: Pentecostalism and Mobility in Rural Mozambique*, Philadelphia: University of Pennsylvania Press

Puntel, J. T. (1994), *A igreja e a democratização da comunicação*, São Paulo: Paulinas.

Pype, K. (2015), "The Heart of Man: Pentecostal Emotive Style in and beyond Kinshasa's Media World," in F. Nyamnjoh R. Hackett and B. Soares (eds), *New Media and Religious Transformations in Africa*, 116–36, Bloomington: Indiana University Press.

Quatremère De Quincy, A-C. (1989), *Lettres à Miranda sur le déplacement des monuments de l'art de l'Italie*, Paris: Persée.

Radde-Antweiler, K. (2019), "Religion as Communicative Figurations: Analyzing Religion in Times of Deep Mediatization," in K. Radde-Antweiler and X. Zeiler (eds), *Mediatized Religion in Asia: Studies on Digital Media and Religion*, 211–24, New York: Routledge.

Radde-Antweiler, K., H. Grünenthal and S. Gogolok (2018), "Blogging Sometimes Leads to Dementia, Doesn't it? The Roman Catholic Church in Times of Deep Mediatization," in A. Hepp, A. Breiter, and U. Hasebrink (eds), *Communicative Figurations: Transforming Communications in Times of Deep Mediatization*, 267–86, Cham, Switzerland: Palgrave Macmillan.

Raichvarg, D. (2017), "Éditorial," *Revue française des sciences de l'information et de la communication*, 13 | 1 juin 2018. http://journals.openedition.org/rfsic/3554

Ramin, B. (2007), "Anthropology Speaks to Medicine: The Case HIV/AIDS in Africa," *McGill Journal of Medicine*, 10 (2): 127–32.

Ramirez, J. (2009), "El campo religioso latinoamericano y caribeño," in A. Alonso (ed.), *America Latina y Caribe: Territorios Religiosos y Desafíos Para el Diálogo*, 83–108, Buenos Aires: Clacso.

Rancière, J. (2004), *The Politics of Aesthetics*, ed. and trans. G. Rockhill, London and New York: Bloomsbury.

Reinhardt, B. (2020), "Atmospheric Presence: Reflections on 'Mediation' in the Anthropology of Religion and Technology," *Anthropological Quarterly*, 93 (1): 1523–53.

Robinson, C. and C. Burnett (2005), "Truck Drivers and Heart Disease in the United States, 1979–1990," *American Journal of Industrial Medicine*, 47 (2): 113–19.

Rockwell, R. (2001), "Finding Power of Hidden Radio Audiences in the Fields of Guatemala," *Journal of Radio Studies*, 8 (2): 425–41.

Rojek, C. (2007), "Celebrity and Religion," in S. Redmond and S. Holmes (eds), *Stardom and Celebrity: A Reader*, 171–80. London: SAGE Publications Ltd.

Rojek, C. (2010), *Celebrity*, London: Reaktion Books.

Rolim, F. C. (1980), *Religião e classes populares*, Petrópolis: Editora Vozes.

Romero, C. (2008), "Religión y espacio público: catolicismo y sociedad civil en el Perú," in Catalina Romero (ed.), *Religión y Espacio Público*, 17–36. CISEPA: Pontificia Universidad Católica del Perú (PCUP).

Rostworowski de Diez Canseco, M. (1992), *Pachacamac y el Señor de los Milagros. Una trayectoria milenaria,* Lima: Instituto de Estudios Peruanos.

Rubino, A. (2016), "Constructing Pseudo-intimacy in an Italo-Australian Phone-in Radio Program," *Journal of Pragmatics*, 103: 33–48.

Rudnyckyj, D. and F. Osella, (2017), "Introduction: Assembling Market and Religious Moralities," in D. Rudnyckyj and F. Osella (eds), *Religion and the Morality of the Market*, 1–28, Cambridge, UK: Cambridge University Press.

Ruiz Baía, L. (1999), "Rethinking Transnationalism: Reconstructing National Identities among Peruvian Catholics in New Jersey," Special Issue *Religion in America*, 41 (4): 93–109.

Ruprecht, L. A. Jr. (2014), "Classics at the Dawn of the Museum Era: The Life and Times of Antoine Chrysostome Quatremère de Quincy (1755–1849)," *Arion: A Journal of Humanities and the Classics,* 22 (1): 133–74.

Sabry, T. (2017), "Mediatization, Suffering and the Death of Philosophy," *Westminster Papers in Communication and Culture*, 12 (1): 28–9.

Sanchez Rodriguez, S. (2002), "Un Cristo moreno 'conquista' Lima - Los arquitectos de la fama pública del Señor de los Milagros (1651–1771)," in S. Carrillo, et al. (eds), *Etnicidad y discriminación racial en la historia del Perú*, 65–92, Lima: Instituto Riva Agüero.

Sbardelotto, M. (2012), *E o verbo se fez bit*, Aparecida: Santuário.

Scarry, E. (1985), *The Body in Pain: The Making and Unmaking of the World*, New York: Oxford University Press.

Scannell, P., ed. (1991), *Broadcast Talk*, London: Sage.

Schlegel, J-L. (2012), "L'Eglise et les médias: entre fascination et réprobation," *Conférence donnée à PAU, le 9 novembre 2012, dans le cadre du Service de formation permanente du Centre diocésain du Béarn.*

Schloesser, S. (2018), "On the Advantage and Disadvantage of History for Life," *The Immanent Frame. Couture and the Death of the Real: A Response to Heavenly Bodies.*

September 28. https://tif.ssrc.org/2018/09/28/on-the-advantage-and-disadvantage-of-history-for-life/.

Schmitt, C. (1922), *Political Theology*, Chicago: University of Chicago Press.

Schmitt, C. ([1923] 1996), *Roman Catholicism and Political Form*, trans. G. L. Ulmen, Westport: Greenwood Press.

Schneider, J. (1991), "Spirits and the Spirits of Capitalism," in Eric Wolf (ed.), *Religious Regimes and State-Formation: Perspectives from European Ethnology*, 181–219, Albany: State University of New York Press.

Schulz, W. (2004), "Reconstructing Mediatization as an Analytical Concept," *European Journal of Communication*, 19 (1): 87–101.

Schwartz, R. M. (2008), *Sacramental Poetics at the Dawn of Secularism: When God Left the World*, Stanford: Stanford University Press.

Scofield, J. (1960), "Easter Week in Indian Guatemala," *National Geographic Magazine*, 117 (3) (March): 406–17. *National Geographic Archive 1888–1994*. tinyurl.gale.com/tinyurl/DjFp76 (accessed May 11, 2020).

Scott, J. C. (1990), *Domination and the Arts of Resistance: Hidden Transcripts*, New Haven and London: Yale University Press.

Sepúlveda, L.V. (2018), "La secularización en el contexto sociocultural latinoamericano," *Albertus Magnus*, 92: 107–18.

Shapiro, L. (2017), "Anatomy of a Russian Facebook Ad," *The Washington Post*, November 1. https://www.washingtonpost.com/graphics/2017/business/russian-ads-facebook-anatomy/ (accessed August 18, 2020).

Sherman, D. J. (1994), "Quatremère/Benjamin/Marx: Art Museums, Aura, and Commodity Fetishism," in D. J. Sherman and I. Rogoff (eds), *Museum Culture: Histories, Discourses, Spectacles*, 123–43, Minneapolis: University of Minnesota Press.

Smythe, P. A. (2004), *The Heaviest Blow: The Catholic Church and the East Timor Issue*, Münster and New Brunswick: Lit. Distributed by Transaction Publishers.

Souza, A. (2005), *Igreja in Concert*, São Paulo: Annablume.

Souza, B. M. (1969), *A experiência da salvação*, São Paulo: Duas Cidades.

Souza, J. (1997), "Multiculturalismo e racismo: uma comparação Brasil – Estados Unidos," *Paralelo* 15: 189–208.

Stahl, M. (1997), *Sometimes I Must Speak Out Strongly*, Sydney: Gillian Film.

Stoler, A.L. (2002), *Carnal Knowledge and Imperial Power: Race and the Intimate in Colonial Rule*, Berkeley: University of California Press.

Stolow, J. (2005), "Religion and/as Media," *Theory, Culture & Society*, 22 (4): 119–45.

Stout, D., and J. M. Buddenbaum (2002), "Genealogy of an Emerging Field: Foundations for the Study of Media and Religion," *Journal of Media and Religion*, 1: 5–12.

Stout, D., and J. M. Buddenbaum (2008), "Approaches to the Study of Media and Religion," *Religion*, 38: 226–32.

Swiatek, L. (2019), "Funded by Philanthropy, Founded for Activism: Nobel Peace Prize Laureates and Their Organisations' Political Endeavours," in N. Farrell (ed.), *The Political Economy of Celebrity Activism*, 35–50, London: Routledge.

Szalai, K. (2000), "From Informal Labor to Paid Occupations: Marketization from Below in Hungarian Women's Work," in S. Gal and G. Kligman (eds), *Reproducing Gender: Politics, Publics, and Everyday Life after Socialism*, 200–24, Princeton: Princeton University Press.

Taiwo, Rotimi. (2015), "Religious Discourse in the New Media: A Case Study of Pentecostal Discourse Communities of SMS Users in South-western Nigeria," in R. I. J. Hackett and B. F. Soares (eds), *New Media and Religious Transformations in Africa*, 190–204, Bloomington: Indiana University Press.

Taylor, J. G. (2003), "Encirclement and Annihilation," in Robert Gellately and Ben Kiernan (eds), *The Specter of Genocide: Mass Murder in Historical Perspective*, 163–88, Cambridge: Cambridge University Press.

Tentler, L. (2004), *Catholics and Contraception: An American History*, Ithaca: Cornell University Press.

Thakur, A., M. Toppo, and R. Lodha (2015), "A Study on Sexual Risk Behaviors of Long-distance Truck Drivers in Central India," *International Journal of Research in Medical Sciences*, 3 (7): 25–48.

"Tízéves az Erdélyi Mária Rádió," (2016a). Szekelyhon.ro. https://szekelyhon.ro/videos/view/4757/tizeves-az-erdelyi-maria-radio.html

"Tízéves az Erdélyi Mária Rádió," (2016b). April 2, 2016. Kronikaonline.ro. https://kronikaonline.ro/eklezsia/tizeves-az-erdelyi-maria-radio.

Tomlinson, M. (2010), "Compelling Replication: Genesis 1: 26, John 3: 16, and Biblical Politics in Fiji," *Journal of the Royal Anthropological Institute*, 16 (4): 743–60.

Tracy, D. (1998), *The Analogical Imagination: Christian Theology and the Culture of Pluralism*, New York: Crossroads.

Tracy, D. (2018), "The Catholic Imagination: The Example of Michelangelo," in A. Bolton (ed.), *Heavenly Bodies: Fashion and the Catholic Imagination*. Volume I: The Vatican Collection. Exhibition Catalogue, 10–16, New York: Metropolitan Museum of Art.

Tsaliki, L., C. A. Frangonikolopoulos, and A. Huliaras (2011), "Conclusion: Making Sense of Transnational Celebrity Activism: Causes, Methods and Consequences," in L Tsaliki, C Frangonikolopoulos, and A Huliaras (eds), *Transnational Celebrity Activism in Global Politics: Changing the World?* 295–312, Bristol: Intellect Books.

Turner, G. (2010), *Ordinary People and the Media: The Demotic Turn*, London: SAGE.

Ukah, A. (2015), "Managing Miracles: Law, Authority, and the Regulation of Religious Broadcasting in Nigeria," in F. Nyamnjoh R. Hackett and B. Soares (eds), *New Media and Religious Transformations in Africa*, 245–65, Bloomington: Indiana University Press.

Ukah, A. F.-K. (2003), "Advertising God: Nigerian Christian Video-Films and the Power of Consumer Culture," *Journal of Religion in Africa*, 33 (2): 203–31.

United Nations Transitional Administration in East Timor (UNTAET) (2005), "Conflict Related Deaths in Timor-Leste 1974–1999: The Findings of the Final Report of the

Commission for Reception, Truth and Reconciliation in East Timor (CAVR)," Dili: United Nations. http://www.cavr-timorleste.org/updateFiles/english/CONFLICT-RELATED%20DEATHS.pdf (accessed October 23, 2021).

United States Conference of Catholic Bishops [USCCB] (1986), "Economic Justice for All: Pastoral Letter on Catholic Social Teaching and the U.S. Economy."

Upton, R. (2016), *Negotiating Work, Family, and Identity among Long-Haul Christian Truck Drivers What Would Jesus Haul?* Lanham: Lexington Books.

Vadnal, J. (2018), "Are Young Women Totally over the Pill?" *Cosmopolitan*, March 12. https://www.cosmopolitan.com/sex-love/a18930043/are-young-women-over-the-pill/

Valderrama Adriansen, C. (2010), "Religion and the Secular State in Peru," *Religion and the Secular State*, 549–57, BYU Law: International Center for Law and Religion Studies.

Valdettaro, S. (2016), "Mediatizaciones: Hacia la consolidación de un campo de estudios," *Inmediaciones de la Comunicación*, 11: 21–9.

Vargas Uguarte, R. (1966), *Historia del Santo Cristo de los Milagros*, Sanmartí: Lima.

Vatican (1971), "Instruction Pastorale Communio et Progressio," *sur les moyens de communication sociale*, mai 23. http://www.vatican.va/roman_curia/pontifical_councils/pccs/documents/rc_pc_pccs_doc3051971_communio_en.html

Vatican News (2020), "Pope Francis Prays for Those Affected by Coronavirus," *Vatican News*, March 8. https://www.vaticannews.va/en/pope/news/2020-03/pope-francis-prays-for-those-affected-by-coronavirus-angelus.html (accessed July 20, 2020).

Verdery, K. (1996), *What Was Socialism, and What Comes Next?* Princeton: Princeton University Press.

Verdery, K. (2003), *The Vanishing Hectare: Property and Value in Postsocialist Transylvania*, Ithaca: Cornell University Press.

Verdery, K. (2013), *Secrets and Truths: Ethnography in the Archive of Romania's Secret Police*, Budapest: Central European University Press.

Verma, N. (2012), *Theater of the Mind: Imagination, Aesthetics, and American Radio Drama*, Chicago: University of Chicago Press.

Verón, E. (1986), *La Mediatización*, Buenos Aires: Buenos Aires University Press.

Villa Y Vásquez, G. and A. Calderón Cruz (2020), "Mensaje de los Obispos de Guatemala ante el estado de calamidad actual." http://www.iglesiacatolica.org.gt/CEG-20200317.pdf (accessed August 10, 2020).

Viscelli, S. (2016), *The Big Rig: Trucking and the Decline of the American Dream*, Berkeley: University of California Press.

Warren, K. B. (1989), *The Symbolism of Subordination: Indian Identity in a Guatemalan Town*, Austin: University of Texas Press.

Weschler, T. (2015), *Taking Charge of Your Fertility: The Definitive Guide to Natural Birth Control, Pregnancy Achievement, and Reproductive Health*, 20th edn, New York: HarperCollins.

Whaites, A. (1999), "Pursuing Partnership: World Vision and the Ideology of Development - A Case Study," *Development in Practice*, 9 (4): 410–23.

Wiegele, K. L. (2005), *Investing in Miracles: El Shaddai and the Transformation of Popular Catholicism in the Philippines*, Honolulu: University of Hawai'i Press.

Wilson, R. (1995), *Maya Resurgence in Guatemala: Q'eqchi' Experiences*, Norman: Oklahoma University Press.

WNPI (What's New In Publishing) (2019), "5 Digital Media Trends in Brazil That Publishers Need to Know," *Whatsnewinpublishing.com*. https://whatsnewinpublishing.com/5-digital-media-trends-in-brazil-that-publishers-need-to-know/ (accessed July 25, 2021)

Woolard, K. A. (1995), "Changing Forms of Codeswitching in Catalan Comedy," *Catalan Review*, IX (2): 223–52.

Worrall, R. (2020), "Battling the 'Pandemic of Misinformation,'" *The Harvard Gazette*, May 8. https://news.harvard.edu/gazette/story/2020/05/social-media-used-to-spread-create-covid-19-falsehoods/ (accessed August 18, 2020).

Zeiler, X. (2019), "Mediatized Religion in Asia: Interrelations of Media, Culture and Society beyond the 'West,'" in K. Radde-Antweiler and X. Zeiler (eds), *Mediatized Religion in Asia: Studies on Digital Media and Religion*, 3–16, New York: Routledge.

Zialcita, F. (1986), "Popular Interpretations of the Passion of Christ," *Philippine Sociological Review*, 34 (1–4): 56–62.

Zires, M. (2006), "Los imaginarios del milagro y la política," *Versión*, 17: 131–60.

Zito, A. (2008), "Can Television Mediate Religious Experience? The Theology of *Joan of Arcadia*," in H. de Vries (ed.), *Religion: Beyond a Concept*, 724–38, New York: Fordham University Press.

Index

abundance 52, 162–4, 169, 173–7, 177
    n.3, 187, 188
Agamben, G. 25, 185, 196
agape (godly love) 103, 104, 110
ambient faith 79–80, 95
ambiguity 19–20
anda 189–92, 200 n.12
Andrade, A. 195
anthropology 5–8
Aráoz, M. 196
Asamoah-Gyadu, J. 75, 77
átérezni 91
attributed celebrity 138, 139
Augustinian sisters 13–14, 22, 26
authority and authorization 22–6

Barker, N. 128
baroque 8, 21, 186
basal body temperature (BBT) 49, 60 n.1,
    60 n.5
Bautista, J. 10, 19, 21, 24, 198, 213
Belo, C. F. X. 25, 132–40
Benedict XV, Pope 175
Benedict XVI, Pope 173, 202, 212
Benjamin, W. 186
Blanton, A. 112
Blatty, W. P. 152, 153, 158, 159
*Body in Pain, The: The Making and
    Unmaking of the World* (Scarry) 123
Boehm, B. 172
Boltanski, L. 81, 86
Boston Globe 114
Bourdieu, P. 92, 207, 208
Bräunlein, P. 128, 129
Brazil 12, 203, 206–10, 213, 215
de Brébeuf, J. 20
Brothers of Faith (2004) 213
Brown, P. 132
bureaucracy 6, 19, 81–8, 95–6, 198
Buttici, A. 177 n.5

Campanella, B. 137
cantoras (hymn-singers) 189

caritatis ordo (order of love) 104, 108,
    118
Catholic
    "celebrified" 19
    hierarchy 23–4, 78 n.3
    identity 50, 54, 55, 66
    "love" 19
    media 5–8
    mediation 12–13
    sensibility 6, 7, 31, 114
    sensorium 7, 8
Catholic Church 5, 11, 15, 20, 23, 25, 42.
    See also Roman Catholic Church
    in Cameroon 75
    in Chad 15, 64–7, 73, 75
    media and 63–4
    in religious field 207–9
Catholicism 3, 111, 117, 205–7, 209
    anthropologists of 6
    emplacement of 7
    globalism 6–7
    Latin America 209
    love and 108
    and mediation 6, 204–5, 213–15
    museums and 164–8
    post-bureaucratic 95–6
    robust anthropology of 119
    sensational form 8
Catholicization 169
Catholicized 164, 168, 175
Catholic radios 19, 23, 66, 67, 69–71, 75,
    95, 193
celebrification 10, 123–7, 130–2, 136–9
celebrity
    culture 126, 138
    effectiveness 141 n.4
    humanism 137
Chad 9, 15, 23, 63–6
    Catholic Church in 15, 64–7, 73,
    75
    Catholicism 64
    Catholics in 9, 23, 73, 74
    clergy 70

communication 74–7
institutional Church in 66–74
law 66
N'Djamena 64, 66, 67, 71, 72, 75
Pala 66, 68
Charismatic Catholics 24, 33, 35, 75, 107, 126, 147, 209
Chartres Cathedral 173
Chen, Y. 141 n.4
Chiapello, E. 81, 86
childhood sponsorship projects 18
Chouliaraki, L. 129
Christian Base Communities (CEB) 32, 35, 42
Christian Foundation for Children 99
Cipriani, R. 194, 200 n.9
civilization 11, 159, 166
Civilizing Rituals (Duncan) 169
Coleman, S. 114, 120 n.2
Comaroff, Jean 174
Comaroff, John 174
communication 33
    child and sponsor 112
    dimensions 119
    media 30, 75, 208
    and obstruction 17–20
    social 64, 67
    and transmission 76
    vertical and horizontal 74–7
community
    in-person 51, 54
    mediated 16
    medical 56, 57
    NFP 48, 49, 53
    online 54, 55, 58
    politics of 9
    problems of 14
    prophetic 16
    radio 67, 68, 75
complexio oppositorum 6
Confederación de Trabajadores del Perú (CTP) 179
Costume Institute, The 11, 161, 163, 172, 175
Covid-19 9, 31, 36–9, 44, 46 n.17, 58, 60 n.2, 212
Csíksomlyó station 80, 84, 85, 90–2, 96 n.1
Csordas, T. 10–11, 19, 20, 22, 24
cucuruchos 29, 30, 37

de Abreu, M. J. 216 n.2
De Certeau, M. 183
De la Cruz, D. 125, 132, 141 n.5
Demeter, C. 96 n.1
Devil and Father Amorth, The (2017) 19, 151–8
De Witte, M. 74
digital media 210, 214
digital religion 52, 55
Distefano, D. 161
documentary film 19, 127, 135, 144–58
Dolce & Gabbana 168, 170
Dugan, K. 9, 14–15, 17, 22, 24, 207
Dulles, A. 95
Duncan, C. 166–9, 175

East Timorese Church 133–6, 140
El Shaddai 126
embodied mediation 21, 102
embodiment 22, 97, 107, 138
Enaje, R. 127–9, 138–40
    Dodong case 131–2
    fanaticism, spectacles of 129–30
    suffering 130–2
    telecommunicated agency 131
Engelke, M. 79, 95, 175–6, 177 n.4
English, J. F. 124
enNobeling 136–7
entextualization 97, 103, 120
Estéreo Gerardi 32, 43
Ethnic Hungarian minority 79–80, 82–4, 95–6
evanescence 30
evangelism/evangelization 7, 10, 19, 24, 46 n.16, 71, 79–82, 86–8, 91–5, 114, 206
exorcism 10–11, 19, 20, 24, 143–4
    ABC News show *20/20* 144–51
    controversial insofar 145
    Devil and Father Amorth, The 151–8
    as mediation 158–9
Exorcism of Emily Rose, The (2005) 143
Exorcist, The (1973) 19, 143–5, 151–3, 158, 159

Facebook 7, 9, 15, 30, 36–40, 42–4, 46 n.16–46 n.17, 47, 51–60, 60 n.2, 70, 116
Farrow, M. 59
fashion

and Catholicism 11, 172–3
 items 163, 164, 168–71
 objects 169
Fehérváry, K. 83–4
fertile window 49
"Fertility Awareness Methods" 57
Fifth Avenue Met 161, 169, 170, 172
Foxeus, N. 175
Francis effect 138
Francis, Pope 38, 58, 102, 121 n.11,
  122 n.17, 137–9, 141 n.9, 173, 209,
  212
Freidenfelds, L. 52
Frente Revolucionária de Timor-Leste
  Independente (FRETILIN) 133
Friedkin, W. 19, 144, 151–9
Fujimori, A. 180, 195, 199 n.2

Gal, S. 83, 84, 96 n.2
García, A. 195
Geiss, M. 106
Georgel, C. 167
Ghanaian Pentecostals 4
Goffman, E. 33, 45 n.6
Goodman, F. 143
Gospel of John 171
Greeley, A. 5, 6, 177 n.5
Guatemala 46 n.12
 Catholics 9, 15, 18, 29–31, 33, 35–6, 40,
  41, 45 n.5, 46 n.12, 207
 Cobán 31, 37, 40, 43, 44, 45 n.3
 Holy Week 35
Guatemalan Episcopal Council 36

Hahn, C. 21, 166
Hall, S. 211
Harvey, D. 81
Heavenly Bodies exhibition 21, 25, 161–4,
  168–76
Heinich, N. 126
Hentzen, B. 99–105, 107, 108, 111, 119,
  120 n.3, 120 n.4, 121 n.9, 121 n.11
Hermandad 31–7, 39–42, 183, 188–91
Hesukristo superstar (Bautista) 127–9
heterotopia 83–4
Hoenes del Pinal, E. 9, 15, 18, 22, 24, 78
  n.6, 212
holistic management theory 81, 86–8, 96
Holy Spirit 4, 7, 174

Holy Week 9, 10, 29, 30, 32, 35, 36, 39,
  127, 213
homenajes 191
Howard Stern Show, The 45 n.9
Humala, O. 193, 195, 197, 199 n.2,
  200–1 n.21
Humanae Vitae 47, 55, 57

immediacy 39, 102, 162, 174, 177 n.4, 186,
  198
Indonesian Bishops Conference (IBC) 134
infertility struggles 49
International Association for Media
  and Communication Research
  (IAMCR) 204
internet 1, 9, 12, 18, 22, 31, 37, 41, 42, 55,
  64, 65, 70–3, 75–7, 116, 143, 210,
  212, 214

John Paul II, Pope 7, 60 n.4, 123, 124, 134,
  137

Kaell, H. 10, 16–18, 21, 95, 206
Karácsony, T. 86
kenosis (self-emptying) 111, 113, 119
Kim, B. 141 n.4
Kligman, G. 82–4, 96 n.1, 96 n.2
Kohen, A. 133, 135
Kotsko, A. 163, 176
Krüger, O. 125
Kuczynski, P. 195, 196

Lado, L. 7, 9, 15, 22, 23, 193
Lanuza, G. 126, 139
Larkin, B. 40–1
Latin America 34, 99, 179, 206, 209
Lebar, J. 144–50
legitimation 25, 163, 182, 183, 185, 191–8
Lent 30–2, 34, 36–9
Liebelt, C. 126, 141 n.5, 141 n.6
Limeños 183, 185, 187, 188
Livingstone, S. 27 n.2, 27 n.3, 210
Loustau, M. 10, 16, 19, 71, 206
love 10, 97–9
 catholic 16, 19, 98
 Christian 206
 God's 106–8, 111, 113, 118
 Hentzen 99–105, 107, 108, 111, 118, 119
 human and divine 98, 104–9, 114, 123

mother 103, 104, 107–13
 organizational principle of 81
 Szatmári and 80, 86, 87
 Tolle and 99, 104–5
 unbound 97–120
love-talk 119, 120
Luckmann, T. 207

McAllister, C. 186
McLuhan, M. 2, 3
Maigret, E. 76
Martino, L. M. S. 11
Massumi, B. 199 n.5
materialism 18, 111, 113
materiality 97, 162, 163, 169
 and embodiment 20–2
Mayblin, M. 113
Mayer, S. 136–7
mechanistic capitalism 86
media 1, 2, 109, 205, 209–13
 catholic 5–8, 23, 25, 27, 63–8, 71–4,
  79, 94, 96, 162–5, 168, 169, 173–5,
  177
 Chadian 66
 communication 30, 32
 environment 211–12, 214
 internet and digital 210
 logic 124, 125, 138
 religion and 1–4, 11, 63, 64, 125, 126,
  138, 141 n.5, 203–5, 208
 spectacle 127, 136
 technologies 1, 2, 4, 5, 7, 8, 14, 18–19,
  23, 40, 43, 64, 65, 70, 116, 125
 Vatican 75
media-centrism 214
media practices 65
 of clergy 70
 of faithful 70–4
mediated authority 24
mediatic forms 1
mediatic turn 27 n.2
mediation 2–9, 12–13, 20, 27 n.3, 64, 65,
  97, 103, 112, 118, 132, 140 n.1,
  143, 162, 166–8, 174, 182, 210–11.
  See also mediatization
mediatization 2–6, 8, 9, 11, 14, 19, 27 n.3,
  30, 40, 64, 65, 101, 123–33, 135–9,
  140 n.1, 141 n.6, 203–5, 211, 212,
  215. *See also* mediation

Meisenzahl, M. 59
Meyer, B. 4, 5, 140 n.1
Meyrowitz, J. 211
Miklos, J. 214
miraculous *(lo milagroso)* 19, 22, 25, 127,
  181, 183, 185, 187, 198
 legitimation, acts of 191–7
 and performances 187
 religious culture 197
 theopolitics of 183–7
miscarriage 49, 51, 52
Mitchell, J. 7–8
Monastère des Augustines 12–13, 20, 26
Montesinos, V. 199 n.2
Morgan, D. 64, 97, 163, 177 n.4
Mother of the Son of God (2003) 213
Mouthe, G. 63, 75
museum
 and Catholicism 163–8
 functions 166
 Met (Metropolitan Museum of Art)
  Cloisters 25, 159, 161, 167, 169–70
 Met (Metropolitan Museum of Art)
  Store 161
 reliquaries and 166
 significance of 167
mutability 52, 53, 55, 56, 58

Nagel, A. 176, 178 n.11
Napolitano, V. 186
Natale, S. 130
National Commission for Social
  Communications 66–7
Natural Family Planning (NFP) 9, 47–51
 exceptional and ordinary experience
  56–8
 intimate and anonymous 51–3
 vulnerable and authoritative 53–6
New Evangelization 7, 71, 79, 84, 92, 94
NFP Facebook Group 48–50, 52–60
Nikunen, K. 137
non-Catholic radio station 69
Norget, K. 7, 11, 15–16, 22, 25, 78 n.7,
  116, 206

occult economies 174
Oliphant, E. 11, 21, 22, 25
Ong, J. C. 127, 129, 130, 132, 139
Orsi, R. 7, 162, 176–7

paradas (procession stops) 179, 192
Pascale, M. 129
Pat McGrath Labs 161
Paul VI, Pope 47, 57
Pentecostal 4, 7, 9, 15, 24, 33, 35, 36, 63,
    72–5, 77, 120 n.2, 174, 175, 209
Peru 177–96
    demographics of 182, 200 n.13
    Lima 11, 16, 22, 179–82, 188, 190, 191,
        193, 200 n.12
Peters, J. 33
Philippines 124, 126–9, 140 n.3
Picketty, T. 178 n.7
Pierucci, A. F. 208
Pius XII, Pope 105
Political Theology (Schmitt) 185, 186
Pontifical Council for Social
    Communication 64
pregnancy 48–53, 59
processions 15, 22, 29–30, 39, 168, 177,
    179–82, 185, 189, 193, 195, 197.
    See also paradas (procession
    stops)
    mediatization of 35, 39, 191
Profane Museum 165
professionalism 87
prosperity 164, 174–5
Pulchérie 71
Pype, K. 74

Q'eqchi'-Mayas 31, 32, 34, 38, 46 n.14
Quatremère de Quincy, A. -C. 165–6

Radde-Antweiler, K. 126
radio
    broadcasts 15, 18, 19, 31, 33–5, 41, 43,
        68, 204
    Catholic and non-Catholic 69
    community 75
    FM 9, 15, 30–2, 35, 43, 78 n.6
    private 66
    program 24, 34, 35, 71
    strengths 41
    ubiquity 35
Radio Arc-en-Ciel (Rainbow radio) 67–8,
    71–3
Radio Maria Transylvania 10, 16, 19, 24,
    25, 71, 79–82
    bureaucracy 85–8, 95–6

    evangelism and trucking 91–4
    finances 87
    history 82–5
    work at 88–90
Radio Presence Antenna 67
Radio Television Presence (RTV-
    Presence) 67
Radio Terre Nouvelle (Radio New Earth)
    68, 70
Radio Voix de l'Espérance 71, 72
Rancière, J. 171
religion 203, 207
    digital 52, 55
    and media 1–4, 11, 63, 64, 125, 126,
        138, 141 n.5, 203–5, 208
    mediatization of 212
    role of 44
    and social media 50
Religion and Media (de Vries and Weber) 3
religious freedom 184
religious practices 4, 43, 52, 59, 74, 131,
    143, 164, 174, 182, 212
reliquaries 20–2, 166–8
reliquary effect 21, 166
resistant spouse 54
"return of religion" 3
Rite, The (2011) 143
Rojek, C. 126
Roman Catholic Church 6, 23, 124, 127,
    129, 133, 163–5, 178 n.8, 194, 204,
    205, 208. *See also* Catholic Church
Romania 16, 71, 82–4, 95
Rossi, M. 213
Ruprecht, L. A. Jr. 165

sahumadoras (incense blowers) 189, 190
San Felipe 30–4, 36–44
Santa Cruz Massacre 135
santo (saint) 11, 15, 22, 25
Sbardelotto, M. 214
Scarry, E. 123
Schloesser, S. 163, 164
Schmitt, C. 6, 185–6
screen 17–19, 38–40, 42, 170, 212
Second Vatican Council 6–7, 23, 31, 63,
    81, 105
Semana Santa (Holy Week) 29, 32, 35–40
semiotic ideology 177 n.4, 177 n.5
Señor de los Milagros (Lord of Miracles)

procession of 179, 184–5, 187–91,
   195–8
Señor de los Milagros (Lord of Miracles)
   7, 11, 15, 22, 25, 78 n.7, 179–85,
   187, 198, 200 n.12
   history of 197
   "*Nothing there for the Senor*" 181
sentimentalism 103, 104, 109, 186
sexual intimacy 49, 55
singing and silence 26–7
social media 1, 9, 14, 24, 31, 36–42, 44, 46
   n.16, 50–2, 54, 55, 65, 72, 75, 116,
   119, 124, 204, 205, 207, 208, 210,
   212–15
social process 212, 214
soga (thick rope) 188–9
sovereignty 7, 25, 182, 185, 186, 197, 198
Spectatorship of Suffering, The
   (Chouliaraki) 129
Stolow, J. 4, 64
suffering 24–5, 31, 112, 123–4, 127–30,
   132–5, 137, 138 n.2, 152–3, 155,
   156, 183, 187
Swiatek, L. 136
Symposium of Episcopal Conferences of
   Africa and Madagascar (SECAM)
   64, 77 n.1
Szatmári, F. 80, 86, 87

television
   broadcast channel 38, 40, 65–7, 72,
      124, 205, 213
   journalists 24, 144, 145
theopolitics 25, 185, 191, 197, 198
Tighe, P. 172, 173
Timor-Leste 124, 127, 132–7, 140, 140 n.3
Tolle, J. 99, 102, 104, 105, 120 n.3, 120 n.4,
   121 n.9, 121 n.11
Tracy, D. 177 n.5

trucking 92–4
Turner, G. 139
Tzolok (to teach, study or learn) 45 n.8

*Understanding Media: The Extensions of
   Man* (McLuhan) 2
United States Conference of Catholic
   Bishops (USCCB) 104–6, 121 n.11
United States of America (USA) 47, 58,
   97, 102, 103, 120 n.2, 133, 141, 142,
   156, 162
   Kansas City 98–100, 116, 120 n.3
   New York 45 n.9, 142–3, 159 (*See also*
      Costume Institute, The)

Vargas, A. 195
Verdery, K. 83, 96 n.4
Versace 175
Via Crucis 38–9, 43, 128–31, 138–40,
   141 n.6
videos on-line 18, 37–40, 46 n.12, 58, 74,
   100–2, 116–17, 142, 210. *See also*
   YouTube
Viscelli, S. 93
de Vries, H. 3
vulnerability 15, 43, 50, 51, 53–7, 60, 100,
   127, 138, 149, 194

Wasserman, S. 99, 106, 121 n.6, 122 n.13
Weber, S. 3
WhatsApp 37, 44
Wiegele, K. 126, 127

YouTube 97, 100, 101, 119, 141 n.9, 212,
   213, 215

Zeiler, X. 125, 126, 131
Zialcita, F. 129
Zito, A. 143

www.ingramcontent.com/pod-product-compliance
Lightning Source LLC
Chambersburg PA
CBHW050417280326
41932CB00013BA/1896